SCRIPT AND IMAGE

PAPERS OF THE 12th WORLD SANSKRIT CONFERENCE
VOL. 11.1

Script and Image

Papers on Art and Epigraphy

Edited by

ADALBERT J. GAIL

GERD J.R. MEVISSEN

RICHARD SALOMON

MOTILAL BANARSIDASS PUBLISHERS
PRIVATE LIMITED ● DELHI

PAPERS OF THE 12TH WORLD SANSKRIT CONFERENCE HELD IN HELSINKI, FINLAND, 13-18 JULY 2003 VOL. 11.1

General editors:
PETTERI KOSKIKALLIO & ASKO PARPOLA

*First Editon : Delhi, **2006***

ISBN: 81-208-2944-1

MOTILAL BANARSIDASS
41 U.A. Bungalow Road, Jawahar Nagar, Delhi 110 007
8 Mahalaxmi Chamber, 22 Bhulabhai Desai Road, Mumbai 400 026
203 Royapettah High Road, Mylapore, Chennai 600 004
236, 9th Main III Block, Jayanagar, Bangalore 560 011
Sanas Plaza, 1302 Baji Rao Road, Pune 411 002
8 Camac Street, Kolkata 700 017
Ashok Rajpath, Patna 800 004
Chowk, Varanasi 221 001

PRINTED IN INDIA
BY JAINENDRA PRAKASH JAIN AT SHRI JAINENDRA PRESS,
A-45 NARAINA, PHASE-I, NEW DELHI 110 028
AND PUBLISHED BY NARENDRA PRAKASH JAIN FOR
MOTILAL BANARSIDASS PUBLISHERS PRIVATE LIMITED,
BUNGALOW ROAD, DELHI 110 007

PREFACE

In traditional India as elsewhere, script and image naturally complement each other. They are the offspring of the same symbolizing spirit and inherently elucidate one another. Paraphrasing a famous statement attributed to Immanuel Kant ("Anschauungen ohne Begriffe sind blind, Begriffe ohne Anschauungen sind leer"), one could say that script without image can be an empty vision, and image without script, a blind composition. For example, the Bharhut stupa, dating from the second to first centuries B.C., provides with its inscribed and labelled reliefs our first clear insight into the world of Indian images – and a particularly happy one it is. Who could have identified Kubera, the god of wealth, among the vast gallery of deities and spirits at Bharhut, were it not for the accompanying label inscription reading *kupiro yakho*, "The yakṣa Kubera"? Similarly, the investigation of art history in India has an intimate connection to the study of literary texts of such genres as *śāstra*, *āgama* and *purāṇa*, as illustrated in several of the papers in this volume.

It is with this principle of the inherent relationship between art history and literary and epigraphic studies in mind that the editors have compiled this collection of essays on Indian art and epigraphy from the 12th World Sanskrit Conference, held at the University of Helsinki, Finland, on 13-18 July, 2003. The first part of the volume contains the art history papers, covering a wide range of periods, regions and traditions, including both Buddhist and Hindu art. As such, they are representative of the continuing breadth, diversity, and sophistication of academic studies of Indian art history. The first section opens with Adalbert Gail's discussion of a new jewel among Buddhist monasteries, only recently excavated at Udayagiri (Cuttack Dist., Orissa), whose name is revealed by an inscription to be *Sinhaprastha-mahāvihāra*. Two articles by Gudrun Bühnemann as well as one by Gerd Mevissen address issues of iconography and textual traditions in the tantric tradition, both Hindu and Buddhist.[1] Finally, Sadananda Das presents an important Āgama text on Hindu architecture, further illustrating the relation between image and written word.

The second part of the present volume exemplifies some new developments in the field of epigraphy. This field has had something of a checkered history in modern Indology. At some periods, particularly during the pioneering phases of Indological studies in the 19th century, epigraphy occupied a position very much in the center of the stage, and it was the efforts of early Indian epigraphists that gradually led to the construction of the chronological and historical framework on which all other subfields of Indology rest, directly or indirectly. For much of the 20th century, however, epigraphy lost its prominence, and has sometimes – especially in the west – been relegated to a marginal status within Indology; this, despite that fact that significant numbers of important new inscriptions have continued to be discovered throughout this period, right down to the present, in India and Pakistan as well as in neighboring countries of South Asia.

In recent years, however, epigraphic studies have begun to come back to the fore, as a result both of new discoveries and of newly developed approaches to and applications of inscriptional data. The three epigraphy papers in this volume provide excellent illustrations of some of these innovative methods. Stefan Baums' article on the development of a system for the encoding of Brāhmī script ably demonstrates some of the promising applications of technology to the paleographic study of Indic scripts. Annette Schmiedchen's paper on the *tulāpuruṣa* ritual illustrates the sophisticated manipulation of a large and varied corpus of inscriptional data to the study of a particular

[1] Although Mevissen's article and Bühnemann's second article were not presented at the 12th World Sanskrit Conference, they have been included in this volume since they are wholly appropriate to its themes and subject matter.

cultural phenomenon, namely the medieval ceremony of the distribution of the king's weight in gold. Finally, Bharati Shelat's detailed study of memorial stones in western India amply demonstrates how inscriptional records can contribute to an understanding of local cultures and folk traditions.

The editors hereby wish to thank the hosts and organizers of the 12th World Sanskrit Conference, including the officers and staff of the University of Helsinki, for their hospitality and efficiency which made the meeting such a success. We also express our gratitude to the Finnish Cultural Foundation for its generous support of the conference.

CONTENTS

LIST OF PLATES

(24 colour plates after p. 98)

BÜHNEMANN: Gaṇeśa

BÜHNEMANN: Tantric Deities

PLATES IV-XVII are reproduced from manuscript 258, preserved in the N.C. Mehta Gallery of the Gujarat Museum Society on the campus of the L.D. Institute of Indology, Ahmedabad.

MEVISSEN: Grahamātṛkā

LIST OF CONTRIBUTORS

STEFAN BAUMS
Asian Languages and Literature
University of Washington
Box 353521, Seattle, WA 98195-3521, U.S.A.

GUDRUN BÜHNEMANN
Dept. of Languages and Cultures of Asia
The University of Wisconsin-Madison
1240 Van Hise Hall, 1220 Linden Drive, WI 53706, U.S.A.

SADANANDA DAS
Alice Boner Institute
B1/159 Assi Ghat, Varanasi – 221 000, INDIA

ADALBERT J. GAIL
Institut für Indische Philologie und Kunstgeschichte der Freien Universität
Königin-Luise-Str. 34a, D-14195 Berlin, GERMANY

GERD J. R. MEVISSEN
Institut für Indische Philologie und Kunstgeschichte der Freien Universität
Königin-Luise-Str. 34a, D-14195 Berlin, GERMANY

ANNETTE SCHMIEDCHEN
Seminar für Geschichte Südasiens
Institut für Asien- und Afrikawissenschaften
Humboldt-Universität zu Berlin
Unter den Linden 6, D-10099 Berlin, GERMANY

BHARATI SHELAT
B.J. Institute of Learning and Research
Ashram Road, Ahmedabad – 380 009, INDIA

Udayagiri 2:
In Praise of a Very Important Excavation of a Buddhist Site in Orissa*

ADALBERT J. GAIL

in memoriam Debala Mitra

One of the most spectacular Buddhist sites in India is at present Udayagiri 2 (Orissa), being excavated since 1997 by the Archaeological Survey of India.[1]

Here, a monastery came to light where considerable parts of the groundfloor are preserved, including the ceiling and the infrastructure of various cells.

The site belongs to the important Buddhist triangle formed by Ratnagiri, Lalitagiri and Udayagiri some 100 km north-east of Bhubaneswar. Udayagiri 1 already surprised by the remnants of a *stūpa* with magnificent Tathāgata niches, each flanked by two Bodhisattvas,[2] and by an extended monastic area with additional sculptures.[3]

The new site Udayagiri 2, some 400 m south-east of the older one, is probably of even more interest. After six campaigns the monastery itself – epigraphically called *Sinha-prastha-mahāvihara* – is fully exposed including an annex on the north-western side (FIGURES 1-3).

---

* My participation in a multidisciplinary research project in Orissa, supported by the German Research Council (DFG), led me several times to the Buddhist triangle Ratnagiri etc., hence my familiarity with Udayagiri 2 since 1999.

[1] See *Indian Archaeology 1997-98 – A Review*. New Delhi, 2003: 134-136

[2] See Donaldson 1995; see further Mitra 1996.

[3] See footnote 1.

Originally, the monastery belongs to ca. 8th cent. A.D. (Bhauma-Kara period). The arched windows of the cells were – for reasons of safety? – closed by bricks in a later period (ca. 10th/11th cent. A.D.; FIGURE 4). The cells are equipped with a podium on the back side functioning as a reclining place (*śayanāsana*) as well as with a larger wall niche for a statue and a smaller one for a lamp (FIGURES 4-6). In addition triangular openings just behind the entrance seem to have functioned as fridges for food (FIGURES 7-8).

In 2002/03 the sacred area in the north-eastern direction from the monastery was the main focus of the excavators. Full-round lion figures as well as socles (podia) with lion reliefs seem to underline the name *Lion Monastery* (FIGURES 9-10).

Votive *caitya*s of small size and middle size are well known from Debala Mitra's stupendous Ratnagiri excavation (Mitra 1981-83). In Udayagiri 2, however, votive *caitya*s of a new type were found where the main *caitya* is encircled by four *(pañcāyatana* type) or even eight smaller *caitya*s (*navāyatana* type). I am inclined to interpret the latter species as an aniconic version of *Buddha surrounded by eight Bodhisattvas*, an image type so familiar from Ratnagiri and also detected at Udayagiri 1 (FIGURES 11-12). This type of relief seems to be a trademark of the Buddhist triangle in Orissa.

An excellent version from Udayagiri 1 with the Buddha (now beheaded) in preaching attitude in the centre and another one with the earth-touching Buddha in the centre (Mitra 1996: pls. 26.28 and 26.30) now find a further counterpart in a partly destroyed specimen from Udayagiri 2 showing the earth-touching Buddha in the centre. In all three cases the distribution of the respective eight Bodhisattvas seems to be similar (FIGURES 13).[4]

A nouveauté, however, from the Udayagiri 2 excavation and from Orissa as a whole is an *Avalokiteśvara* as the central figure (instead

[4] Here we see on the Buddha's proper right side from above: Samantabhadra, Maitreya, Avalokiteśvara, Sarvanivaraṇaviṣkambhin. The proper left originally displayed: Kṣitigarbha, Vajrapāṇi, Mañjuśrī, and Ākāśagarbha. Ākāśagarbha in the pedestal and traces of Mañjuśrī above are still visible.

of Buddha) accompanied by eight Bodhisattvas (FIGURE 14). This sculpture displays all the virtues of Bhauma-Kara art: superb workmanship, a roundish, almost heavy plasticity, and a calm and peaceful expression.

The distribution of the eight Bodhisattvas and their main emblems are as follows:

Samantabhadra	**Vajrapāṇi**
(*utpalastha-khaḍga*)	(*vajra*)
Maitreya	**Mañjuśrī**
(*nāgakesara*)	(*pustaka*)
Avalokiteśvara	**Kṣitigarbha**
(*padma*)	(*abjastha-kalpadruma*)[5]
Sarvanivaraṇaviṣkambhin	**Ākāśagarbha**
(*patākā*)	(*cintāmaṇi*)[6]

The most exciting middle-size *caitya* (about 3 m high) was being unearthed when I saw the site twice in spring 2003 (FIGURES 15-16). In an upper register of niches three Tathāgatas (the eastern one missing) were unveiled while the larger lower register offered perfectly preserved images of a two-armed Avalokiteśvara (west, FIGURE 17), a four-armed Cundā (south, FIGURE 18), a four-armed Bhṛkuṭī (east, FIGURE 19),[7] and the Buddha himself (north, FIGURE 20).[8] This configuration of images encircling a *caitya* seems to be unique in the Buddhist world. It is, furthermore, a good testimony for the tendency of that period not to

[5] Three branches ending with three jewels; see Mitra 1996: pls. 26.13 and 26.19.

[6] See Mitra 1996: pl. 26.17. — My identifications are based on *Niṣpannayogāvalī*, *maṇḍala* 21, and are in harmony with Mitra 1996. They differ from the three schemes offered by Cl. BAUTZE-PICRON 1997: 53. The iconographic variants and problems are discussed by Mitra 1997: 63-65.

[7] Textual references are given in Mallmann 1975; v. Index des Noms Propres: 483-492.

[8] This meditating Buddha was not yet fully unearthed, as you can see. In the meantime it has been stolen.

exaggerate both regarding the overall embellishment and the amount of arms that rarely exceeds four.

The preference attributed to the earth-touching Buddha at Udayagiri etc. (FIGURES 3 and 13, and Mitra 1981: 216ff.) can well be explained as an hommage to the enlightend Buddha at Bodh Gayā, a site that was the most prominent sacred place for Buddhist pilgrims from Orissa, resp. from the Buddhist triangle.

Summing up my short introduction to the site of Udayagiri 2 I would like to congratulate the excavation team branch IV of ASI for an excellent work. Orissa, formerly better known from the Jagannāth cult, the sun temple at Koṇārka, or the Jaina caves near Bhubaneswar (Udayagiri-Khandagiri) is now occupying the Buddhist map of India with quick and firm steps. Udayagiri 2 surpasses all other constructed monasteries in India by the amount of meticulously elaborated and well preserved architectural details. Its sculptural treasure is characterised both by original ideas and masterly execution.

REFERENCES

BAUTZE-PICRON, Claudine 1997. Le groupe des huit grands Bodhisatva en Inde; genése et développement. In: Natasha Eilenberg, M.C. Subhadradis Diskul, Robert L. Brown (eds.), *Living a life in accord with dhamma: Papers in honor of Professor Jean Boisselier on his eightieth birthday*: 1-55. Bangkok.

DONALDSON, Thomas Eugene 1995. Probable Textual Sources for the Buddhist Sculptural Maṇḍalas of Orissa. *East and West* 45: 173-204.

MALLMANN, Marie-Thérèse de 1975. *Introduction à l'Iconographie du Tântrisme Bouddhique*. Paris.

MITRA, Debala 1981-83. *Ratnagiri (1958-61)*, 2 vols., New Delhi (Memoirs of the Archaeological Survey of India, No. 80).

—— 1996. An iconographic study of the figures of eight great Bodhisattvas in Lalitagiri, Udayagiri and Ratnagiri in Orissa. In: Debala Mitra (ed.), *Explorations in Art and Archaeology of South Asia. Essays Dedicated to N. G. Majumdar*: 353-391. Calcutta.

—— 1997. A brief survey of the representations of *Aṣṭa-Mahābodhisattva-Maṇḍala* in India and Bangladesh. In: *Journal of Bengal Art* 2: 59-77.

All photographs are by the author.

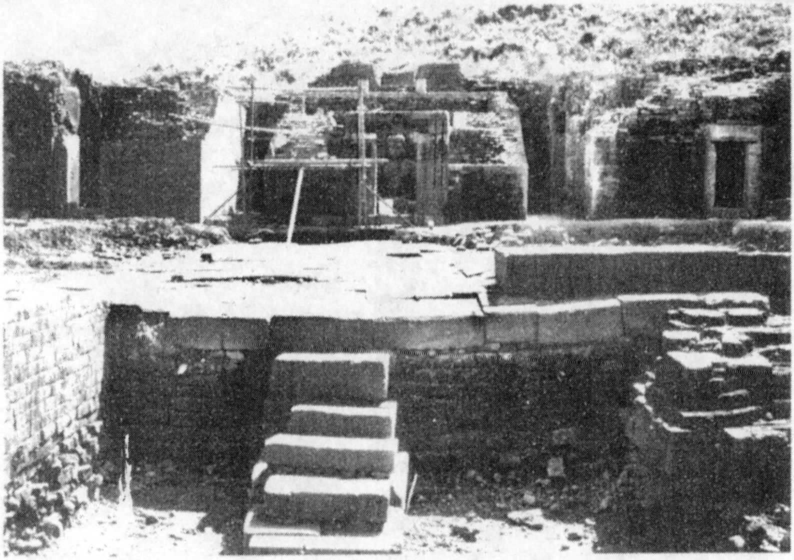

FIGURE 1 Entrance to monastery Udayagiri 2 from north

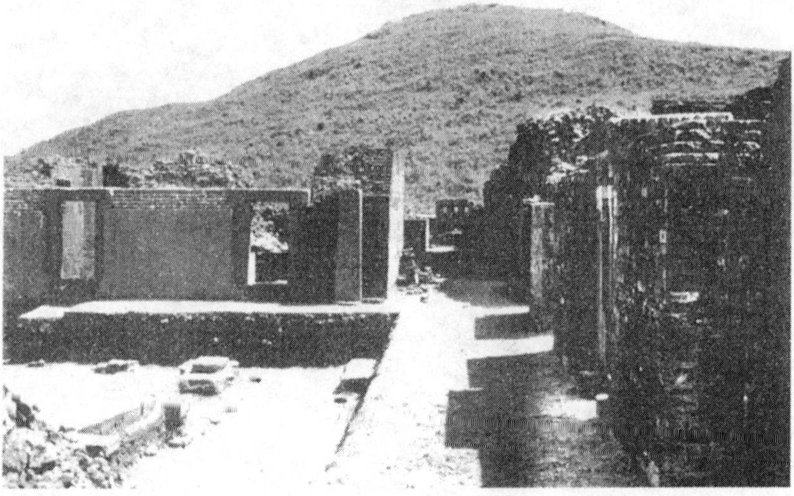

FIGURE 2 Monastery, courtyard, south-east corner

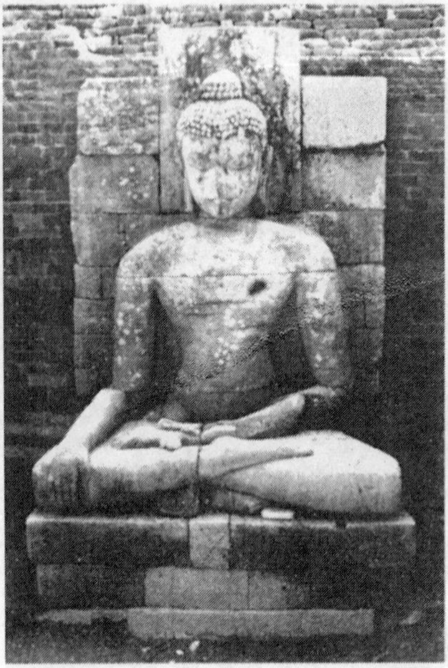

FIGURE 3 Monastery, sanctum: Buddha in bhūsparśamudrā

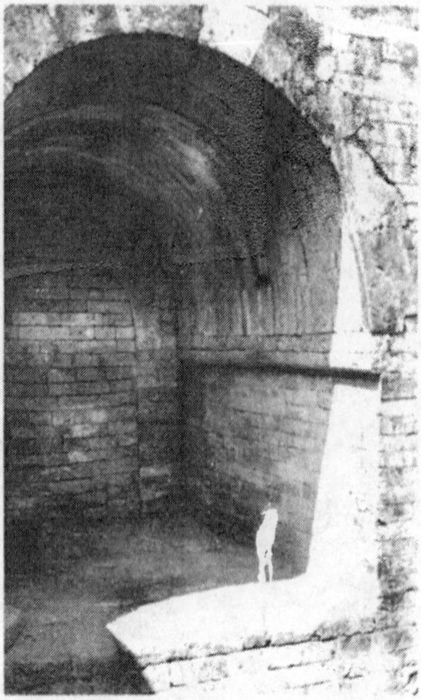

FIGURE 4 Monastery, backside of monk's cell: arched podium and blocked-up window

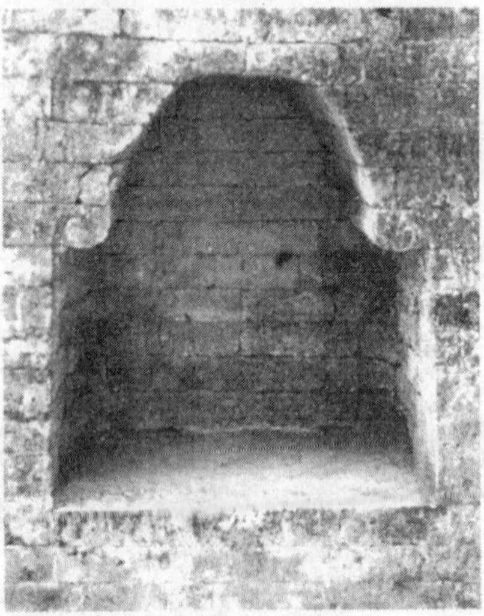

FIGURE 5 Monastery, niche for image (ca. 60 cm high)

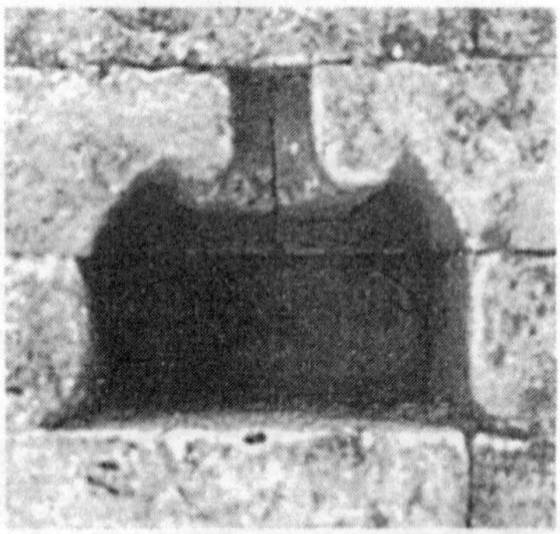

FIGURE 6 Monastery, niche for lamp (ca. 13 cm high)

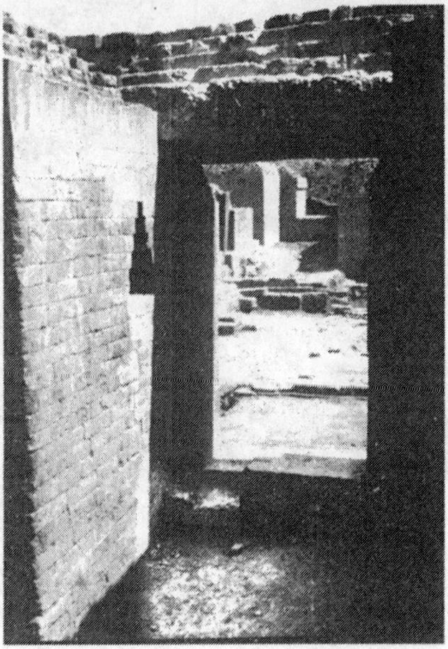

FIGURE 7 Monastery, view from cell to courtyard; left: triangular hole

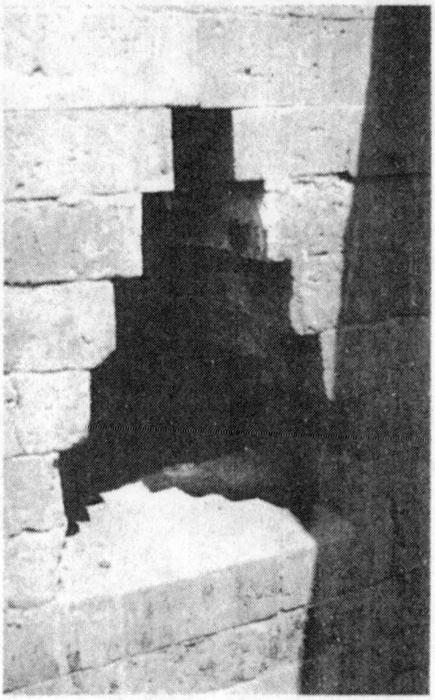

FIGURE 8 Detail of FIG. 7: triangular hole

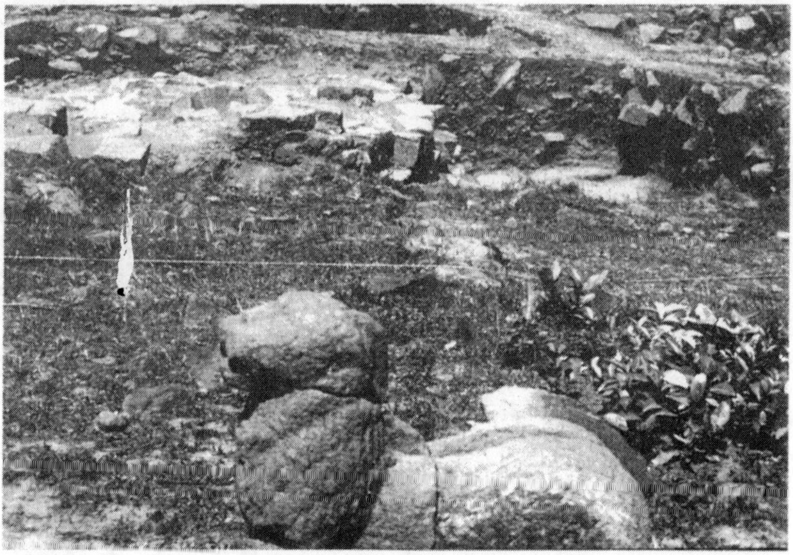

FIGURE 9 Sacred area: full-round lion figure

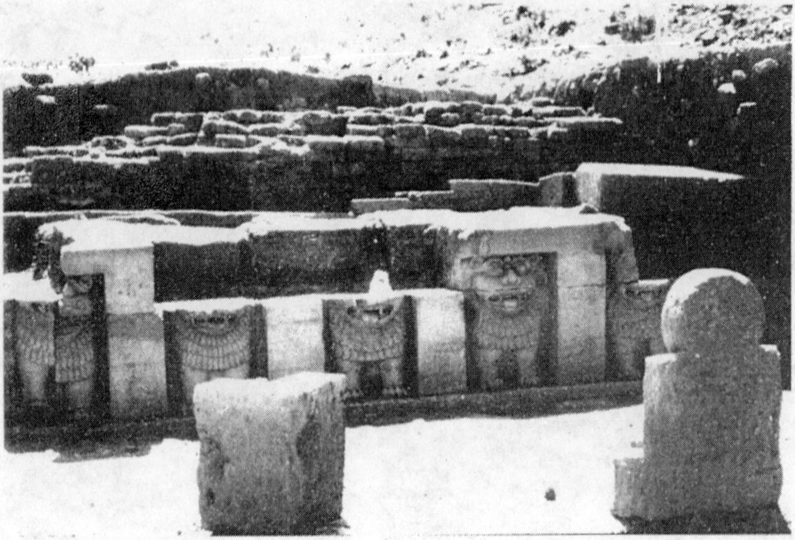

FIGURE 10 Sacred area: podium with lion reliefs

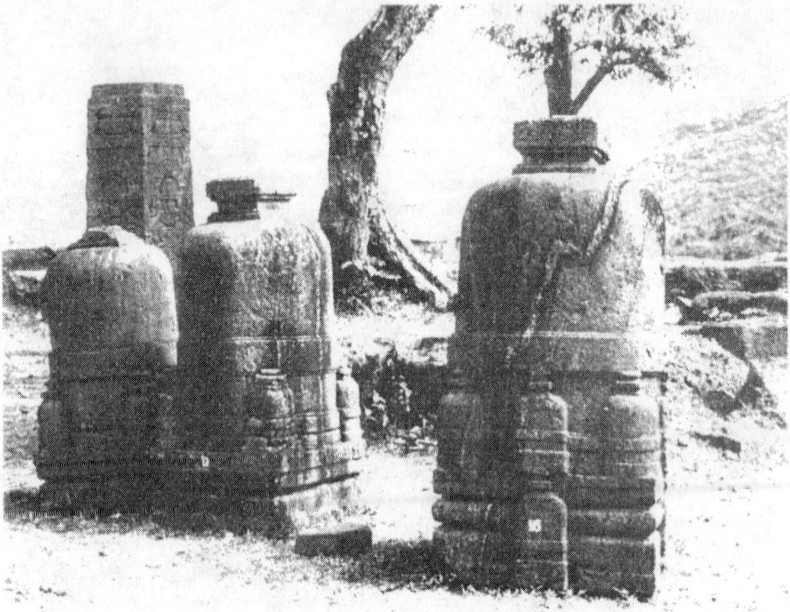

FIGURE 11 Annex to monastery: pañcāyatana-caitya and navāyatana-caitya

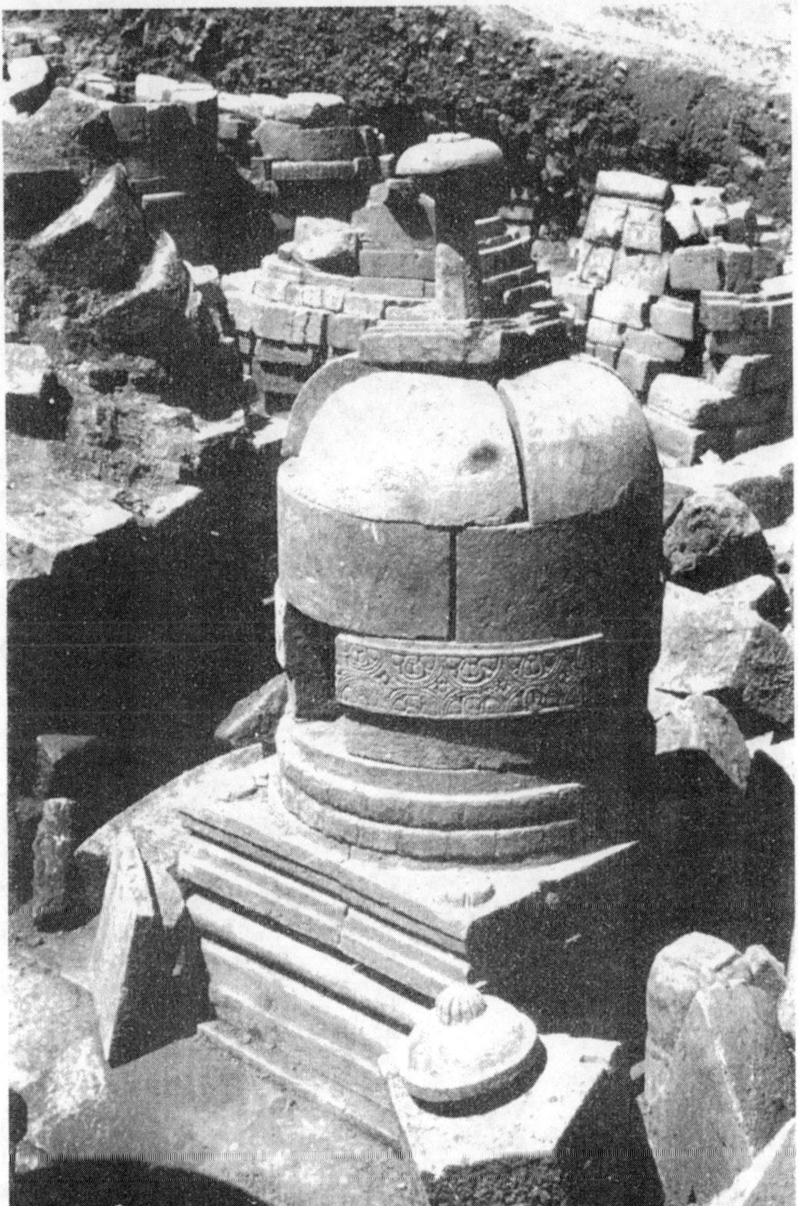

FIGURE 12 Sacred area: caitya with ekachattra finial

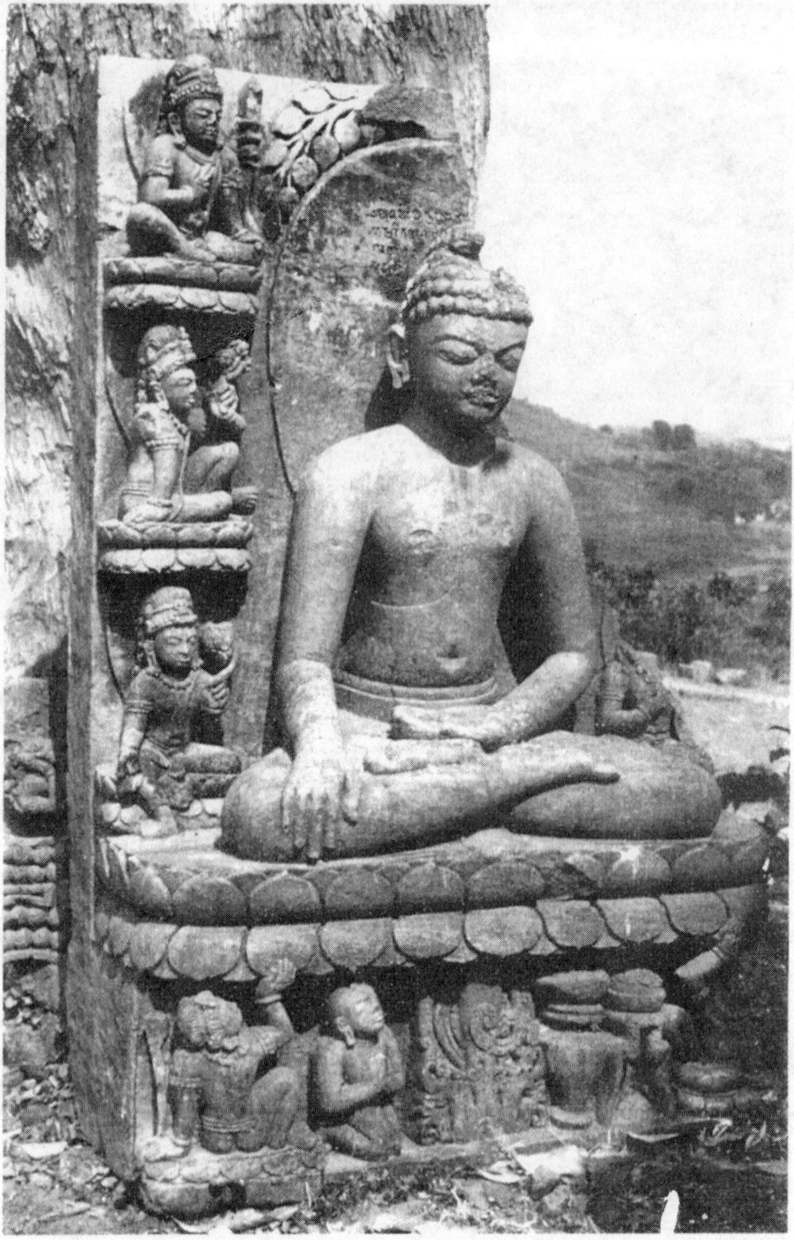

FIGURE 13 Sacred area to the north of monastery: Buddha with eight Bodhisattvas

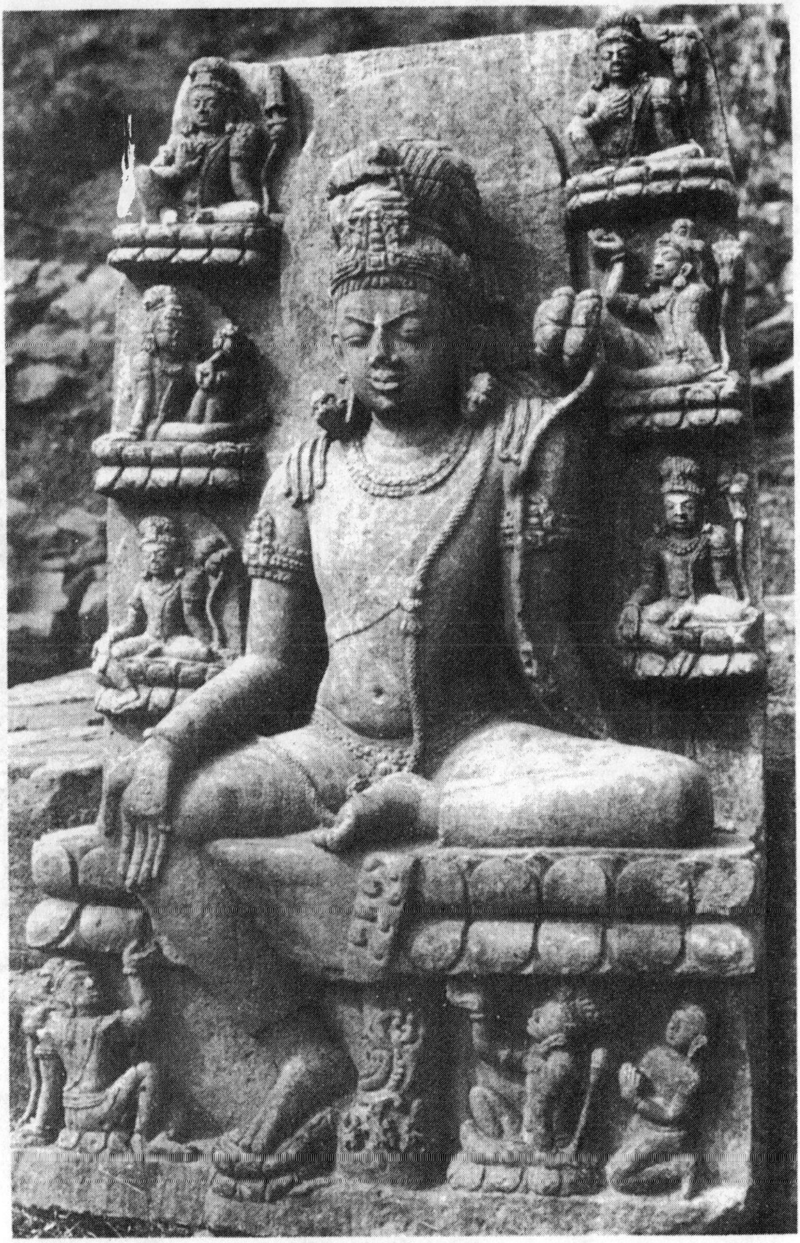

FIGURE 14 Sacred area: Avalokiteśvara with eight Bodhisattvas

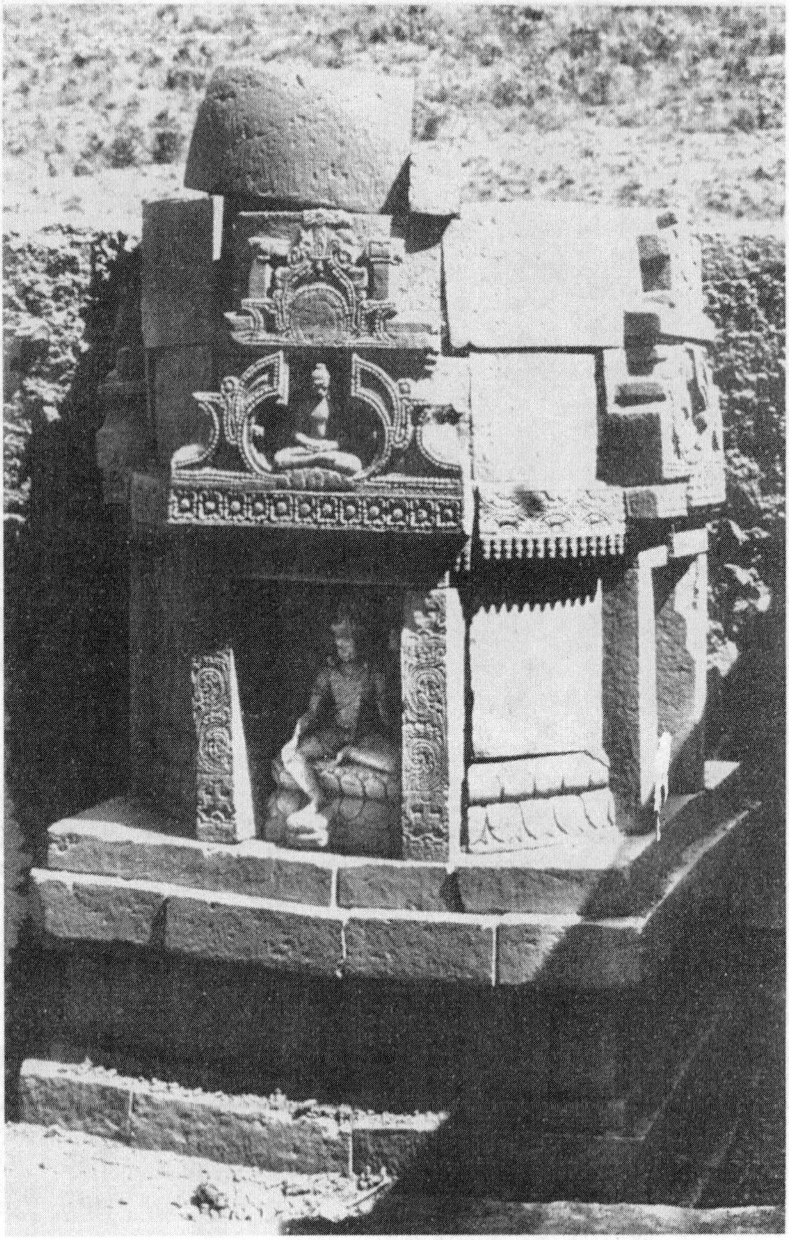

FIGURE 15 Sacred area: caitya with two registers of niches

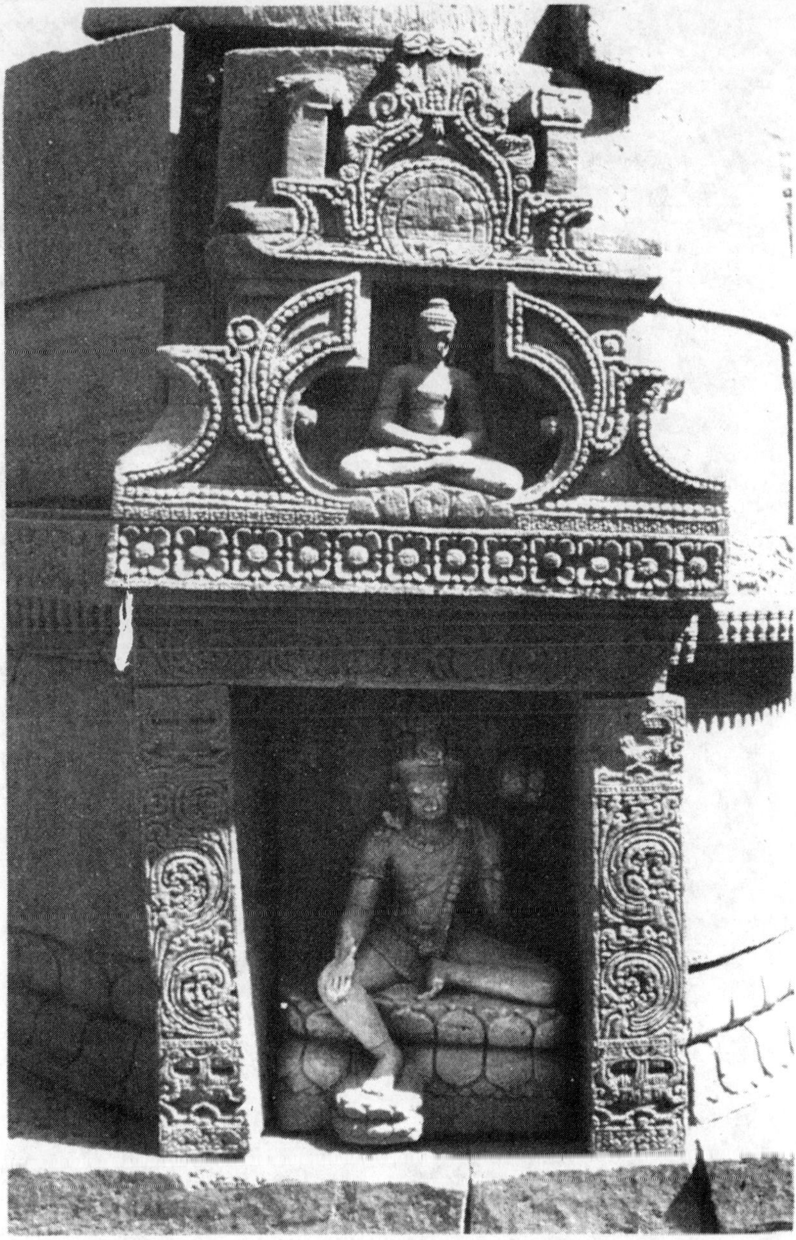

FIGURE 16 Detail of FIG. 15: Amitābha (above) and Avalokiteśvara on west side

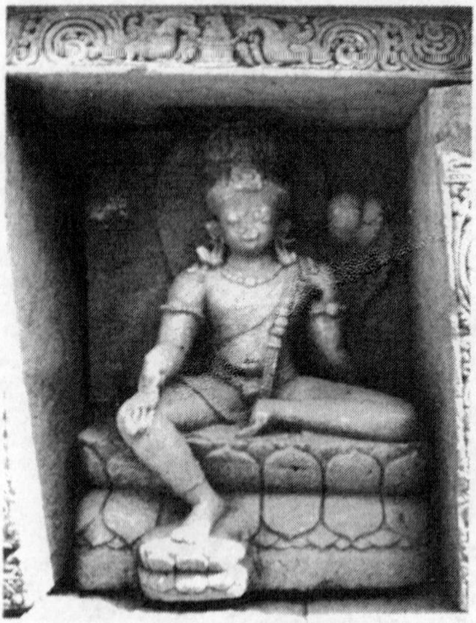

FIGURE 17 Detail of FIG. 16: *Avalokiteśvara in Lokeśvara form*

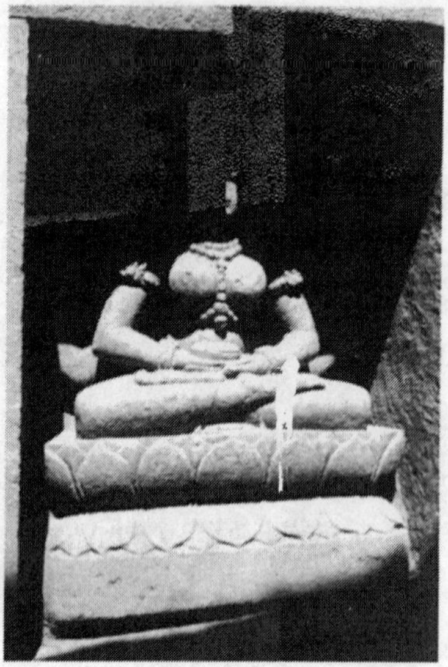

FIGURE 18 Detail of FIG. 15: *four-armed Cundā on south side*

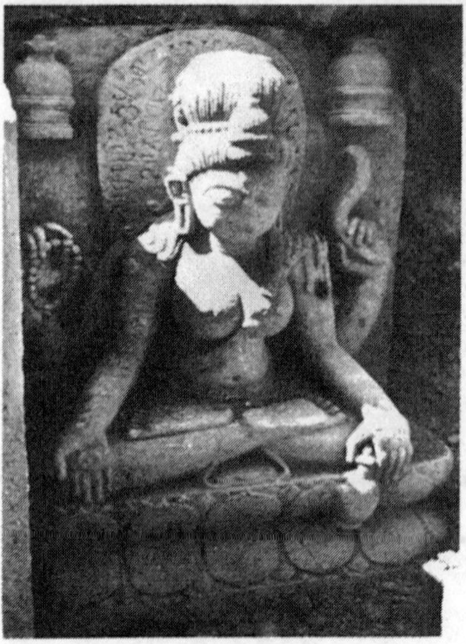

FIGURE 19 Detail of FIG. 15: *four-armed Bhṛkuṭī on east side*

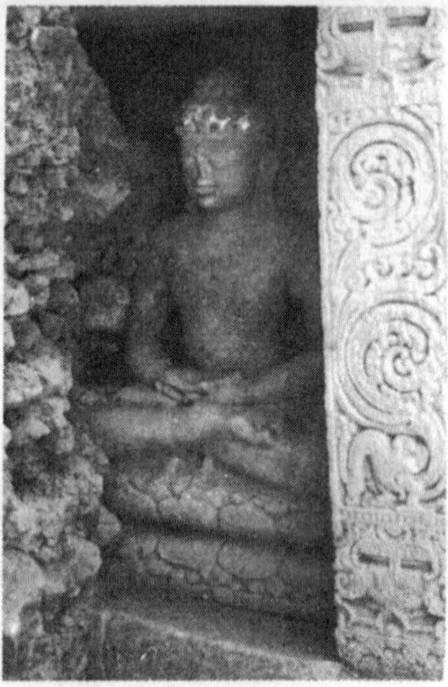

FIGURE 20 Detail of FIG. 15: *Samādhi-Buddha on north side*

Erotic Forms of Gaṇeśa in Hindu and Buddhist Iconography*

GUDRUN BÜHNEMANN

Like that of no other deity, the iconography of Gaṇapati/Gaṇeśa is extremely varied. In addition to different forms of one-headed multi-armed icons, various multi-headed and multi-armed representations of the deity are described in texts and represented in Indian art. Groups of Gaṇeśas, including 16 or 32 figures, are also found. Outside India the deity is represented in Central, Southeast and East Asia in a variety of styles. While Purāṇic texts describe mostly a one-headed four-armed Gaṇeśa and emphasize the deity's role as a remover of obstacles and ensurer of auspicious beginnings (a notion still popular in South Asia), in Hindu Tantric texts and icons a different aspect of Gaṇeśa is more prominent. Gaṇeśa appears in the company of a consort (*śakti*), with whom he attempts intercourse. This erotic aspect of the deity manifests itself in various ways in icons, whether those of the Hindu Tantric Gaṇeśa from India and Nepal or in Buddhist forms of the god from Tibet and East Asia. This paper explores the lesser known erotic icons of the deity in Tantric texts and art, and inquires into their significance.

---

* An earlier version of this article was presented as a lecture at the 12th World Sanskrit Conference, Helsinki, on July 17, 2003. Conference support was provided by the Graduate School Research Committee of the University of Wisconsin-Madison, using income earned through the efforts of University of Wisconsin-Madison faculty and staff filing successful patents with the Wisconsin Alumni Research Foundation (WARF).

EROTIC FORMS OF THE HINDU GAṆEŚA IN INDIA

Indian sculptures of Gaṇeśa with a consort date from the sixth[1] century onwards. In addition to representations of the deity with his consort seated on his left thigh, one finds South Indian sculptures depicting Gaṇeśa and his consort as fondling each other, such as the three sculptures from Tamilnadu in FIGURES 1-3. This type is also represented in other parts of South Asia, two examples being an 18th-century North Indian miniature painting (PLATE I.A) and a line drawing from Nepal (FIGURE 4). In Indian icons, the use of Gaṇeśa's trunk in sexual activity is noteworthy. It is not only attested in Tantric texts and in iconography but also referred to in at least one later literary work.[2] This iconographic type of Gaṇeśa and his consort touching each other's sex organs is often classified by art historians as Ucchiṣṭagaṇapati ("Gaṇeśa [fond] of the polluted"). Textual support can be found in descriptions in the 10th/11th-century Śāradātilakatantra,[3] which are most likely based on unidentified older sources and have influenced a number of later texts. Depending on the attributes the deity holds and on the mantra with which he is identified, the Śāradātilaka classifies this iconographic type as Śakti-Gaṇapati, Bhogātilola-Gaṇapati ("Gaṇapati extremely eager for sexual enjoyment") or Viri-Gaṇapati ("Gaṇapati [whose mantra is] connected with [the word] *viri*"). Tantric texts such as the 16th-century Mantramahodadhi[4] describe the deity as actually engaging in intercourse

---

[1] See Getty 1936: 27.

[2] An incomplete Telugu poem in 61 stanzas titled Gaṇapatīyamu, attributed to "an old poet" and ascribed to the Skanda-Purāṇa, describes Gaṇapati as having sexual intercourse with his mother Pārvatī using his trunk. This composition, which may possibly be based on an older manuscript, was published in Pondicherry as a fascicle in the series Kāmagranthamālā. Publisher and publication date are not indicated. I thank Prof. V. Narayana Rao of the University of Wisconsin-Madison for this information and for showing me a copy of the text.

[3] See Lakṣmaṇadeśika's Śāradātilaka 13.70 (Viri-Gaṇapati), 13.79 (Śakti-Gaṇapati) and 13.86 (Bhogātilola-Gaṇapati) (= Bühnemann 2000-2001, 2: 230-233). Rao 1914-1916, 1: 54 refers to a similar description from the Uttarakāmikāgama.

[4] Mantramahodadhi 2.61 (see Bühnemann 2000-2001, 1: 84-85).

with his naked consort. The Mantramahodadhi refers to this form of the deity as Ucchiṣṭagaṇapati. To date no such representation of the deity in art has been found.

Although sexual motifs, portrayals of erotic figures and copulation of human couples are commonly found in various parts of temples all over India and Nepal, explicitly erotic portrayals of deities like this are rare in Hindu Tantric traditions and remind one vaguely of the Buddhist *yab-yum* icons, in spite of the differences. One wonders why Gaṇeśa is represented in this way and whether this could possibly be due to some Buddhist influence.

EROTIC FORMS OF THE BUDDHIST GAṆAPATI IN THE INDO-TIBETAN AND TIBETAN TRADITIONS

Let us now look at representations of the Buddhist Gaṇeśa in the Indo-Tibetan tradition for comparison's sake. Some Tibetan *sādhana* texts portray Gaṇapati as engaging in oral sex, and that with an animal-faced goddess. The oldest two *sādhana* texts, preserved in the Tibetan canon as translations of lost Sanskrit texts,[5] identify this iconographic type as Ājñāvinivarta-Gaṇapati (Rāgavajra).[6] Both are associated with the name of Dīpaṃkaraśrījñāna/Atiśa (who flourished in the 11th century) as the translator or compiler.[7] This Gaṇapati is also described in the Rin-lhan (vol. 2, fol. 369,5-373,3) of the Fourth Panchen Lama (1781-1854),[8] and

[5] The two *sādhanas* are: 1) Śrī-ajñāvinivartagaṇapatisādhana (P 4563; D 3741; omitted in Narthang) written by Indrabodhi and translated by Dīpaṃkaraśrījñāna (Atiśa) and rGya brTson 'grus Seṅ ge; and 2) Āryagaṇapatirāgavajrasamayastotra (P 4561; D 3739; omitted in Narthang) written by Dīpaṃkaraśrījñāna (Atiśa) and translated by him in collaboration with Tshul khrims rGyal ba.

[6] The significance of the name, which can be translated as "authority-averting Gaṇapati" (Willson & Brauen 2000: 334), is unclear.

[7] In Bühnemann 1994 I have dealt with Ājñāvinivarta-Gaṇapati in more detail and have discussed textual sources. The two *sādhana* texts are translated in Wilkinson 1991: 256-258, 265-266. These translations, however, need some revision.

[8] The Rin-lhan is based on Tāranātha's 17th-century Rin-byuṅ brgya-rtsa. The deity's *sādhana* according to the Rin-lhan is summarized in Willson & Brauen 2000: 334.

based on the Rin-lhan's description, the deity was illustrated in the 19th-century set of miniature paintings of Tibetan Buddhist deities titled Bris-sku mthoṅ-ba don-ldan (no. 334), now in the Völkerkundemuseum of Zürich University (PLATE I.B).[9]

According to the *sādhanas*, the deity has three heads. The central head is that of an elephant, the other two being one of a cat (in PLATE I.B, a pig) and one of a monkey. His six hands hold the pairs of attributes: the (Japanese) radish and sweetmeat ball (*laḍḍu*), the jewel and the skull vessel filled with liquor, and the axe and sword. The deity has four legs. The first pair is in a standing position, with one leg stretched out and the other retracted. The other pair of legs is in a crossed-legged posture (*paryaṅka*). This Gaṇapati is supported by a goddess with a monkey's head (in PLATE I.B, by a monkey) who performs fellatio on the deity.

The deity is further represented in a Himalayan bronze (FIGURE 5) which has been assigned to the 15th or 17th century.[10] A seated female with possibly a monkey's head performs fellatio on Gaṇeśa. His central head is an elephant's and his left head is a monkey's, while his right head may be a cat's or rat's head. Other representations of this type include a 19th-century Tibetan painting in the Nyingma tradition ascribed to the Karma Gardri Painting School (PLATE II),[11] although some details vary from earlier representations described above. The deity has only one head, two legs and four (not six) arms. His four arms hold a plate of sweetmeats, an elephant goad, a (Japanese) radish and a rosary. He stands with legs apart, his heels supported by the hands of a dark cat-headed

---

[9] See Willson & Brauen 2000: 143. For different wood-block editions and block-print sets of this collection, see Willson & Brauen 2000: 7-11 (introduction), 425-426 (bibliography), 431ff. (concordances).

[10] The bronze was first published by Mookerjee 1985, no. 107, who assigned it to the 17th century and to Nepal. Mookerjee describes it as "Gaṇeśa ... combined with Hanumān the monkey-god and the boar incarnation of Vishṇu." The same bronze was recently reproduced in Sotheby's catalogue, Indian & Southeast Asian Art (New York, Thursday, March 21, 2002), no. 140, where it is identified as a c. 15th-century Tibetan statue of Ājñāvinivarta-Gaṇapati.

[11] Also published in Mullin & Watt 2003: 193.

female who performs fellatio on him. Her menstrual blood is being collected in a skull vessel by two kneeling females who support the cat-headed female. Gaṇapati is surrounded by four naked menstruating attendants. This representation of Gaṇeśa is remarkable because no other deity in the Buddhist pantheon seems to be represented undergoing fellatio. The three animal heads clearly indicate a syncretistic form. The significance of the cat's head is not quite clear, whereas the deity's association with monkeys is quite common. Monkeys are featured in several of his *sādhanas*.[12] Gaṇeśa's mantra specifies the acquisition of jewels (*ratna*) and wealth as the objectives for which he is worshipped and allows us to place the image in the tradition of Tibetan wealth-granting icons.

A later post-canonical 19th-century Tibetan painting of Gaṇapati portrays the deity in a state of sexual excitement with an erect penis and wide-open eyes. He is again shown in the company of a monkey (PLATE III), but this time the monkey, who presents him with a (Japanese) radish, has assumed the role of his female consort on the left side of Gaṇapati's lap. We get the impression that Gaṇapati is about to engage in sexual intercourse with the consort. The deity holds an elephant goad topped by a double *vajra* (right) and a noose (left). A vase couched in his right arm showers wish-granting jewels and other precious objects.

EROTIC FORMS OF THE BUDDHIST GAṆAPATI IN JAPAN

Buddhist forms of Gaṇapati worshipped in Japan include a different form of the erotic Gaṇapati. The dual icon of Gaṇapati (FIGURE 6) called Kangiten/Nandikeśvara ("God of Bliss") consists of a male and a female figure, both with elephant heads. The dual icon continues to be on sale today in the shops around Hōzanji Temple on Mt. Ikoma (near Nara) in Japan and is worshipped by members of the business community. Rice wine (*sake*), radishes and the so-called "bliss buns" (*kangi-dan*), the equivalent of the Indian *moduka* sweetmeats, are

[12] For more information, see Bühnemann 1994: 209.

offered during the ritual. The icon is kept under a cover in the form of a phallus, known as the *liṅga-koṣa*, when not receiving worship.[13]

CONCLUDING REMARKS

The Tantric forms of Gaṇeśa discussed here are esoteric and therefore less familiar to the public. They reveal the sexual aspect of the deity in a way unknown in the iconography of other deities. The Hindu Tantric texts describe the deity either as attempting or engaging in intercourse with his female consort. Such representations of deities are unusual in Hindu Tantric traditions, although they are quite common in Indian Buddhist Tantric sources. Like the Hindu Tantric representations, the Tibetan representations of Gaṇeśa included in this article (which are partially based on Indian Buddhist *sādhana* texts) are also unusual, since in the Tibetan Buddhist tradition no other deity seems to be depicted undergoing fellatio, and that from an animal-headed goddess. The Japanese dual icon of Gaṇeśa is unique as well. Its iconographic development is still unclear. Sanford 1991: 314-315 traces it back to four-legged icons of Gaṇeśa and to Indian icons of "Ucchiṣṭagaṇapati", but this is not likely because the iconography is too different. The Tibetan and Japanese representations of Gaṇeśa introduced here do not derive from the known Hindu Tantric forms but from separate iconographic traditions. But although they have each their own peculiar features, they all emphasize the erotic aspect of the deity.

How are we to explain that it is specifically Gaṇeśa who is portrayed in this way? One may think of Gaṇeśa's origin as a Yakṣa and thus his association with the concept of fertility. However, the fertility concept does not account for the representations of Gaṇeśa undergoing fellatio, that is, sexual activity for pleasure and not procreation. The Tantric traditions apparently portray Gaṇeśa as an enjoyer (*bhogin*) of worldly pleasures, including sexual ones, and emphasize his elephant nature. Obviously, Gaṇeśa's head evokes the image of an uncontrolled elephant

---

[13] See Sanford 1991 and Strickmann 1996: 265-266 for more details.

in rut often described in literature, namely the image of the elephant as a prototype of virility. Another factor contributing to the development of the erotic representations of the deity may be that Gaṇeśa is the (adopted) son of Śiva, who is commonly represented by the *liṅga*. As Strickmann 1996: 266 notes, it would then be natural for Gaṇeśa to manifest the virility of his father. Finally, one may also recall Gaṇeśa's origin as a *vināyaka*, a wild and evil demon. These factors may explain why there was less inhibition in depicting erotic aspects of the deity.

REFERENCES

BAKSHI, D.N. *Hindu Divinities in Japanese Buddhist Pantheon. A Comparative Study*. Calcutta: Benten Publishers.

BÜHNEMANN, G. 1989. *Forms of Gaṇeśa: A Study based on the Vidyārṇavatantra*. Wichtrach: Institut für Indologie.

—— 1994. Two Forms of Gaṇapati in the Indo-Tibetan Buddhist Tradition. *Wiener Zeitschrift für die Kunde Südasiens* 8: 201-211.

—— 1995. Aspects of Tantric Ganesh in India. In: P. Pal (ed.), *Ganesh, the benevolent*: 27-40. Bombay: Marg Publications. Second impression, 2001.

—— 2000-2001. *The Iconography of Hindu Tantric Deities*. 2 vols. Groningen: Egbert Forsten.

D = *The Nyingma Edition of the sDe-dge bka'-'gyur and bsTan-'gyur, sponsored by the Head Lama of the Tibetan Nyingmapa Meditation Center, published by Dharma Maudraṇālaya under the direction of Tarthang Tulku*. Vols. 117 and 118. Oakland, California: Dharma Press, 1981-1982.

GETTY, A. 1936. *Gaṇeśa: A Monograph of the Elephant-faced God*. Oxford: Clarendon Press.

MOOKERJEE, A. 1985. *Ritual Art of India*. New York: Thames and Hudson.

MULLIN, G.H. with J.J. WATT 2003. *Female Buddhas: Women of Enlightenment in Tibetan Mystical Art. Art from the Collection of the Shelley & Donald Rubin Foundation*. Santa Fe, New Mexico: Clear Light Publishers.

NAGEL 2005. *Nagel Auktionen. 30. Spezialauktion Asiatische Kunst (30 A), Vol. IV/IV (Fine Asian Art)*. 16.11.2005, 9.00 am. Stuttgart: Nagel.

P = *The Tibetan Tripiṭaka: Peking Edition*, reprinted under the Supervision of the Otani University, Kyoto, edited by D.T. Suzuki. 168 vols. Tokyo/Kyoto, 1955-1961.

Rin-lhan. *Sadhana-Mala of the Panchen Lama Bstan-paḥi-ñi-ma-phyogs-las rnam-rgyal entitled Yi-dam-rgya-mtshoḥi sgrub-thabs rin-chen-ḥbyuṅ-gnas-kyi lhan-thabs rin-ḥbyuṅ don gsal*, reproduced by Lokesh Chandra from the Collections of Prof. Raghu Vira. Parts I-II. New Delhi: International Academy of Indian Culture, 1974.

RAO, T.A. Gopinatha 1914-1916. *Elements of Hindu Iconography*. 2 ols. in 4 parts. Madras: Law Printing House.

SANFORD, J.H. 1991. Literary Aspects of Japan's Dual-Gaṇeśa Cult. In: R.L. Brown (ed.), *Ganesh: Studies of an Asian God*: 287-335. Albany, New York.

STRICKMANN, M. 1996. *Mantras et mandarins: Le bouddhisme tantrique en Chine*. Paris: Gallimard.

WILKINSON, Ch. 1991. The Tantric Gaṇeśa: Texts Preserved in the Tibetan Canon. In: R.L. Brown (ed.), *Ganesh: Studies of an Asian God*: 235-275. Albany, New York.

WILLSON, M. & M. BRAUEN (eds.) 2000. *Deities of Tibetan Buddhism*. The Zürich Paintings of the *Icons Worthwhile to See* (Bris sku mthoṅ ba don ldan). Boston: Wisdom Publications.

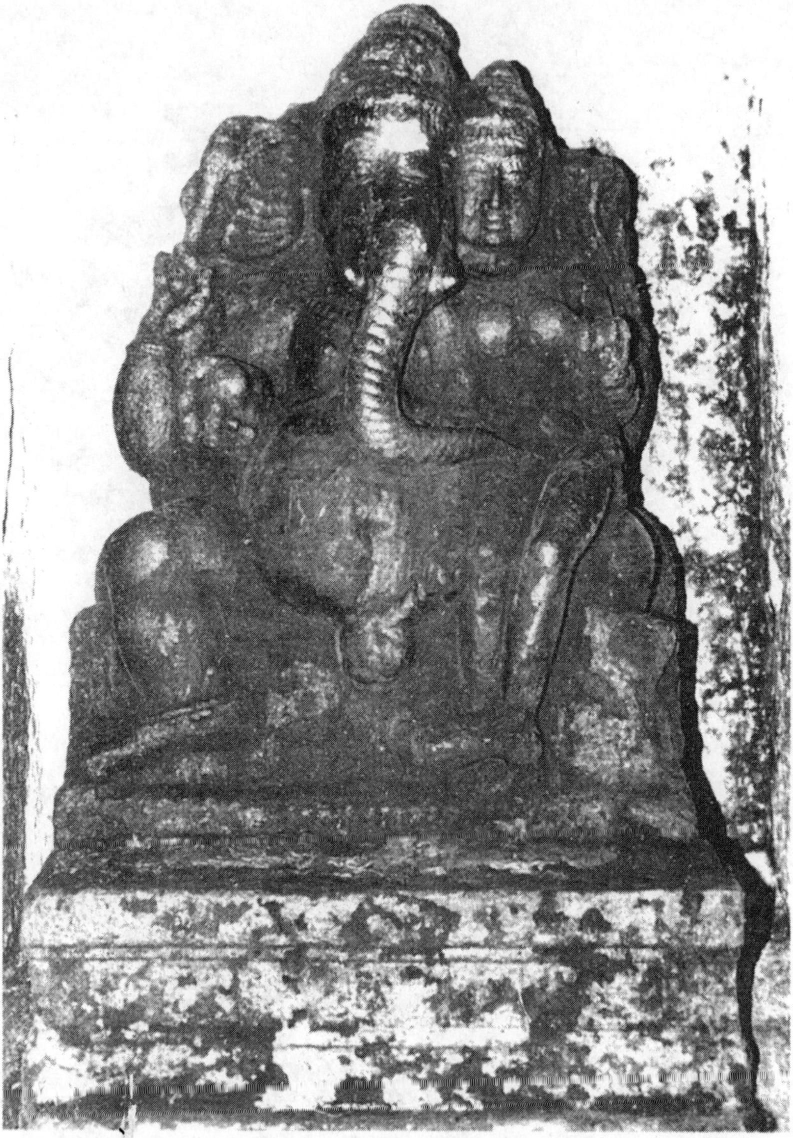

FIGURE 1 *Ucchiṣṭagaṇeśa, sculpture from the Nāgeśvarasvāmin Temple, Kumbhakonam; photograph by the author*

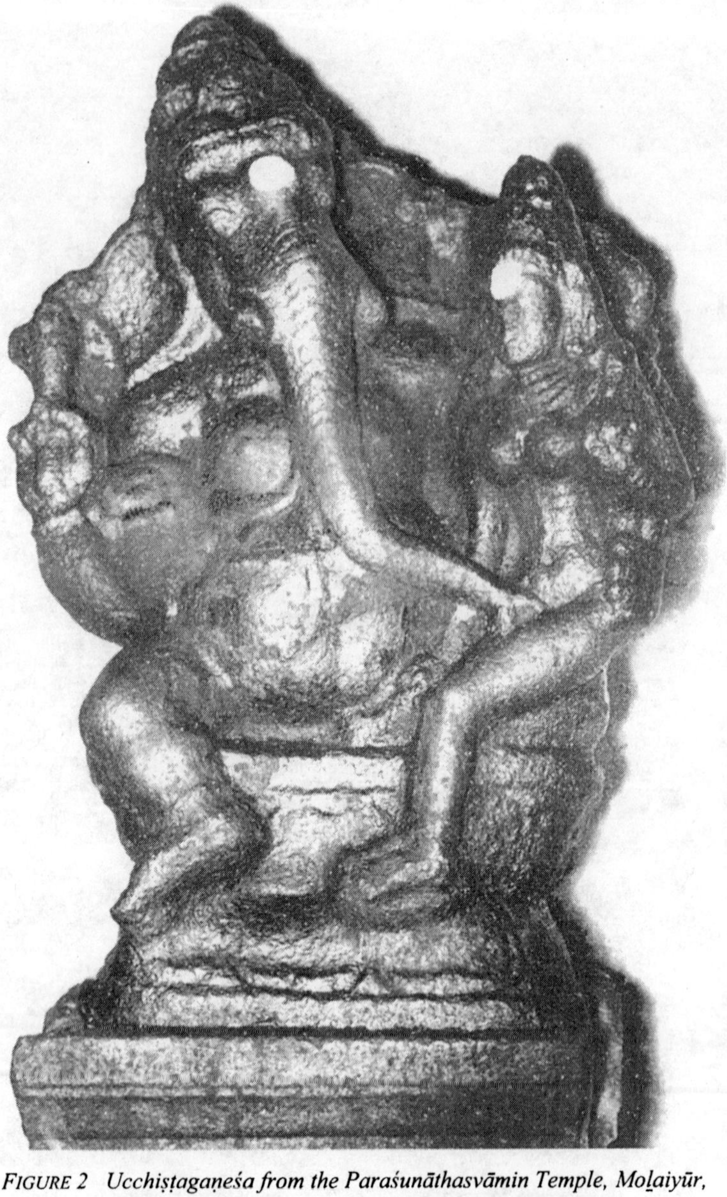

FIGURE 2 Ucchiṣṭagaṇeśa from the Paraśunāthasvāmin Temple, Moḻaiyūr, Tanjāvūr district; photo courtesy of the Institut Français de Pondichéry/École Française d'Extrême-Orient

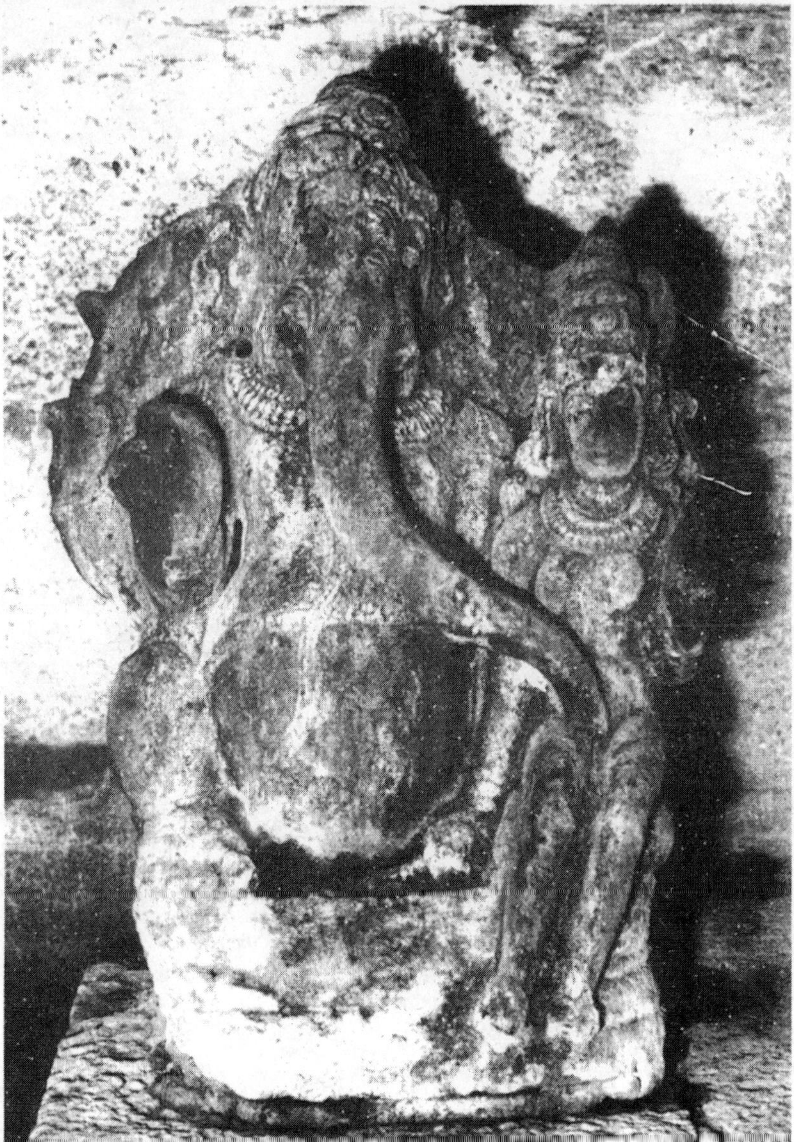

FIGURE 3 Ucchiṣṭagaṇapati from the Tirumūlanāthasvāmin Temple, Tirumūlasthānam, South Arcot district; photo courtesy of the Institut Français de Pondichéry/École Française d'Extrême-Orient

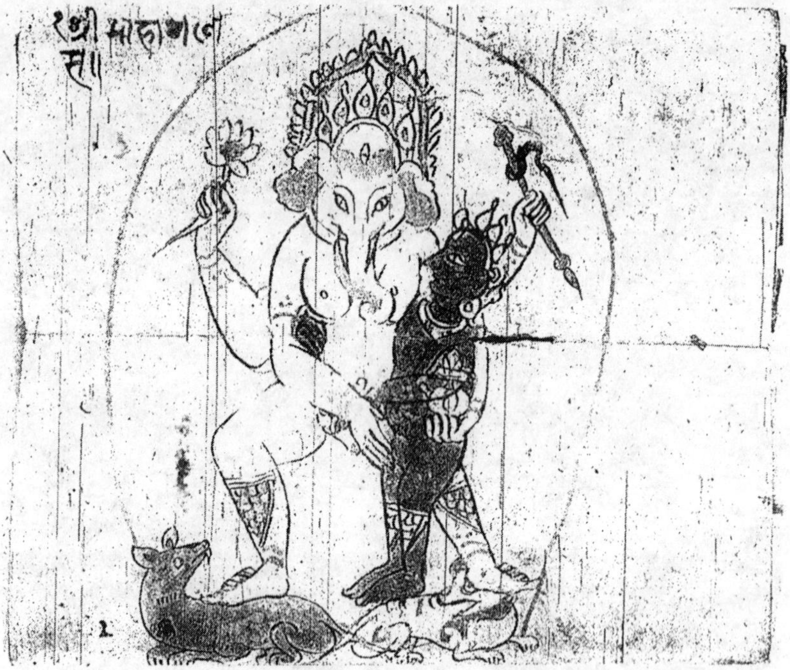

FIGURE 4 Nepalese line drawing from a manuscript titled Kāmakalācitra; reproduced from a manuscript microfilmed by the Nepal-German Manuscript Preservation Project, reel no. G38/13, running no. 776

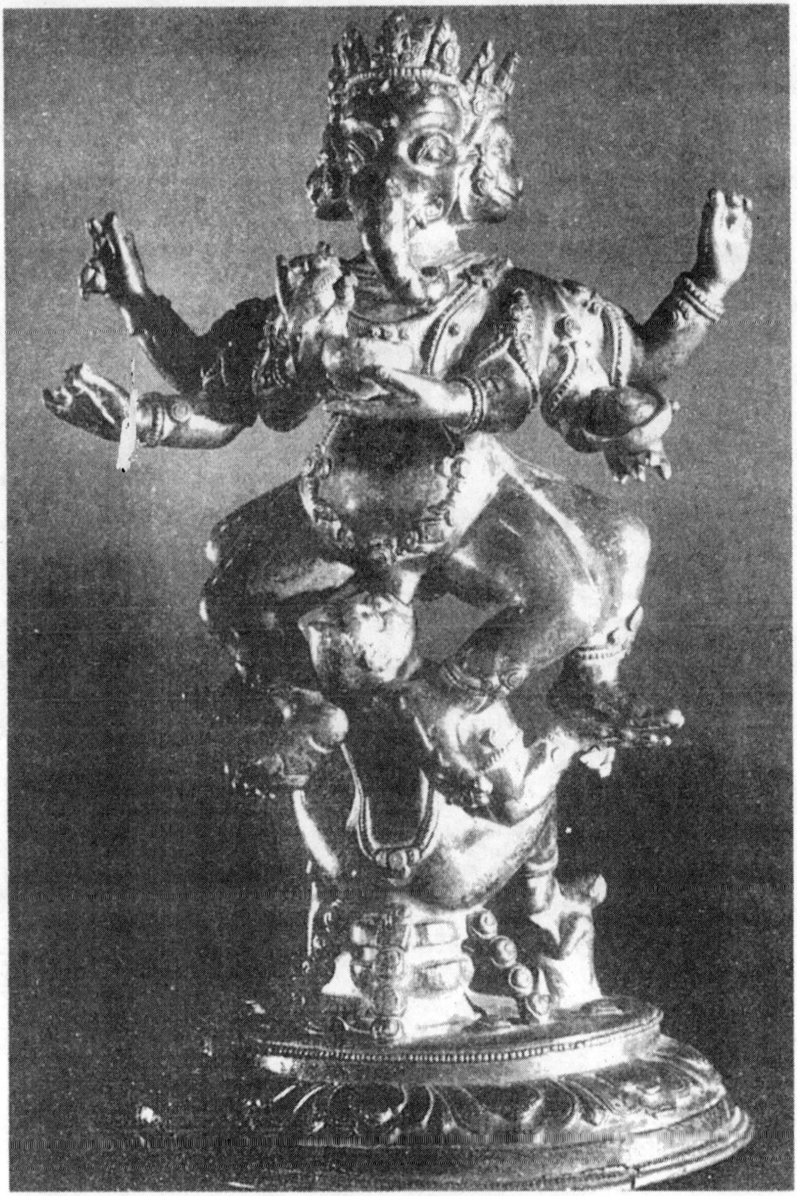

FIGURE 5 Bronze of Ājñāvinivarta-Gaṇapati; reproduced from Mookerjee 1985, no. 107

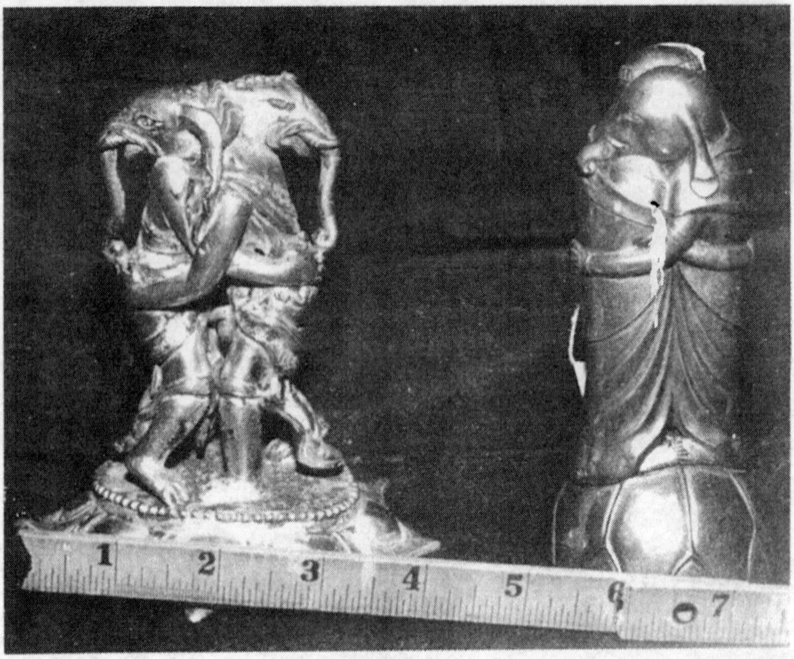

FIGURE 6 Dual forms of Gaṇeśa, Kangiten; antique shop, Kyoto, Japan; photograph by the author. For similar wooden sculptures from the Hōzanji Temple, see Bakshi 1979, plates XXXVIII.3, XXXIX.2-3, XL.1, XLI.1. For a similar bronze image from Japan, formerly in a Scandinavian private collection, see Nagel 2005: 180, no. 3335.

Tantric Deities in an Illustrated Dhāraṇī Manuscript from Nepal*

GUDRUN BÜHNEMANN

1. GENERAL REMARKS ON THE MANUSCRIPT

Of the extant corpus of *dhāraṇī* texts only a small portion has been critically edited. This less frequently studied genre of literature is closely connected with popular religious practice, as shown, for example, in the study by Reis-Habito (1993), which explores popular beliefs, functions and practices associated with the *dhāraṇī* of the thousand-armed Avalokiteśvara in China. In this article I wish to contribute to the study of illuminated *dhāraṇī* manuscripts from Nepal by providing a description, iconographic analysis and reproduction of the miniature paintings in an unpublished illustrated manuscript. In this connection special attention is given to the deities associated with the seven days (*saptavāra*) of the week, including Gaṇapatihṛdaya.

While I was going through an extensive list of manuscripts kept in storage at the N.C. Mehta Gallery of the Gujarat Museum Society on the campus of the L.D. Institute of Indology in Ahmedabad, one manuscript, numbered 258, caught my attention. It is described as an unidentified 18th-century Nepalese Buddhist manuscript with yellow letters on blue paper. For security reasons, the curator of the collection was not

* I would like to thank the Gujarat Museum Society – N.C. Mehta Gallery for granting permission to reproduce the extant folios of the manuscript. I am indebted to G.J.R. Mevissen, M.A., for valuable suggestions, to M. Kropf for providing some reference material and to P. Pierce, M.A., for editing this article for English style.

allowed to open the storage and show the manuscript to me. In this article I therefore base my description of it on colour photographs and information provided by the curator, Amitabh Madia.

The manuscript consists of 14 folios of text in Rañjanā characters, each containing one miniature painting. The backsides of the extant folios are blank. Of the paintings, 13 depict individual deities of the Buddhist pantheon, and one miniature features a *caitya*. An analysis of the Sanskrit text shows that the manuscript consists of several individual texts expounding mantras. Some mantras are specified as *dhāraṇīs*, others as *vidyārājñīs* or *mahāvidyās*, while others are termed heart (*hṛdaya*) mantras. Fragments of a hymn, a so-called *dhāraṇīstotra* with a litany of 108 names of the goddess Vasudhārā, are also included. The mantras were deified, the corresponding visual forms being represented in the miniature paintings of this manuscript.

The numbering of the folios indicates that the manuscript is incomplete. The first folio is preserved, but there are lacunae in the middle and at the end. It is likely that only the folios with miniature paintings have been preserved. The sequence of the extant folios can partly be established with the help of the folio numbers (where available). The unnumbered folios can be placed in proper order with the help of the text inscribed on them. The collection of texts begins with the *dhāraṇīs* of the Pañcarakṣā goddesses in the sequence commonly found in Nepal. Then follow mantras of a group of seven deities, which appear in other Nepalese manuscripts in almost identical order.[1] Next is a folio with a miniature of Vajravārāhī, which somewhat differs in style from the other paintings. The last extant folio of this incomplete manuscript is likely to be the folio depicting a *caitya*.

[1] See, for example, manuscript 10741, preserved in the Asiatic Society of Bengal, Kolkata, and described in Shāstri 1917: 48-49 (no. 10741); Bendall 1883: 44 (Add. 1315) and 66 (Add. 1356); manuscripts Cod. sanscr. 423 and 511, preserved in the Bayerische Staatsbibliothek, Munich, and described in Grönbold 2001; manuscript 66.13.4, preserved in the Watson Collection of Indian Miniatures at the Elvehjem Museum of Art, Madison, Wisconsin, and 'Sanscrit 1814' of the Bibliothèque Nationale, Paris; see also the discussion in Tsukamoto, Matsunaga & Isoda 1989: 67.

2. THE PAÑCARAKṢĀ GODDESSES

Folios 1-5 contain *dhāraṇīs* and miniature paintings of the Pañcarakṣā goddesses. Different iconographic concepts of these goddesses were examined in great detail by G.J.R. Mevissen (1989a, 1989b, 1990-1991/ 1992, 1992, 1998). While the goddesses' complexions in the paintings of this manuscript are in accordance with the description in Sādhanamālā 206 (see Mevissen 1989a: 353), their attributes correspond only roughly to the description in the *sādhana*. There are deviations which do not seem to be found elsewhere, being previously still unrecorded, and so endow this manuscript with special importance. Following a Nepalese tradition, all the Rakṣās ride mounts (*vāhana*). These mounts are described neither in the *sādhanas* of the Sādhanamālā (= SM) nor in Abhayākaragupta's Niṣpannayogāvalī. However, four of them can be shown to have been borrowed from the Tathāgatas who are associated with the Rakṣā goddesses.[2] The Pañcarakṣā goddesses (in the reconstructed sequence of the manuscript), their complexions, mounts and Tathāgatas are:

RAKṢĀ GODDESS	COLOUR	MOUNT	TATHĀGATA
1) Mahāpratisarā	white	lion	Vairocana
2) Mahāsāhasrapramardanī	blue	man[3]	Akṣobhya
3) Mahāmāyūrī	yellow	horse	Ratnasaṃbhava
4) Mahāśītavatī	green	Garuḍa	Amoghasiddhi
5) Mahāmantrānusāriṇī	red	peacock	Amitābha

[2] See D.C. Bhattacharyya 1972: 88 and Mevissen 1989a: 359-360.

[3] As Mevissen 1989a: 360 notes, Mahāsāhasrapramardanī is the only Rakṣā goddess who does not borrow the mount of her respective Tathāgata: Akṣobhya rides an elephant.

3. GENERAL REMARKS ON THE SAPTAVĀRA DEITIES

Next follow the mantras and miniature paintings of a group of seven deities. Based on the sequence of the texts in the manuscript which I established they are:

1) Vasudhārā
2) Vajravidāriṇī
3) Gaṇapati(hṛdaya)
4) Uṣṇīṣavijayā
5) Mārīcī
6) Parṇaśavarī
7) Grahamātṛkā

This group is known from *dhāraṇī* collections[4] and is represented on wooden struts in Chuṣya Bāhā, also called Guṇākara(mahā)vihāra, Kathmandu, as Kooij 1977: 60-66 documented.[5] Kooij also mentions the presence of the group in a monastery called 'Chun-Bāhā' in Kathmandu. He probably means Khuñ Bāhā, also known as Pinchẽ Bāhā, Manijū Bāhā or Jāmbūnadavana Vihāra in Wotu Tole, Kathmandu,[6] where the deities are carved on wooden struts. The group of seven mantra deities is referred to as Saptavāra in some manuscripts. Two Saptavāra manuscripts (Cod. sanscr. 423 and 511) from the Bayerische Staatsbibliothek, Munich, were recently described by Grönbold 2001. As the name Saptavāra indicates, these mantra deities became associated with the seven days (*saptavāra*) of the week, so that a specific *dhāraṇī* was recited on a particular weekday. This religious practice is

---

[4] See Tsukamoto, Matsunaga & Isoda 1989: 67 and Grönbold 2001: 369-370 for references to manuscripts in other collections. Saptavāra manuscripts are often catalogued as 'Grahamātṛkādhāraṇī', because the colophon signalling the end of Grahamātṛkā's *dhāraṇī* appears at the very end of the seven mantra texts. An example is the manuscript catalogued as Sacitra-Grahamātṛkāstotradhāraṇī (= Nepal-German Manuscript Preservation Project, reel no. C39/8).

[5] See also Kooij 1978: 26-27 with plates XLV-XLVI. A detailed description of the Bāhā is also found in Bajracharya 2004.

[6] For a description of this *bāhā*, see Locke 1985: 249, no. 47, an also p. 352. Pruscha 1975, volume 2: 51 dates the *bāhā* to 1591 CE.

briefly mentioned in Gellner 1992: 127, who notes that it is now in a state of decline. It seems to be peculiar to Nevār Buddhism (Grönbold 2001: 373), since it is not documented in Indian manuscripts. The practice may have been current already in the 15th century, when the wood carvings of Chuṣya Bāhā are said to have been executed (Kooij 1978: 41). Several Nepalese manuscripts add the names of the days in the margin of the texts,[7] suggesting the following correspondences:

DAY OF THE WEEK	DEITY/MANTRA
Sunday	Vasudhārā (also called Vasundharā in some texts)
Monday	Vajravidāriṇī (also written Vajravidāraṇī)
Tuesday	Gaṇapati/Gaṇapatihṛdaya (also Gaṇapatihṛdayā)
Wednesday	Uṣṇīṣavijayā
Thursday	Parṇaśavarī or Prajñāpāramitā[8]
Friday	Mārīcī
Saturday	Grahamātṛkā

The peculiarity of the Saptavāra group of deities as represented in our manuscript is that Mārīcī and Parṇaśavarī swap positions. Whereas in Chuṣya Bāhā's carvings, in several *dhāraṇī* collections (see Tsukamoto, Matsunaga & Isoda 1989: 67) and in Dharmarāj Bajrācārya 1997/1998 Parṇaśavarī precedes Mārīcī, in our manuscript Parṇaśavarī follows Mārīcī. This unusual order is clearly indicated by the colophon of Mārīcī's *dhāraṇī* being followed by Parṇaśavarī's *dhāraṇī* on the same folio. One would have to examine a large number of Saptavāra manuscripts to determine whether this sequence is just an error or whether it represents a different tradition.

---

[7] See, for example, the manuscripts referred to by Kooij 1977: 61 and Grönbold 2001: 371, and the two manuscripts reprinted in Lokesh Chandra 1981, nos. 249-314 and 316-353.

[8] See Kooij 1977: 63. Dharmarāj Bajrācārya 1997/1998 adds Prajñāpāramitā's *dhāraṇī* as an option.

In addition to the days of the week (which are presided over by seven of the heavenly bodies), the Nevār Buddhist tradition also assigned Buddhist deities to the entire group of nine heavenly bodies, as evident from the following list in Hemrāj Śākya 1991: 8 (I retain the original orthography of the deities' names):

HEAVENLY BODY	DEITY
Āditya	Vasundharā
Soma	Vajravidāriṇī
Maṅgala	Gaṇapati
Budha	Uṣṇīṣavijayā
Bṛhaspati	Dhvajāgrakeyūrī
Śukra	Māricī
Śani	Grahamātṛkā
Rāhu	Parṇaśavarī
Ketu	Pratyaṅgirā

In this list Dhvajāgrakeyūrī is the deity associated with Bṛhaspati/Jupiter and not Parṇaśavarī, as before, which shows that different traditions of connecting Buddhist deities with the heavenly bodies existed.

Let us now take a closer look at the Saptavāra deities. Hodgson 1874 (1972): 19 mentions a text titled Saptavāradhāraṇī,[9] which he describes as "an account of the seven Devís (Buddha Saktis) called Vasundhará, Vajra Vidáriní, Ganapati Hridayá, Ushnisha Vijayá, Parna Savarí, Maríchi, Graha Mátriká, together with their Vija mantras." The unusual term Buddhaśakti[10] shows that Hodgson regarded the deities of the Saptavāra

[9] The information is based on Amṛtānanda's Dharmakośasaṃgraha, fol. 67b.5-7: *saptavāradhāraṇī tantradhāraṇī, vasundharādevī vajravidāriṇīdevī gaṇapatihṛdayādevī uṣṇīṣavijayādevī parṇaśavarīdevī mārīcīdevī grahamātṛkādevī, saptānāṃ devīnāṃ dhāraṇīsaṃgrahatvāt, saptavāradhāraṇīdeva[ṃ]devīvarṇanaṃ vaktā* ....

[10] Padmagiri's Vaṃśāvalī (Hasrat 1970: 17) refers to the consorts of the Tathāgatas, such as Locanā, Māmakī and the others, as Buddhaśaktis. This is understandable, but the term Prajñās of the Tathāgatas would be more appropriate.

group as female. In this Hodgson is followed by many others. Kooij 1977: 60 and 1978: 26, for example, describes the Saptavāra group as consisting of seven goddesses.[11] He thereby takes the inscription Gaṇapati on a strut of Chuṣya Bāhā (Kooij 1977, Fig. 32)[12] as a short form of Gaṇapatihṛdayā. However, this is not necessary or even desirable, since the deity does not exhibit female features. Similarly, the two carvings of Gaṇapati on the struts of Khuñ Bāhā bear no such features. The short fragment of the text of our manuscript corresponds to the text edited by Iwamoto 1937b: 10-12 under the title Gaṇapatihṛdaya.[13] As evident from Iwamoto's edition, the text teaches several mantras referred to as heart mantras of Gaṇapati, which invoke aspects of the deity. There is no reference to a female deity called Gaṇapatihṛdayā. Based on manuscript evidence, Tsukamoto, Matsunaga & Isoda 1989: 67 include the male Gaṇapatihṛdaya among the deities of the Saptavāra group.[14] I therefore assume that actually only six of the seven deities of the group are (or were originally) goddesses. However, the Tantric tradition of associating females with male deities must have led some individuals to associate the seven deities with the heavenly bodies presiding over the weekdays, and this must have led in turn to the creation of a goddess Gaṇapatihṛdayā. The miniature painting in our manuscript, which accompanies the mantra text, shows the regular iconography of a male Gaṇapati, as do

---

[11] Kooij 1977: 61 even considers the possibility that the Saptavāra group was formed on the analogy of another well-known group of seven goddesses, the Brahmanical group of Saptamātṛkās.

[12] The two statues of Gaṇapati in the *bāhā* shown in Fig. 4 (Gaṇapati) and Fig. 32 (supposedly Gaṇapatihṛdayā but inscribed Gaṇapati) are rather similar, as I could verify during a visit to Chuṣya Bāhā in 2003. One of the carvings of Gaṇapati (Kooij's Fig. 4: Gaṇapati) has now been replaced by a new wooden statue.

[13] The Gaṇapatihṛdayadhāraṇī is also listed in Moriguchi 1989: 30 (no. 118) and described with a short extract from the text in Mitra 1882 (1971): 87-88 (no. 816 A).

[14] See also Mitra 1882 (1971). 289-290 (no. D 5), where the following names are listed: Vasundharā, Vajravidāraṇa (sic), Gaṇapatihṛdaya (sic), Ushṇīshavijaya (sic), Marīchī, Parṇaśavarī, Gṛhamātrikā (sic), followed by Dhvajāgrakeyurī (sic), the five Rakṣās and others. In this list the masculine gender is assigned not only to Gaṇapatihṛdaya but erroneously also to Vajravidāraṇī and Uṣṇīṣavijayā.

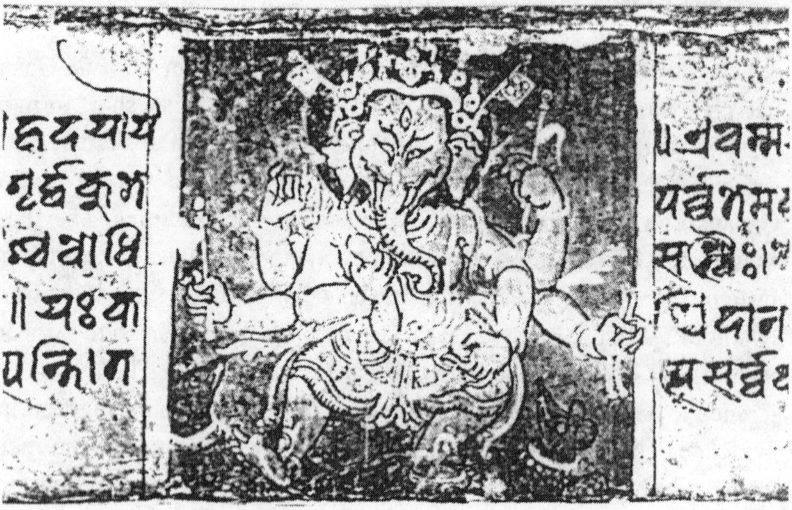

FIGURE 1 *The goddess Gaṇapatihṛdayā; painting in a dhāraṇī manuscript catalogued as Ādityādigrahamātṛkā, dated N.S. 763 = 1642/43 CE; National Archives, Kathmandu, acc.no. 4-1483; Nepal-German Manuscript Preservation Project, reel no. B 107*

all other illustrated *dhāraṇī* manuscripts which I examined,[15] with one exception. This is a 17th-century miniature painting (FIGURE 1) in an unedited illustrated *dhāraṇī* collection catalogued as Ādityādigrahamātṛkā, which contains the Saptavāra group of deities.[16] The painting shows a female Gaṇapati dancing on two mice. The goddess holds the rosary, axe and Japanese radish in her right hands, and the elephant goad, noose and possibly a sweetmeat in her left hands. The deity can

[15] See, for example, the Nepalese illustrated manuscript reproduced in Lokesh Chandra 1981, no. 266, and the illustrated 19th-century manuscript from the Bayerische Staatsbibliothek, Munich, Cod. sanscr. 423 (= Janert & Poti 1985: 947-948, no. 2865; also described by Grönbold in: *Bayerische Staatsbibliothek: Erwerbungen aus drei Jahrzehnten 1948-1978: Abendländische und orientalische Handschriften, Inkunabeln und seltene Drucke, Noten und Landkarten. Ausstellung April-Juli 1978*. Wiesbaden: Dr. Ludwig Reichert Verlag, 1978: 171, no. 190).

[16] The manuscript is preserved in the National Archives, Kathmandu, accession no. 4-1483 (= Nepal-German Manuscript Preservation Project, reel no. B 107/18). It is dated N.S. 763 = 1642/1643 CE.

easily be identified as female by the two small flags marked with four-petalled rosettes found on either side of the headgear, which are characteristic of females. Otherwise no female features can be discerned. Some manuscripts of the text use the feminine dative of the noun Gaṇapatihṛdaya in their initial invocation *āryagaṇapatihṛdayāyai namaḥ*, while the others invoke the male Gaṇapatihṛdaya with the formula *āryagaṇapatihṛdayāya namaḥ*. The feminine form Gaṇapatihṛdayā found in the invocation appears occasionally in the colophons of the text. In both cases it modifies the feminine noun *dhāraṇī*: *iti gaṇapatihṛdayā dhāraṇī samāptā*.[17] In some texts the masculine and feminine forms alternate. Thus Dharmarāj Bajrācārya 1997/1998 begins with an invocation of the female Gaṇapatihṛdayā, then includes several stanzas in praise of the male Gaṇapati, continues with the text of the Gaṇapatihṛdaya, but then refers to the *gaṇapatihṛdayā dhāraṇī* in the colophon. The accompanying line-drawing shows the male Gaṇapati.[18]

4. THE SPECIAL CASE OF GAṆAPATIHṚDAYĀ

However, Amṛtānanda's Dharmakośasaṃgraha, written in 1826 CE, and – based on that text – Hodgson 1874 (1972): 19 clearly assume a goddess Gaṇapatihṛdayā as evident from a reference to Gaṇapatihṛdayādevī on fol. 67b.6. In the Dharmakośasaṃgraha Gaṇapatihṛdayā's description appears as part of a group of nine goddesses listed as Vasundharā, Vajravidāriṇī (written Vajravidrāviṇi), Parṇaśavarī, Mārīcī (written Mārici), Dhvajāgrakeyūrī, Gaṇapatihṛdayā, Uṣṇīṣavijayā, Grahamātṛkā and Pratyaṅgirā. Seven of the nine deities (except for Dhvajāgrakeyūrī and Pratyaṅgirā) also appear in the Saptavāra group listed on fol. 67b.5-7. The description of Gaṇapatihṛdayā on fol. 44a.4-5 is as follows:

gaṇapatihṛdayā ekamukha dvibhuja varada abhaya nṛtyāsana.

Here and elsewhere the text lacks case endings. No specific female characteristics, such as breasts, appear in the short description. The only

[17] See, for example, Lokesh Chandra 1981, nos. 272,2 and 331,1.

[18] Recent research has shown that also the gender of some goddesses of the Pañcarakṣā group was originally male (Hidas 2003: 266-267, 272, note 34).

indication of the deity's female gender is the name Gaṇapatihṛdayā. Here the feminine form cannot be explained as modifying the word *dhāraṇī*, which confirms that Amṛtānanda assumed a female Gaṇapatihṛdayā analogous to the other six goddesses in the group. The fact that Amṛtānanda was Hodgson's informant explains the above-mentioned reference to the seven Buddhaśaktis (including Gaṇapatihṛdayā) in Hodgson's work.

Based on the text of the Dharmakośasaṃgraha, whose Sanskrit grammar he improved upon by adding case endings, B. Bhattacharyya 1924: 157-158 described Gaṇapatihṛdayā as part of the Buddhist pantheon in his widely-known book *The Indian Buddhist Iconography*. The description is found in the following rather short paragraph:[19]

> Like Gaṇapati himself Gaṇapatihṛdayā, who, in all probability, is his Śakti, does not bear any image of a Dhyānī Buddha. She is described in the work as: — [158]
>
> "Gaṇapatihṛdayā ekamukhā dvibhujā varadā abhayā nṛtyāsanā."
>
> Dharmakoṣasaṅgraha, Fol. 43.
>
> "Gaṇapatihṛdayā is one-faced, two-armed, exhibits the Varada and the Abhaya poses, and a dancing attitude."
>
> The miniature, (Plate XLII,d) however, does not tally with the above description. In this miniature she has sixteen arms and one face. The symbols, beings (sic) indistinct, cannot be recognised in all details.

The last paragraph was not included in the second edition of Bhattacharyya's book.

Other authors of iconographic handbooks and studies have adopted B. Bhattacharyya's description of or reference to the goddess Gaṇapatihṛdayā. These include D.C. Bhattacharyya 1974: 9-10 and 1978: 20, Agrawala 1978: 2, 33-34, Mallmann 1975: 167, Getty 1936: 37, Grönbold 1984: 353, Kirfel 1948: 64, Liebert 1976: 89, Nagar 1989: 119, and Kooij 1977: 61, note 49. However, Mallmann 1975: 167 has already noted that the description of Gaṇapatihṛdayā in the Dharmakośa-

[19] See also the second revised edition of his work, 1958: 349, for a similar description.

saṃgraha does not specify the deity's colour, her presiding Tathāgata or the presence of the elephant's head. She adds (1975: 167, note 6) that the Nepalese painting reproduced in B. Bhattacharyya's book (from the collection of W.Y. Evans-Wentz)[20] does not correspond to the description cited from the Dharmakośasaṃgraha but that it shows the regular iconography of (a male) Gaṇapati as found, for example, in manuscript Sanscrit 1814 in the Bibliothèque Nationale, Paris. That the illustration in Bhattacharyya's book does not correspond to the Dharmakośasaṃgraha's description is obvious, since it shows a multiple-armed dancing Gaṇapati. It appears to be the twelve-armed dancing Gaṇapati known from Buddhist iconography and described in Bühnemann 1994: 201-204,[21] and not a sixteen-armed female Gaṇapati as B. Bhattacharyya states, since female features cannot be discerned. The only reason why the painting was identified as Gaṇapatihṛdayā seems to be that it appears in a manuscript with the mantras of the Saptavāra deities.

Another Nepalese painting identified as 'Gaṇapatihṛdayā (Śakti-Gaṇapati)' is published in D.C. Bhattacharyya 1980, Fig. 25.[22] It shows a four-armed seated deity, whose iconography does not correspond to that of the dancing two-armed form described in the Dharmakośasaṃgraha. This miniature can be identified as belonging to manuscript 10741 ('A number of Dhāraṇīs with illustrations') in the Asiatic Society of Bengal, Calcutta (Kolkata), dating from 1843 CE. The icon does not exhibit any female features. As before, the reason why the painting was labelled Gaṇapatihṛdayā is that it accompanies the text of the Gaṇapati-

[20] The painting is also reproduced in Sharma 1979, plate 34, and again labelled Gaṇapatihṛdayā.

[21] For this identification, see also Bhattacharya 1995: 68, who attributes it to Getty. Getty, however, seems to refer to a different Nepalese painting (Getty 1936, plate 1b, labelled Gaṇapati-Heramba). Getty 1936: 37 (referring to Mitra 1882 [1971]: 87-88 [no. 816 A]) erroneously states that the mantra text contains an iconographic description of the red twelve-armed dancing Gaṇapati. The description of the twelve-armed deity is not found in the *dhāraṇī* but in SM 37. The text of this *sādhana* is re-edited in Bühnemann 1994: 205-206.

[22] See also the description in D.C. Bhattacharyya 1980: 34 and in Sharma 1979: 41-42 with illustration 35.

hṛdayadhāraṇī, which in the manuscript begins with the invocation *namo bhagavatyai āryagaṇapatihṛdayāyai.*

The text of the *dhāraṇī* printed in Dharmarāj Bajrācārya 1997/1998: 12-19 begins with the same invocation as the manuscript from Kolkata. However, the *dhyāna* verses prefixed to the text of the *dhāraṇī* describe the male Gaṇapati. The body of the *dhāraṇī* text clearly refers to male forms of the deity, but the text is corrupt in many places.[23]

In contrast, the *dhāraṇī* in manuscript Cod. sanscr. 423, preserved in the Bayerische Staatsbibliothek, Munich, fol. 11b invokes a male Gaṇapati, while the colophon names the text as *gaṇapatihṛdayā* (*nāma*) *dhāraṇī*. As stated before, the form Gaṇapatihṛdayā here modifies the feminine noun *dhāraṇī*. The miniature on fol. 11b shows an eight-armed male Gaṇapati, not a female form as stated in Grönbold 2001: 373.

Sharma 1979: 48 quotes Lokesh Chandra as having informed him that Gaṇapatihṛdayā is mentioned in the Hevajratantra. However, according to Lokesh Chandra[24] this is an error and no such reference is found in the Tantra.

We know of female forms of Gaṇeśas in other traditions. A Brahmanical goddess Vināyakī/Gaṇeśvarī is described by Agrawala 1978, and an (East-Asian) Buddhist Vināyakī in Sanford 1991: 315-316 and 325-326. However, the conception of these goddesses is different. None of them is a personification of Gaṇapati's heart mantra(s).

5. SEQUENTIAL DESCRIPTION OF THE TEXTS AND MINIATURES IN THE MANUSCRIPT

In the following, I shall describe the extant folios of the manuscript in the reconstructed sequence. I have identified the individual *dhāraṇī* texts as far as possible and provided references to published materials. However, some Japanese articles and books referred to in Tsukamoto,

[23] Thus we read: *yaḥ kaścid ānanda imāni* (sic) *gaṇapatihṛdayā nāma dhāraṇī dhārayiṣyanti* (sic) instead of *yaḥ kaścit kulaputra ānanda imāni gaṇapatihṛdayāni dhārayiṣyati* (Iwamoto 1937b: 10, 9-10).

[24] Written communication by Lokesh Chandra, dated June 18, 2002.

Matsunaga & Isoda 1989 were inaccessible to me. In the short extracts from the *dhāraṇī* texts, which often display grammatical inaccuracies I have not attempted to correct, I have standardized the orthography of the transliterated Sanskrit text, taking into consideration that in Nevārī manuscripts long and short vowels are frequently interchanged, as are the letters *l/r*, *n/r*, *j/y*, *v/b*, *kh/ṣ* and *ś/ṣ/s*.[25]

5.1 Mahā ratisarā

The text begins on fol. 1b.1 as follows:

> *oṃ namo bhaga<va>tyai āryap<r>atisarāyai // evaṃ mayā śrutam ekasmi<n> samaye bhagavān vajrameruśikharakūṭāgāre viharati sma // tad idānīṃ pravakṣyāmi bhūtasaṅgho śṛṇotu me // namo buddhāya // namo dharmāya // namo <saṅ>ghāya // nama<ḥ> sarvatathāgatānāṃ namo namaḥ [//] sarvabuddhabodhisat<t>vadharmasaṅghebhyaḥ // tadyathā // oṃ vipulagarbhe vimale jayagarbhe ....*

A similar but much longer version of the text is printed in Iwamoto 1938: 1, 4-5 and 7, 14ff. Information about manuscripts of this *dhāraṇī* can be found in Tsukamoto, Matsunaga & Isoda 1989: 82-83, and a detailed discussion of the different versions in Hidas 2003. Hidas is preparing a critical edition of the *mahāpratisarāmahāvidyārājñī* with an English translation.

The miniature painting (PLATE IV) depicts the white-complexioned Mahāpratisarā seated on a white lion. She has four heads (coloured yellow, blue, white and red) and holds with her eight hands:

RIGHT	LEFT
sword	banner
arrow	bow
vajra	bell
wheel	noose

[25] For the unique orthographical features of Nevārī manuscripts, see Lienhard & Manandhar 1988: XXVII-XXVIII.

The attributes here correspond roughly to the description in SM 206 (see also Mevissen 1989a: 363), except for the banner replacing an axe; and the bell, a trident. Mevissen 1989b (colour plates 11b, 20c and 22d) provides three examples from manuscript paintings that support the above iconography of Mahāpratisarā which deviates from the description in SM 206.[26]

5.2 Mahāsāhasrapramardanī

After a lacuna the next extant folio is fol. 6b. The mantra of Mahāpratisarā, called the 'great queen of *vidyās*' (*mahāvidyārājñī*), ends in line 1 with *svāhā // āryamahāpratisarāyā mahāvidyārājñī samāptā //*
The next section, on Mahāsāhasrapramardanī, begins in line 2:

> *oṃ namo bhagavatyai āryamahāsāhasrapramardanyai // evaṃ mayā śrutam ekasmin samaye bhagavān rājagṛhe viharati sma // gṛdh<r>akūṭaparvate dakṣiṇe pārśve buddhagocare ....*

A similar but longer version of the text appears in the *āryamahāsāhasrapramardanī nāma mahāyānasūtra* printed in Iwamoto 1937: 1, 2ff. Manuscripts of this *dhāraṇī* are described in Tsukamoto, Matsunaga & Isoda 1989: 85-86.

The miniature (PLATE V) depicts the blue-complexioned Mahāsāhasrapramardanī kneeling on a man. Her three heads are green, blue and red. The goddess holds with her eight hands:

---

[26] The three examples are found in (1) palm-leaf manuscript 105, preserved in the Keśar Library, Kathmandu (= Nepal-German Manuscript Preservation Project, reel no. C11/2); see Mevissen 1989a: 369, no. 17 and Mevissen 1989b: Kat. M.I.B.16b, colour plate 11b; (2) fol. 1a of a 19th-century paper manuscript, kept in the Staatsbibliothek Berlin, Hs.or.1932; see Janert & Poti 1970, colour plate 17, Mevissen 1989a: 371, no. 33 and Mevissen 1989b: Kat. M.II.A.35c, colour plate 20c; (3) fol. 96b of a 19th-century paper manuscript in the Staatsbibliothek Berlin, Hs.or.2384; see Mevissen 1989a: 372, no. 36 and Mevissen 1989b: Kat. M.II.A.38d, colour plate 22d.

RIGHT	LEFT
sword	skull-topped staff
trident	axe
goad	sixteen(-edged) jewel on a lotus (?)[27]
vajra	noose

The iconography is similar to the description in SM 206, except that the number and the colours of the heads are different, the trident replaces an arrow in the SM, and the skull-staff is found in place of a bow.

5.3 Mahāmāyūrī

The next extant folio is fol. 8b. The text begins:

> ... *namo mahāmāyūryai / vidyārājayā tadyathā // iḍi viḍi hiḍi miḍi niḍi // āḍe ghāḍe ....*

This text presents the 'queen of *vidyās*' (*vidyārājayā*[28] or *vidyārājñī*, as in the colophon) Mahāmāyūrī. A longer version of this *vidyārājñī* is published in Minayeff & Oldenburg 1983: 191-234 and in Takubo 1972. Manuscripts of this *dhāraṇī* are described in Tsukamoto, Matsunaga & Isoda 1989: 87-90.

The goddess (PLATE VI) is seated on a green horse. She is of yellow complexion, has three heads (coloured blue, yellow and red) and holds with her eight hands:

RIGHT	LEFT
sword	banner
wheel	white flower
vajra	noose
wish-granting gesture	a monk in a begging bowl

---

[27] The attribute is somewhat unclear and almost looks like a white flower. SM 206 prescribes a sixteen(-edged) jewel on a lotus.

[28] For this term, see Waddell 1912: 171.

A similar miniature painting is found in palm-leaf manuscript 105, preserved in the Keśar Library, Kathmandu (= Nepal-German Manuscript Preservation Project, reel no. C11/2); see Mevissen 1989a: 369, no. 17 and Mevissen 1989b: Kat. M.I.B.16f, colour plate 11f. The iconography is somewhat similar to SM 206, but three of the attributes differ. While the SM lists these as (1) a pot with jewels, (2) a double *vajra* on a pot[29] and (3) a peacock feather, the miniature shows a *vajra*, white flower and noose.

5.4 Mahāśītavatī

The next folio is unnumbered. It is in the proper sequence, since it contains the final part of the Mahāmāyūrī mantra and the colophon in line 3 (*āryamahāmāyūrīvidyārājñī samāptā*), followed by the mantra of Mahāśītavatī:

> *oṃ namo bhagavatyai āryaśītavatyai // u<d>gṛhna tvaṃ rāhula imāṃ śītavatī<ṃ> nāma dhāraṇī<ṃ> mahāvidyāmantrapadā°*

Only a small part of Mahāśītavatī's mantra (called *dhāraṇī mahāvidyā*) is preserved on the folio. A longer version of the *dhāraṇī* is printed in Iwamoto 1937b: 2, 8ff. Manuscripts of this *dhāraṇī* are described in Tsukamoto, Matsunaga & Isoda 1989: 90-92.

The miniature (PLATE VII) represents the green-complexioned Mahāśītavatī seated on Garuḍa. The goddess has three heads (coloured white, green and red) and holds with her six hands:

RIGHT	LEFT
arrow	bow
sword	banner
gesture of protection	noose

The attributes correspond to the description in SM 206 but for the sword being found instead of a *vajra*. This deviation is also attested to

[29] The attribute is a double *vajra* on a pot (not on a bell); see Mevissen 1989a: 358.

in miniature paintings in a number of other manuscripts; see, for example, the paintings in Mevissen 1989b: Kat. M.I.B.3b, colour plate 9b; Kat. M.I.B.16h, colour plate 11h; Kat. M.II.A.16d, colour plate 16d; Kat. M.II.36e, colour plate 21e and Kat. M.II.A.43d, colour plate 23d.

5.5 Mahāmantrānusāriṇī

Another unnumbered folio is next in sequence, preserving as it does the final section of Mahāśītavatī's *dhāraṇī*, there specified as *mahāvidyā*: *āryamahāśītavatī nāma dhāraṇī mahāvidyā samāptā //*
Mahāmantrānusāriṇī's *dhāraṇī* begins in line 2 with:

> *namo bhagavatyai āryamahāmantrānusāriṇyai // tatra khalu bhagavān āyuṣmān ānandam āmantrayate sma / imāni mahāmantrānusāriṇī mantrapadāni ....*

For a somewhat similar text, see Mahāmantrānusāriṇīsūtra (= Skilling 1994: 609-610). References to manuscripts of this *dhāraṇī* can be found in Tsukamoto, Matsunaga & Isoda 1989: 92-93.

The miniature (PLATE VIII) shows the red-complexioned Mahāmantrānusāriṇī, the last in the group of the five Rakṣās. The goddess is seated on a peacock. She has three heads (coloured white, red and blue) and holds with her 12 hands:

RIGHT	LEFT
arrow	bow
sword	cluster of jewels[30]
gesture of protection	white flower/lotus
wish-granting gesture	vase

gesture of turning the *dharma* wheel (*dharmacakramudrā*)
gesture of meditation (*samādhimudrā*), holding a bowl

[30] According to SM 206, the goddess holds a cluster of jewels. The painting is not quite clear. An identical attribute is held by Parṇaśavarī (see 5.11 and PLATE XIV).

Four miniature paintings are known whose iconography is similar to this painting.[31] The iconography is somewhat similar to the description in SM 206, but in the painting the sword replaces a *vajra*, and there is no noose held with a threatening gesture, as specified in the SM.

5.6 Vasudhārā

An unnumbered folio is likely to follow here in sequence. It begins with an invocation of Vasudhārā in line 1, which continues with the litany of the goddess's 108 names:

> *oṃ namo bhagavatyai āryaśrīvasudhārāyai // namo ratnatrayāya //*
>
> *divyarūpī surūpī ca saumyarūpī varapradā (v.l. bala°) /*
> *vasudharī vasudhārī [ca[32]] vasuśrī śrīkarī varā // ....*

The text was published in *Dhīḥ* 3 (1987): 3-4 and 6 (1988); 1-2 from an unpublished collection of hymns (*stotra*) preserved in the Śāntarakṣita Library. It is also printed in Bauddhastotrasaṃgraha, pp. 220-221 [titled *vasudhārā nāma dhāraṇīstotra*], in Mahendraratna Śākya 1994: 36-37 and in Dharmarāj Bajrācārya 1997/1998: 1-5. The verses preserved in our manuscript correspond to verses 1-4c and, after a lacuna, to verses 23c-24 of the *stotra*.

This litany of names of Vasudhārā is found in a number of manuscripts, such as Add. 1356 (labelled "Dhāraṇīs") in the University Library, Cambridge. Short extracts are printed in Bendall 1883: 66, and references to other manuscripts and related materials gathered in Tsukamoto, Matsunaga & Isoda 1989: 117-118.

---

[31] I thank G.J.R. Mevissen for the following information on similar paintings: (1) manuscript OMPB Or.14000, preserved in the British Library (with some deviations); (2) palm-leaf manuscript 105, preserved in the Keśar Library, Kathmandu (= Nepal-German Manuscript Preservation Project, reel no. C11/2); see Mevissen 1989b, colour plate 11j; (3) fol. 168b of manuscript Hs.or.1932, kept in the Staatsbibliothek Berlin; see Mevissen 1989b, colour plate 21c (with deviations); and (4) unnumbered folio in paper manuscript Hs.or.2384, kept in the Staatsbibliothek Berlin; see Mevissen 1989b, colour plate 23a (with deviations).

[32] The syllable *ca* is metrically redundant.

The miniature (PLATE IX) shows the yellow-complexioned Vasudhārā seated on a lotus. The goddess has one head and six arms with the following attributes:

RIGHT	LEFT
gesture of veneration (*tathāgatavandanā*)	manuscript
jewel	ear of corn
wish-granting gesture	vase

A similar iconographic type is described in the Vasundharoddeśa, quoted in Mallmann 1975: 441-442 and D.C. Bhattacharyya 1974: 35-36. Similar representations are a Nepalese miniature painting published in Getty 1928, plate LXIb,[33] and described in Mallmann 1975: 442; a miniature in manuscript Cod. sanscr. 423, preserved in the Bayerische Staatsbibliothek, Munich, fol. 1b (also Grönbold 2001: 373); a painting in manuscript 66.13.4, fol. 1b, preserved in the Watson Collection of Indian Miniatures at the Elvehjem Museum of Art, Madison, Wisconsin; and line drawing 85 in the Bauddhadevatācitrasaṃgraha and line drawing 127 in Nepalese sketchbook LC; see also the inserted colour plate in Mahendraratna Śākya 1994: 22+. This iconographic type is referred to in B. Bhattacharyya 1958: 245 (with Fig. 188) and appears in Bris-sku mthoṅ-ba don-ldan, no. 504 (Willson & Brauen 2000: 202-203, 414-415)[34].

[33] Getty gives no details about the manuscript but merely specifies it as a 'Nepalese book'. Mallmann 1975: 178, 442 refers to it as 'BN', i.e., a manuscript from the Bibliothèque Nationale, Paris, with the accession number 'Sanscrit 1814'. The illustrated manuscript belongs to the Getty bequest now preserved in the Bibliothèque Nationale. It consists of 31 folios of blue paper, with the text written in gold.

[34] See also the concordance on p. 435 for block prints and other sources depicting this form of the deity.

5.7 Vajravidāriṇī

An unnumbered folio which preserves the final part of Vasudhārā's mantra in lines 2/3 follows:

āryaśrīvasudhārā nāmāṣṭottaraśataṃ buddhabhāṣitaṃ samāptam //

The section on Vajravidāriṇī begins in line 3:

oṃ namo bhagavatyai āryavajravidāriṇyai // evaṃ mayā śrutam ekasmin samaye bhagavān vajreṣu viharati sma // sarvaśarīraṃ vajramayam adhiṣṭhāya ....

The text of this *dhāraṇī* is printed in Iwamoto 1937b: 7, 2ff. under the title *śrīvajravidāraṇā nāma dhāraṇī hṛdayopahṛdayaṃ mūlasūtram*; see also Dharmarāj Bajrācārya 1997/1998: 6-11. References to manuscripts can be found in Tsukamoto, Matsunaga & Isoda 1989: 148-149. Along with the form Vajravidāriṇī, which is also found in Bendall 1883: 44 (Add. 1315) and Dharmarāj Bajrācārya 1997/1998, the forms Vajravidāraṇā and Vajravidāraṇī also appear in the literature. Amṛtānanda's Dharmakośasaṃgraha refers to the goddess once as Vajravidrāviṇī (fol. 43b.7, but as Vajravidāriṇī on fol. 67b.6), which may be a scribal error.

The miniature (PLATE X) shows the red-complexioned Vajravidāriṇī on a lotus in the act of stepping to her right. The goddess has five heads (coloured white, yellow, red, blue and green) and ten arms. She holds:

RIGHT	LEFT
sword	shield
goad	axe
arrow	bow
wish-granting gesture	gesture of protection
double *vajra*	noose

A similar iconographic description appears in Amṛtānanda's Dharmakośasaṃgraha, fol. 43b.7-8 (a banner is found in place of the axe), summarized in B. Bhattacharyya 1958: 205 and Mallmann 1975: 430-431. The miniature reproduced in B. Bhattacharyya 1924, Fig. XLIIe and in

B. Bhattacharyya 1958, Fig. 150, is too unclear for iconographic details to be discerned.

5.8 Gaṇapati(hṛdaya)

After a lacuna the next extant folio is fol. 21b, which begins as follows:

> *oṃ namo ratnatrayāya // evaṃ mayā śrutam ekasmin samaye bhagavān rājagṛhe viharati sma // gṛdhrakūṭaparvate ....*

This section introduces Gaṇapati's heart (*hṛdaya*) mantras, which are referred to as *gaṇapatihṛdayāni* (fol. 21b.4). The short extant fragment corresponds to the text published in Iwamoto 1937b: 10, 2-11 under the title Gaṇapatihṛdaya. From Iwamoto's edition of the remaining text it becomes clear that several heart mantras of Gaṇapati are taught and several forms of Gaṇapati invoked, including Mahāgaṇapati, Gaṇapati, Gaṇādhipa, Gaṇeśvara and Gaṇapūjita. Wilkinson 1991: 242 attempted an English rendering of the Tibetan translation of a text titled Ārya-gaṇapatihṛdaya, which is a shorter version of Iwamoto's text. References to manuscripts of this text can be found in Tsukamoto, Matsunaga & Isoda 1989: 119. The *dhāraṇī* is also published in Dharmarāj Bajrācārya 1997/1998: 12-19.

The miniature (PLATE XI) shows the red-complexioned Gaṇapati seated on a mouse. His four arms hold:

RIGHT	LEFT
rosary	axe
Japanese radish	vessel (with sweet meats)

Similar iconographic representations of Gaṇapati from Nepal, which date from the 16th to the 19th centuries, are reproduced in Bangdel 1995: 101 (no. 8), 250 (no. 5), 319 (no. 29) and 469 (no. 13). Two of these lack the mouse, and one shows the figure standing on two mice.[35]

---

[35] Two mice are also found in the miniature painting illustrated in FIGURE 1, p. 36.

5.9 Uṣṇīṣavijayā

After a lacuna the next folio is fol. 23b, which presents Uṣṇīṣavijayā's mantra:

> *bhagavatyai āryoṣṇīṣavijayāyai // evaṃ mayā śrutam ekasmin samaye bhagavān sukhāvatyā<ṃ> dharmasaṃgītimahāguhya-prāsāde bhavane viharati sma /....*

Only a short section of the introductory section of the well-known *dhāraṇī* is preserved; for the complete text of this version of Uṣṇīṣa-vijayā's *dhāraṇī*, see Dharmarāj Bajrācārya 1997/1998: 20-24. For the text of the *dhāraṇī* (without the introductory and concluding sections) as reconstructed from one Nepalese Saptavāra manuscript, which is re-printed in Lokesh Chandra 1981, nos. 332-336, see Yuyama 2000: 171-174.[36] References to manuscripts can be found in Filliozat 1941: 55 (with a short extract of the text) and Tsukamoto, Matsunaga & Isoda 1989: 67, 101.

The miniature (PLATE XII) shows the white-complexioned Uṣṇīṣa-vijayā seated on a lotus. She has three heads (coloured yellow, white and blue) and eight arms which hold:

RIGHT	LEFT
Buddha icon <of Amitābha> on a lotus	gesture of protection
arrow	bow
wish-granting gesture	vase
double *vajra* (*viśvavajra*)	noose

An identical iconographic type is described in SM 191.[37] It is repre-sented in line drawing 105 in the Bauddhadevatācitrasaṃgraha, in line drawing 135 in Nepalese sketchbook LC, in a painting in manuscript

---

[36] Yuyama has studied different versions of this *dhāraṇī*. For a somewhat similar version of the text, which was transliterated by Tz'u-hsien, see Yuyama 1997: 733-734.

[37] See also B. Bhattacharyya 1958: 214-215 with Fig. 155-156, Mallmann 1975: 389-390, with references to iconographic representations accompanied by plate XII-1, and Lokesh Chandra 1992: 56-61.

66.13.4, fol. 21a, preserved in the Watson Collection of Indian Miniatures at the Elvehjem Museum of Art, Madison, Wisconsin, and in illustrated manuscript 4-1482 in the National Archives, Kathmandu (Kooij 1977: 63); see also Bris-sku mthoṅ-ba don-ldan, nos. 183 and 425 (Willson & Brauen 2000: 90-91, 286, 383)[38].

5.10 Mārīcī [39]

Folio 26b follows in sequence, containing as it does a fragment of Mārīcī's *dhāraṇī*:

> *°śataiḥ saṃbahulaiś ca mahāśrāvakai<ḥ> bodhisat<t>vai<ḥ> mahāsat<t>vaiḥ / tatra khalu bhagavān bhikṣūn āmantrayate sma / asti bhikṣavo mārīcī nāma devatā / sā sūryacandramaso*[40] *purato 'nugacchati /....*

For the edited text of this *dhāraṇī*, see Ashikaga 1960: 136-137; see also Dharmarāj Bajrācārya 1997/1998: 31-34. For Mārīcī's *dhāraṇīs*, see Filliozat 1941: 55 and Tsukamoto, Matsunaga & Isoda 1989: 93-95.

The red-complexioned goddess (PLATE XIII) is riding a chariot drawn by pigs. The number of pigs associated with the goddess Mārīcī is not always seven but can vary from one to nine (for a table listing 51 images with two to nine pigs, see Table 1 in Mevissen 2004c). This miniature associates the goddess with three pigs, just as drawings 151-153 in the Bauddhadevatācitrasaṃgraha do. For a comprehensive article on Mārīcī, see Bautze-Picron 2001. In this painting Mārīcī has three heads (coloured white, red and blue), one of which is a boar's. The goddess is shown shooting an arrow. Her six arms hold:

---

[38] See also the concordance on pp. 433 and 435 for block prints and other sources depicting this form of the deity.

[39] I adopt the standardized spelling Mārīcī recorded in Edgerton's *Buddhist Hybrid Sanskrit Dictionary* and the Monier-Williams *Sanskrit-English Dictionary*, not the form Māricī found in the manuscript and, for example, in Mitra 1882 (1971): 169 (no. B. 4).

[40] The manuscript erroneously reads *candrasūryamaso*. The reading *sūryacandramaso* is found in Ashikaga 1960: 136 and in manuscript 66.13.4 (catalogued as *āryagrahamātṛkā nāma dhāraṇī*), fol. 24b.5, preserved in the Watson Collection of Indian Miniatures at the Elvehjem Museum of Art, Madison, Wisconsin. The correct reading (according to Classical Sanskrit) would be *sūryācandramasoḥ*.

RIGHT	LEFT
arrow	bow
vajra	flowering branch of an Aśoka tree
needle (?)	string

This iconographic type appears in line drawing 152 in the Bauddhadevatācitrasaṃgraha and in illustrated manuscript 4-1482 in the National Archives, Kathmandu (Kooij 1977: 64).

5.11 Parṇaśavarī

An unnumbered folio is next in sequence; its first line indicates the end of Mārīcī's *dhāraṇī*:

> *<mu>khaṃ bandha bandha svāhā // āryamārīcī nāma dhāraṇī samāptam* (read: *samāptā*) *iti*.

At the end of line 1 Parṇaśavarī's *dhāraṇī* begins:

> *oṃ namo bhagavatyai āryaparṇaśavarītārāyai // namo ratnatrayāya / namo amitābhāya tathāgatāyārhate samyaksambuddhāya / namo āryāvalokiteśvarāya bodhisat<t>vāya....*

For a similar *dhāraṇī*, see Dharmarāj Bajrācārya 1997/1998: 25-30, and for an extract from this *dhāraṇī*, see Filliozat 1941: 40. Manuscripts of this *dhāraṇī* are described in Tsukamoto, Matsunaga & Isoda 1989: 140-141.

The miniature (PLATE XIV) shows the yellow-complexioned Parṇaśavarī kneeling on a lotus. The goddess has three heads (coloured white, yellow and blue). Her six arms hold:

RIGHT	LEFT
axe	cluster of jewels (?)[41]
arrow	bow
gesture of turning the *dharma* wheel (*dharmacakramudrā*)	gesture of turning the *dharma* wheel (*dharmacakramudrā*)

[41] A similar object is also held by Mahāmantrānusāriṇī (see 5.5 and PLATE VIII).

A similar miniature painting from Nepal appears in manuscript Cod. sanscr. 423, preserved in the Bayerische Staatsbibliothek, Munich, fol. 20b. An iconographic type holding somewhat similar attributes appears in the Bauddhadevatācitrasaṃgraha (107), in Nepalese sketchbook LC (137) and in Bris-sku mthoṅ-ba don-ldan, nos. 218 and 441 (Willson & Brauen 2000: 102-103, 298-299, 389-390)[42]. However, in these sources the goddess holds a cluster of leaves instead of a cluster of jewels, and a *vajra* and noose instead of displaying the gesture of turning the wheel.

5.12 Grahamātṛkā

Then follows fol. 29b, which preserves the end of Parṇaśavarī's *dhāraṇī* in the first line:

> *<parṇaśava>rī hrīḥ hūṃ phaṭ piśācī svāhā / āryaparṇaśavarī mahāmārīpraśamanī nāma dhāraṇī samāptā //*

The *dhāraṇī* of Grahamātṛkā begins in line 2:

> *oṃ namo bhagavatyai āryagrahamātṛkāyai // evaṃ mayā śrutam ekasmin samaye bhagavān aḍa<ka>vatyā<m> ....*

For the text of Grahamātṛkā's *dhāraṇī*, see Dharmarāj Bajrācārya 1997/1998: 35-43; extracts are printed in Mitra 1882 (1971): 91-93 (no. 816 B) and Filliozat 1941: 44, and manuscript materials described in Tsukamoto, Matsunaga & Isoda 1989: 114-115.

The goddess Grahamātṛkā is also called Navagrahamātṛkā (Bendall 1883: 66 [Add. 1356]), 'mother of the nine *grahas*'. The word *graha*, literally 'seizer', can designate two different entities:

1) a 'heavenly body' and

2) a demon (*bālagraha*) associated with children's diseases.

The heavenly bodies commonly total nine, while the number of demons associated with children's diseases may differ in texts. The third/fourth-century medical text Suśrutasaṃhitā (Kalpasthāna, chapter 27. 4-5), for example, lists the following nine: Skanda, Skandāpasmāra, Śakuni, Revatī, Pūtanā, Andhapūtanā, Sītapūtanā, Mukhamaṇḍikā and

---

42 See also the concordance on p. 433 for block prints and other sources depicting this form of the deity.

Naigameṣa.[43] Rāvaṇa's Kumāratantra (=Filliozat 1935) describes twelve demons called *mātṛkā* associated with children's diseases: Nandā, Sunandā, Pūtanā, Mukhamuṇḍikā/Mukhamaṇḍitikā, Kaṭapūtanā, Śakunikā, Śuṣkarevatī, Aryakā, Bhūsūtikā, Nirṛtā, Pilipicchikā and Kāmukā.[44] Instead of the names *graha* and *mātṛkā* used in the texts to designate the (mostly) female demons, Bagchi 1941: 270 suggests *grahamātṛkā* but is unable to cite evidence for the use of this term in Sanskrit texts.

The text of the *dhāraṇī* itself clearly teaches the mantras of the nine *grahas* beginning with Āditya and ending with Ketu. Therefore the interpretation of the goddess's name as 'mother of the heavenly bodies'[45] seems appropriate, while that of 'mother of demons' found in Kirfel 1948: 75 and Liebert 1976: 97 should be discarded.

Grahamātṛkā is featured as a goddess in individual paintings and in Grahamātṛkā maṇḍalas. She also appears in a subordinate position in maṇḍalas of other deities. More details on the iconography of this goddess can be found in Lokesh Chandra 1999–, volume 4: 1,288-1,292 and in articles by Mevissen (2004a, 2004b, 2004c, and in this volume).

The miniature (PLATE XV) shows the white-complexioned Grahamātṛkā. The goddess is seated on a lotus and has three heads (coloured yellow, white and red). Her six arms hold:

RIGHT	LEFT
arrow	bow
vajra	white lotus

añjali gesture

A similar miniature appears in manuscript Cod. sanscr. 423, preserved in the Bayerische Staatsbibliothek, Munich, fol. 26b (PLATE XIX.B; see Grönbold 2001: 374). For a similar iconographic type, which displays

[43] For a recent discussion of the term *graha* in the Suśrutasaṃhitā, where it can designate either a heavenly body or demon, see Yano 2003: 380.

[44] Bagchi 1941 also refers to lists of sixteen names of demons.

[45] See also Pal & Bhattacharyya 1969: 42-43 for this translation.

the gesture of turning the *dharma* wheel instead of the *añjali* gesture, see Amṛtānanda's Dharmakośasaṃgraha, fol. 44[46] and Bris-sku mthoṅ-ba don-ldan, no. 223 ('Grahamātṛkā Vidyārājñī') (Willson & Brauen 2000: 104-105, 300)[47]. In the Bris-sku mthoṅ-ba don-ldan (PLATE XXIII.A) the heads are coloured blue, white and red. For an iconographic form of the goddess holding a peacock feather or a small peacock-feathered dagger (*śakti*) instead of a *vajra* and a flower bouquet instead of the white lotus, see Getty 1928, plate LXIa[48] and the description in Mallmann 1975: 178.

5.13 Vajravārāhī

Another folio, whose text and folio number are partially broken off on the right side, may follow here in sequence. The text in line 1 begins with an invocation of Vajravārāhī and the following partially corrupt text:

oṃ namo vajravārāhyai //

bhagavati digambare muktakeśārdhapāde
dinakarakarabhāse muṇḍitāmaṇḍitāṅge /
nikhilabhavanihantri siddhisambodhidātri
praṇamitajinadh<ā>tri vajravārāhīkalpe //

athāto bhagavatīnāṃ guhyeśvarīnāṃ sadevatīnām ....

This text can be identified in the Vajravārāhīkalpa(mahā)tantra(rāja), an extract of which is printed in Filliozat 1941: 78-79 and Bṛhatsūcīpatra 7/3: 19. For material on Vajrayoginī's (= Vajravārāhī's) *dhāraṇī*, see Tsukamoto, Matsunaga & Isoda 1989: 161.

The red-complexioned goddess Vajravārāhī (PLATE XVI) is shown dancing in *ardhaparyaṅka* within a downward-pointing triangle

---

[46] See also B. Bhattacharyya 1958: 224-225 with Fig. 165 (= Mevissen [this volume], FIGURE 3) and Mallmann 1975: 178.

[47] See also the concordance on p. 433 for block prints and other sources depicting this form of the deity.

[48] As Mallmann 1975: 178, 442 notes, this miniature belongs to manuscript 'Sanscrit 1814', now preserved in the Bibliothèque Nationale, Paris.

(*dharmodaya*) on a naked male body. A boar's head is visible on the right side of her head. The goddess holds:

RIGHT	LEFT
chopper	skull-cup

She holds a skull-topped staff in the crook of her left arm. The tip of her staff appears to be pointing at the male's sex organ. This painting was seemingly executed over the text, unlike the other miniatures in this manuscript, which are separated from the text by lines.

The two-armed Vajravārāhī in a dancing pose is described in SM 220; see also B. Bhattacharyya 1958: 219 ('Vaśya-Vajravārāhī')[49] with Fig. 159, Mallmann 1975: 427, 429 and English 2002: 50-54. Of the many similar extant illustrations, see, for example, line drawing 169 in the Bauddhadevatācitrasaṃgraha.

5.14 Caitya

The last folio, whose text and folio number are partially broken off on the right side, begins as follows:

oṃ namaḥ śrīdharmadhātave //

natvārkabandhuṃ jagadekabandhuṃ
svayambhūbhaṭṭārakam ādideva<m> /
jarārujāmṛtyuharaikadakṣa
vakṣye taduddeśam aha<ṃ> samastam //

nepāle jagati khyāte gośṛṅgo nāma parvataḥ /
bhedo 'sti ca yuge tasya nāmasya yugaladvayam //[50]

....

[49] For a critique of the term Vaśya-Vajravārāhī, which is not found in original texts, see English 2002: 50, 401.

[50] For a somewhat similar stanza, see the edited Svayambhū-Purāṇa, p. 8,13-14.

This text fragment can be identified as belonging to the Svayambhū-caityabhaṭṭārakoddeśa (a recension of the "Svayambhū-Purāṇa"),[51] an extract of which is printed in Bṛhatsūcīpatra 7/3: 131.

The folio contains a miniature painting of a *caitya* (PLATE XVII) with an attendant on either side, one being a monk. The *caitya* can be identified as Svayambhūnāth Mahācaitya in Kathmandu, located on a hill as indicated by the bushes in front. For a similar painting of Svayambhūnāth Mahācaitya, see painting 14 of the Jucker Collection (Kreijger 1999: 54-55).

6. CONCLUSION

Although *dhāraṇī* manuscripts are extremely widespread in Nepal, only a few illustrated ones have been published and studied which do not focus exclusively on the Pañcarakṣā goddesses.[52] Among the illustrated *dhāraṇī* manuscripts we find manuscripts exclusively devoted to the Saptavāra deities.[53] The Nepalese manuscript published here is among the few manuscripts that include miniature paintings of the Pañcarakṣā goddesses, the Saptavāra deities, and other paintings. Although incomplete, it is a fine example of an 18th-century Nepalese *dhāraṇī* manuscript that teaches mantras of different deities. Of special interest are the somewhat unusual iconography of the Pañcarakṣā goddesses and

---

[51] For the different recensions of the "Svayambhū Purāṇa", see Brinkhaus 1993.

[52] For a list of 37 illustrated Pañcarakṣā manuscripts, see Mevissen 1989a: 366-372.

[53] Illustrated *dhāraṇī* manuscript exclusively devoted to the Saptavāra group are manuscript 4-1483 (B 107/18) of the National Archives, Kathmandu, catalogued as Ādityādigrahamātṛkā (it is erroneously referred to as 4-1482 in Kooij 1977: 60-61); manuscript 10741 in the Asiatic Society of Bengal, Kolkata (Shāstri 1917: 48-49); 'Sanscrit 1814' in the Bibliothèque National, Paris; manuscript Cod. sanscr. 423 in the Bayerische Staatsbibliothek, Munich, described in Grönbold 2001 and Janert & Poti 1965: 947-948, no. 2865; manuscripts CH 552 and CH 557 referred to in Takaoka 1981, and manuscript 66.13.4 in the Watson Collection of Indian miniatures at the Elvehjem Museum of Art, Madison, Wisconsin, catalogued as *āryagrahamātṛkā nāma dhāraṇī* (= Vajracharya 2002: 56-57). Two illustrated Saptavāra manuscripts are reproduced in Lokesh Chandra 1981 (the name Saptavāra is not mentioned).

features in the iconography of some of the other deities which deviate from recorded patterns. The unusual sequence of the Saptavāra deities is also noteworthy.

In connection with the Saptavāra deities, I have discussed the case of Gaṇapatihṛdaya in detail. It appears that originally Gaṇapati or the personification of his heart mantra, Gaṇapatihṛdaya, featured as a member in this group of mantra deities. However, a few individuals took the deity to be a female Gaṇapatihṛdayā, in line with the gender of the other members of the group. In fact, some people seem to have associated the seven deities with the heavenly bodies presiding over the days of the week, in the same way that the Tantric tradition often pairs females with male deities. The grammatically feminine gender of the word *dhāraṇī* must have contributed to this development too. In a similar fashion, the goddesses of the Pañcarakṣā group were loosely associated with the Tathāgatas whose complexions and mounts they adopt (D.C. Bhattacharyya 1972: 88), although the Tathāgatas have their own female partners, called Prajñās. It seems, however, that the goddess Gaṇapatihṛdayā had no significance outside the group of Saptavāra deities. Even as a member of that group, she was acknowledged only by a few individuals.

REFERENCES

AGRAWALA, P.K. 1978. *Goddess Vināyakī: The Female Gaṇeśa.* Varanasi: Prithivi Prakashan.

ASHIKAGA, A. 1960. Marishiten-Darani no Bonpon. On the Sanskrit Text of Ārya-mārīcī-nāma-dhāraṇī (in Japanese). In: Planning Committee for the Commemoration of Dr. Gishô Nakano's Seventieth Birthday (ed.), *Nakano-Kyôju Koki-Kinen Ronbunshû. Studies in Indology and Buddhology Presented in Honour of Professor Gishô Nakano on the Occasion of His Seventieth Birthday*: 135-143. Koyasan: Seminar of Buddhism of Koyasan University.

BAGCHI, P.C. 1941. New materials for the Study of the Kumāratantra of Rāvaṇa. *Indian Culture* 7/3: 269-286.

BAJRACHARYA, Y.R. 2004. *The Gunakar Mahavihar (Chhusya Baha).* Kathmandu: Gunakar Mahavihar Conservation Committee.

BANGDEL, L.S. 1995. *Inventory of Stone Sculptures of the Kathmandu Valley*. Kathmandu: Royal Nepal Academy.

Bauddhadevatācitrasaṃgraha. See BÜHNEMANN 2003.

Bauddhastotrasaṃgraha. *Bauddhastotrasamgraha*. Ed. by Janardan Shastri Pandey. Delhi: Motilal Banarsidass, 1994.

BAUTZE-PICRON, C. 2001. Between Śākyamuni and Vairocana: Mārīcī, Goddess of Light and Victory. *Silk Road Art and Archaeology (Journal of the Institute of Silk Road Studies)* 7: 263-310.

BENDALL, C. 1883. *Catalogue of the Buddhist Sanskrit Manuscripts in the University Library, Cambridge*. Cambridge: University Press.

BERNHARD, F. 1967. Zur Entstehung einer Dhāraṇī. *Zeitschrift der Deutschen Morgenländischen Gesellschaft* 117: 148-168.

BHATTACHARYA, G. 1995. The Dual Role of Ganesh in the Buddhist Art of South Asia. In: P. Pal (ed.), *Ganesh, the Benevolent*: 65-80. Bombay: Marg Publications.

BHATTACHARYYA, B. 1924. *The Indian Buddhist Iconography Mainly Based on the Sādhanamālā and Other Cognate Tāntric Texts of Rituals*. London: Humphrey Milford, Oxford University Press.

—— 1958. *The Indian Buddhist Iconography Mainly Based on the Sādhanamālā and Cognate Tāntric Texts of Rituals*. Calcutta: Firma K.L. Mukhopadhyay (second edition, revised and enlarged).

BHATTACHARYYA, D.C. 1972. The Five Protective Goddesses of Buddhism. In: P. Pal (ed.), *Aspects of Indian Art: Papers Presented in a Symposium at the Los Angeles County Museum of Art, October, 1970*: 85-92. Leiden: E.J. Brill.

—— 1974. *Tantric Buddhist Iconographic Sources*. New Delhi: Munshiram Manoharlal Publishers.

—— 1978. *Studies in Buddhist Iconography*. New Delhi: Manohar Book Service.

—— 1980. *Iconology of Composite Images*. New Delhi: Munshiram Manoharlal Publishers.

Bṛhatsūcīpatra 7/3. *Nepālarājakīya-vīrapustakālayasthapustakānāṃ bṛhatsūcīpatram*. Volume 7/3. Ed. by Pūrṇaratnavajrācārya. Kāṭhmāṇḍū: Vīrapustakālaya, 1966.

BRINKHAUS, H. 1993. Textual History of the Different Versions of the "Svayambhū-Purāṇa". In: G. Toffin (ed.), *Nepal, Past and Present. Proceedings of the Franco-German Conference Arc-et-Senans, June 1990*: 63-71. Paris: CNRS Éditions.

BÜHNEMANN, G. 1994. Two Forms of Gaṇapati in the Indo-Tibetan Buddhist Tradition. *Wiener Zeitschrift für die Kunde Südasiens* 38: 201-211.

—— 2003. *Buddhist Deities of Nepal: Iconography in Two Sketchbooks*. Lumbini: Lumbini International Research Institute.

Deva, Raja Radha Kanta 1961. *Sabda-Kalpadrum: An Encyclopedic Dictionary of Sanskrit Words.* 5 parts. Varanasi: Chowkhamba Sanskrit Series Office.

Dharmakośasaṃgraha. *Dharmakoṣasaṅgraham* <by Amṛtānanda.> [Manuscript no. 8055 in the library of the Asiatic Society, Calcutta] <reproduced> by Lokesh Chandra. New Delhi: no publisher, 1973. (For a description of this manuscript, written in 1826 CE upon the request of Brian H. Hodgson, see Shāstri 1917: no. 119 [8055], pp. 191-193.)

Dharmakośasaṃgraha (2). *Paṃ. Amṛtānandako Dharmakośa-Saṅgraha (bauddha padāvalīko mūrtiko paribhāṣā).* Ed. by Mukundarāj Arjyāl. Kāṭhmāḍauṃ: Nepāl Rājakīya Prajñā-Pratiṣṭhān, 2002.

Dharmarāj Bajrācārya (ed.) 1997/1998. *Saptavāra Grahamātṛkā Pustakam.* Yala: Dharmarāj Bajrācārya (second edition).

Dhavalikar, M.K. 1970. Gaṇeśa Beyond the Indian Frontiers. In: Lokesh Chandra et al., *India's Contribution to World Thought and Culture. A Vivekananda Commemoration Volume:* 1-16. Madras: Vivekananda Rock Memorial Committee.

English, E. 2002. *Vajrayoginī: Her Visualizations, Rituals, & Forms. A Study of the Cult of Vajrayoginī in India.* Somerville, Massachusetts: Wisdom Publications.

Filliozat, J. 1935. Le Kumāratantra de Rāvaṇa. *Journal Asiatique* 226: 1-66.

—— 1941. *Catalogue du Fonds Sanscrit. Fascicule I – N° 1 à 165.* Paris: Adrien-Maisonneuve.

Gellner, D.N. 1992. *Monk, Householder, and Tantric Priest: Newar Buddhism and its Hierarchy of Ritual.* Cambridge: Cambridge University Press.

Getty, A. 1928. *The Gods of Northern Buddhism: Their History, Iconography and Progressive Evolution through the Northern Buddhist Countries.* Oxford: Clarendon Press (second edition)

—— 1936. *Gaṇeśa: A Monograph of the Elephant-faced God.* Oxford: Clarendon Press.

Grönbold, G. 1984. *Die Mythologie des indischen Buddhismus.* In: H.W. Haussig (ed.), *Götter und Mythen des indischen Subkontinents:* 285-508. Stuttgart: Klett-Cotta.

—— 2001. "Saptavāra". A Dhāraṇī Collection from Nepal. In: R. Torella (ed.), *Le Parole e i Marmi: Studi in Onore di Raniero Gnoli nel suo 70° Compleanno:* 369-375. 2 volumes. Rome: Istituto Italiano Per l'Africa e l'Oriente.

Hasrat, B.J. (ed.) 1970. *History of Nepal as Told by Its Own and Contemporary Chronicles.* Hoshiarpur: V.V. Research Institute Book Agency.

Hemrāj Śākya 1991. *Bauddha vidhikathaṃ jaṃkuyā. Saṃkṣipta paricaya.* Yala: Rājendra va Ramila Śākya.

HIDAS, G. 2003. Preliminary Notes on the Mahāpratisarā Mahāvidyārājñī, a Buddhist Protective Text from the Pañcarakṣā-collection. *Berliner Indologische Studien* 15/16/17: 263-284.

HODGSON, B.H. 1874 (1972). *Essays on the Languages, Literature and Religion of Nepal and Tibet together with Further Papers on the Geography, Ethnology and Commerce of Those Countries. Corrected and Augmented Edition of Two Earlier Collections of Essays ... With a Supplement of Additions and Corrections From the Author's Copy.* Ed. by M.P. Saha and with Other Additions, Omitted in the Former Edition. Amsterdam: Philo Press.

IWAMOTO, Y. (ed.) 1937a. *Mahāsāhasrapramardanī.* Kyoto: no publisher.

—— 1937b. *Kleinere Dhāraṇī Texte.* Kyoto: no publisher.

—— 1938. *Mahāpratisarā.* Kyoto: no publisher.

JANERT, K.L. & N.N. POTI 1970. *Indische und nepalesische Handschriften.* Teil 2. Wiesbaden: Franz Steiner Verlag.

—— 1985. *Indische Handschriften.* Teil 7. Wiesbaden: Franz Steiner Verlag.

KANE, P.V. 1968-1977. *History of Dharmaśāstra (Ancient and Medieval Religious and Civil Law in India).* 5 volumes. Poona: Bhandarkar Oriental Research Institute (second edition).

KIRFEL, W. 1948. *Die dreiköpfige Gottheit: Archäologisch-ethnologischer Streifzug durch die Ikonographie der Religionen.* Bonn: F. Dümmlers Verlag.

KOOIJ, K.R. van 1977. The Iconography of the Buddhist Wood-carvings in a Newar Monastery in Kathmandu (Chuṣya-Bāhā). *Journal of the Nepal Research Centre* 1: 39-82.

—— 1978. *Religion in Nepal.* Leiden: E.J. Brill.

KREIJGER, H.E. 1999. *Kathmandu Valley Painting: The Jucker Collection.* London: Serindia Publications.

LC. See BÜHNEMANN 2003.

LEWIS, T.T. 2000. *Popular Buddhist Texts from Nepal: Narratives and Rituals of Newar Buddhism.* Albany, New York: State University of New York Press.

LIEBERT, G. 1976. *Iconographic Dictionary of the Indian Religions: Hinduism – Buddhism – Jainism.* Leiden: E.J. Brill.

LIENHARD, S. & T.L. Manandhar 1988. *Nepalese Manuscripts. Part 1: Nevārī and Sanskrit, Staatsbibliothek Preussischer Kulturbesitz, Berlin.* Stuttgart: Franz Steiner Verlag Wiesbaden.

LOCKE, J.K. 1985. *Buddhist Monasteries of Nepal: A Survey of the Bāhās and Bahīs of the Kathmandu Valley.* Kathmandu: Sahayogi Press.

LOKESH CHANDRA (ed.) 1981. *Kāraṇḍavyūha and Other Texts: Sanskrit Manuscripts from Nepal reproduced from the Collection of Prof. Raghuvira.* New Delhi: Jayyed Press.

—— 1992. Iconography of the Goddess Uṣṇīṣavijayā. In: T. Chandrika (ed.), *Cultural Horizons of India:* 50-62. Volume 2. New Delhi: International Academy of Indian Culture and Aditya Prakashan. [Almost identical with: Iconography of the Goddess Uṣṇīṣavijayā. *Journal of the Indian Society of Oriental Art* (New Series) 10. 1978-1979: 17-29.]

—— 1999–. *Dictionary of Buddhist Iconography.* New Delhi: International Academy of Indian Culture and Aditya Prakashan.

MAHENDRARATNA ŚĀKYA 1994. *Vasundharā devī chagū adhyayan: A Study of Vasundhara Devi.* Lalitpur: Lotus Research Centre (in Nevārī).

MALLMANN, M.-Th. de 1975. *Introduction à l'iconographie du tântrisme bouddhique.* Paris: Adrien-Maisonneuve.

Manuscript 66.13.4, catalogued as *āryagrahamātṛkā nāma dhāraṇī*, dated 1635 CE, preserved in the Watson Collection of Indian Miniatures at the Elvehjem Museum of Art, Madison, Wisconsin (see also VAJRACHARYA 2002: 56-57).

Manuscript Cod. sanscr. 423, preserved in the Bayerische Staatsbibliothek, Munich (see also GRÖNBOLD 2001).

Manuscript 'Sanscrit 1814', preserved in the Bibliothèque Nationale, Paris.

MEVISSEN, G.J.R. 1989a. Studies in Pañcarakṣā Manuscript Painting. *Berliner Indologische Studien* 4/5: 339-374.

—— 1989b. *Ikonographie der Pañcarakṣā-s: Eine Studie über Ursprung und Verbreitung der bildlichen Darstellung der fünf weiblichen Schutzgottheiten im nördlichen Buddhismus* (unpublished M.A. thesis, submitted to the Freie Universität Berlin).

—— 1990-1991/1992. The Indian Connection: Images of Deified Spells in the Arts of Northern Buddhism. 2 parts. *Silk Road Art and Archaeology (Journal of the Institute of Silk Road Studies)* 1.1990: 227-246, 2.1991/1992: 351-382.

—— 1992. Transmission of Iconographic Traditions: Pañcarakṣā Heading North. In: C. Jarrige, J.P. Gerry & R.H. Meadow (eds.), *South Asian Archaeology 1989: Papers from the Tenth International Conference of South Asian Archaeologists in Western Europe, Musée national des Arts asiatiques–Guimet, Paris, France, 3-7 July 1989*: 415-424. Madison, Wisconsin: Prehistory Press.

—— 1998. Deliberate Coincidence or Accidental Purpose? Pañcarakṣā Sequences in Xylographs and Sketchbooks. *Berliner Indologische Studien* 11/12: 307-364.

—— 2004a. The Earliest Image of Grahamātṛkā. Buchmalerei aus Nepal. *Indo-Asiatische Zeitschrift (Mitteilungen der Gesellschaft für indo-asiatische Kunst)* 8: 47-62.

—— 2004b. Ladies and Planets. Images of Female Deities Accompanied by Graha Figures. In: C. Jarrige (ed.), *South Asian Archaeology 2001*. Paris (in press).

—— 2004c. Images of Buddhist Goddesses Accompanied by Astral Deities. In: G. Bhattacharya et al. (eds.), *Kalhāra-Mālikā: Adhyāpak Enamul Haque Abhinandan Grantha (Professor Enamul Haque Felicitation Volume)*. Delhi: Kaveri Books (in press).

—— (this volume) Iconography of Grahamātṛkā. In: A.J. Gail, G.J.R Mevissen & R. Salomon (eds.), *Papers of the 12th World Sanskrit Conference held in Helsinki, Finland, 13-18 July 2003. Vol. 11.1*: 65-97, pls. XVIII-XXIV. Delhi: Motilal Banarsidass.

MINAYEFF, I.P. & S. OLDENBURG 1983. *Buddhist Texts from Kashgar and Nepal*. New Delhi: International Academy of Indian Culture (reprint).

MITRA, R.L. 1882 (1971). *The Sanskrit Buddhist Literature of Nepal*. Calcutta: Sanskrit Pustak Bhandar (reprint).

MORIGUCHI, M. 1989. *A Catalogue of the Buddhist Tantric Manuscripts in the National Archives of Nepal and Kesar Library*. Tokyo: Sankibou Busshorin.

NAGAR, S.L. 1989. *Composite Deities in Indian Art and Literature*. Delhi: Criterion Publications.

Niṣpannayogāvalī. *Niṣpannayogāvalī of Mahāpaṇḍita Abhayākaragupta*. Ed. by B. Bhattacharyya. Baroda: Oriental Institute, 1949.

PAL, P. & D.C. BHATTACHARYYA 1969. *The Astral Divinities of Nepal*. Varanasi: Prithivi Prakashan.

PRUSCHA, C. (ed.) 1975. *Kathmandu Valley: The Preservation of Physical Environment and Cultural Heritage: A Protective Inventory. Prepared by His Majesty's Government of Nepal in Collaboration with the United Nations and Unesco*. 2 volumes. Vienna: Anton Schroll & Co. Publishers.

PRZYLUSKI, J. 1923. Les Vidyārāja: Contribution à l'histoire de la magie dans les sectes mahāyānistes. *Bulletin de l'École Française d'Extrême-Orient* 23: 301-318.

REIS-HABITO, M.D. 1993. *Die Dhāraṇī des grossen Erbarmens des Bodhisattva Avalokiteśvara mit tausend Händen und Augen: Übersetzung und Untersuchung ihrer textlichen Grundlage sowie Erforschung ihres Kultes in China*. Nettetal: Steyler Verlag.

Śabdakalpadruma. See DEVA, Raja Radha Kanta 1961.

SANFORD, J.H. 1991. Literary Aspects of Japan's Dual-Gaṇeśa Cult. In: R.L. Brown (ed.), *Ganesh: Studies of an Asian God*: 287-335. Albany, New York: State University of New York Press.

SHARMA, B.N. 1979. *Iconography of Vaināyakī*. New Delhi: Abhinav Publications.

ṢHĀSTRI, H.P. 1917. *A Descriptive Catalogue of Sanscrit Manuscripts in the Government Collection. Under the Care of the Asiatic Society of Bengal. Vol. I. Buddhist Manuscripts*. Calcutta: Baptist Mission Press.

SKILLING, P. 1994. *Mahāsūtras: Great Discourses of the Buddha. Volume I: Texts*. Oxford: The Pali Text Society.

SM. *Sādhanamālā*. Ed. by B. Bhattacharyya. 2 volumes. Baroda: Oriental Institute, 1925-1928.

Svayambhū-Purāṇa. *The Vṛhat Svayambhú Puráṇam. Containing the Traditions of the Svayambhu Kshetra in Nepal*. Ed. by Haraprasád Sástrí. 5 fascicles. Calcutta: Baptist Mission Press, 1894-1896.

TAKAOKA, H. (ed.) 1981. *A Microfilm Catalogue of the Buddhist Manuscripts in Nepal*. Volume 1. Nagoya: Buddhist Library.

TAKUBO, S. (ed.) 1972. *Ārya-Mahā-Māyūrī Vidyā-Rājñī*. Tokyo: Sankibo.

TSUKAMOTO, K., Y. MATSUNAGA & H. ISODA 1989. *Bongo Butten no Kenkyū IV: Mikkyō Kyoten Hen (A Descriptive Bibliography of the Sanskrit Buddhist Literature. Volume 4: The Buddhist Tantra)*. Kyoto: Heirakuji-Shoten (in Japanese).

VAJRACHARYA, G.V. 2002. *Watson Collection of Indian Miniatures at the Elvehjem Museum of Art: A Detailed Study of Selected Works*. Madison, Wisconsin: Elvehjem Museum of Art.

WADDELL, L.A. 1912. The "Dhāraṇī" Cult in Buddhism: Its Origin, Deified Literature and Images. *Ostasiatische Zeitschrift* 1: 155-195.

WILKINSON, C. 1991. The Tantric Gaṇeśa: Texts Preserved in the Tibetan Canon. In: R.L. Brown (ed.), *Ganesh: Studies of an Asian God*: 235-275. Albany, New York: State University of New York Press.

WILLSON, M. & M. BRAUEN 2000 (eds.). *Deities of Tibetan Buddhism: The Zürich Paintings of the Icons Worthwhile to See (Bris sku mthoṅ ba don ldan)*. Translated by M. Willson. Introduced by M. Brauen. Boston: Wisdom Publications.

YANO, M. 2003. Calendar, Astrology, and Astronomy. In: G. Flood (ed.), *The Blackwell Companion to Hinduism*: 376-392. Oxford: Blackwell Publishing.

YUYAMA, A. 1997. The Uṣṇīṣa-vijayā Dhāraṇī Transliterated by Tz'u-hsien. In: P. Kieffer-Pülz & J.-U. Hartmann (eds.), *Bauddhavidyāsudhākaraḥ: Studies in Honour of Heinz Bechert on the Occasion of His 65th Birthday*: 729-742. Swisttal-Odendorf: Indica et Tibetica Verlag.

—— 2000. An Uṣṇīṣa-Vijayā Dhāraṇī Text from Nepal. *Annual Report of the International Research Institute for Advanced Buddhology at Soka University for the Academic Year 1999*: 165-175. Tokyo: The International Research Institute for Advanced Buddhology, Soka University.

Iconography of Grahamātṛkā

GERD J.R. MEVISSEN

The goddess Grahamātṛkā, the "Mother of the [nine] heavenly bodies",[1] also called Mahādevī or Mahāvidyā, appears quite late on the stage of the Buddhist pantheon. According to Lokesh Chandra (2002: 1290) the "Grahamātṛkā-dhāraṇī was translated [from Sanskrit] into Tibetan by an anonymous person (Toh 661), and into Chinese by Fa-t'ien in AD 990 (K 1180, T 1303). [...] This is the earliest date of a text on the goddess".[2]

Grahamātṛkā is not mentioned among the innumerable deities described in the *Sādhanamālā* (compiled up to the 12th/13th century), nor does she take shape in one of the twenty-six complex *maṇḍalas* designed and systematized by Abhayākaragupta in his opus magnum *Niṣpannayogāvalī* in the beginning of the 12th century.[3] The concept of Grahamātṛkā, which provides the group of male Hindu planetary deities (Navagraha) collectively with a Buddhist *mātṛkā*, seems to have gained prominence shortly after the final redaction of the above two texts.

---

[1] For a discussion on the different interpretations of the name "Grahamātṛkā" see Bühnemann (this volume): 53-54. I am indebted to Gudrun Bühnemann for valuable suggestions.

[2] A work titled *Ārya-graha-mātṛkā-nāma-dhāraṇī* is mentioned on a *dKar chag* (Table of Contents) folio listing *dhāraṇī* texts, discovered in 1993 among the manuscript remains at Tabo; the *dhāraṇī* text itself is only partially extant. The manuscript remains have been tentatively dated "to the middle of the 9th century [...] or [...] the 11th"; cf. Harrison 1996: 49, 56-57 (no. 22, with further references to the occurrence of this text), 68.

[3] For Abhayākaragupta's life and works see Bühnemann 1992.

TEXTUAL DESCRIPTIONS

The earliest description of the iconography of Grahamātṛkā is found in the *Kriyāsamuccaya* of Jagaddarpaṇa, who must have lived between the latter half of the 12th and the middle of the 13th century (Bühnemann 1992-93: 18), i.e. roughly a century after Abhayākaragupta's time. Descriptions are also found in several Tibetan texts and in later *dhāraṇī* collections from Nepal.[4]

All the known texts describe the goddess as white-complexioned, with three heads and six arms, and displaying with her main pair of hands the gesture of exposition (*vyākhyānamudrā* or *dharmacakramudrā*). These features can be regarded as her principle marks of identification. However, the texts differ in the colour of the lateral heads and in the attributes held in the remaining two pairs of hands. Thus, two major types (Types I and II) can be discerned.

Type I is described in Jagaddarpaṇa's *Kriyāsamuccaya* as follows:[5] *vāyau bhaṭṭārikā mahāvidyā sitanīlāruṇatrimukhā mūlabhujābhyā[ṃ]*[6] *vyākhyānamudrā savye padmaratnachaṭā vāme pāśaśaktidharā(ḥ) ratnamukuṭinī vajraparyaṅkinī candrāsanā dviraṣṭābdā sarvālaṃkāravatī //* "In the northwest [of the Navagraha-*maṇḍala*] is the venerable Mahāvidyā. She has three heads, white, blue and red. With the main hands (she displays) the gesture of exposition. On the right is a lotus and *ratnacchaṭā* (cluster of jewels), on the left (her hands) hold a noose and *śakti* (spear/lance). She wears a jewelled diadem, is (seated) in *vajraparyaṅka* on a moon (disk), is two times eight (= sixteen) years old (and) possessed of all kinds of ornaments". Several *Dhāraṇīsaṃgraha* manuscripts contain an almost identical description of the goddess but use slightly different vocabulary.[7]

---

[4] Pal & Bhattacharyya 1969: 42, 71; Mallmann 1975: 178; Chandra 2002: 1288-1292.

[5] Quoted from a manuscript dated 1965/66 AD, published in Chandra 1977: 431, lines 2-4. I am grateful to Gudrun Bühnemann for providing a xerox of the text and for her help in translating the passage. Cf. also Willson & Brauen 2000: 415, no. 505.

[6] The manuscript reads "... *mūlabhūjābhyā* ".

[7] E.g. *śvetanīlāruṇatrimukhā*; cf. Pal & Bhattacharyya 1969: 71.

The main iconographic features can be summarized in the following table:

TABLE 1:	**Type I**	
Colour of heads	blue - white - red	
attributes	(right)	(left)
	cluster of jewels	noose
	lotus	spear/lance
	gesture of exposition	
sitting posture	*vajraparyaṅka*	

Type II can be devided into sub-types a and b; the only difference between a and b concerns the colour of the left lateral head. Type II(a) is found in several Tibetan sources, e.g. in the *Rin-lhan* and in Tāranātha's *Rin-'byuṅ*,[8] in Bu-ston's treatise on the Kriyātantra,[9] in the collection of *sādhana*s titled *rGyud-sde kun-btus*,[10] and in a Tibetan blockprint titled *Yi dam lha srung ma dang bcas pa'i sgrub thabs dang rjes gnang zur kha brgya rtsa dngos grub 'byung gnas zhes bya ba bzhugs so.*[11]

Type II(b) is described in the 19th-century Nepalese text *Dharmakoṣasaṃgraha* of Amṛtānanda as follows:[12] *grahamātṛkā trimukhā śvetapītaraktā ṣaḍbhujā dakṣe dharmacakramudrā vajraśara vāme kamalacāpa sahasradalapadme vajrāsanā* // "Grahamātṛkā has three heads, white, yellow and red. She is six-armed. On the right she displays the gesture of exposition (and holds) a *vajra* and an arrow, on the left a

[8] Cf. Willson & Brauen 2000: 300, no. 223; and 433, no. 223, cols. "*R*" and "Tār." for references.

[9] Fol. 23[illegible], cf. Tucci 1941/1989, I: 190.

[10] Cf. Dagyab 1991: 54.

[11] Fol. 34b; cf. Nebesky-Wojkowitz 1956/1975: 262-263, 598.

[12] Fol. 44A; quoted *verbatim* from Pal & Bhattacharyya 1969: 58, note 67.

lotus and a bow. She is (seated) in *vajrāsana* on a thousand-petalled lotus." According to Bhattacharyya (1974: 9) Amṛtānanda, when composing the *Dharmakoṣasaṃgraha* at the request of Brian Hodgson in Newari era 946 (= 1826 AD), used materials from various other sources, among these the *Kriyāsamuccaya*. However, he obviously did not copy the iconography of Grahamātṛkā from the latter text but rather took note of the images of the goddess that were current and wide spread in 19th-century Nepal.

The main iconographic features of Type II (a and b) can be summarized in the following table:

TABLE 2:	Type II(a)		Type II(b)	
Colour of heads	blue - white - red		yellow - white - red	
attributes	(right)	(left)	(right)	(left)
	arrow *vajra*	bow lotus	arrow *vajra*	bow lotus
	gesture of exposition		gesture of exposition	
sitting posture	*vajraparyaṅka*		*vajrāsana*	

IMAGES

Only few representations of Grahamātṛkā have been hitherto published,[13] and modern standard works on Buddhist iconography deal with the goddess rather casually.[14] As many as 49 images have been listed in the catalogue below. The earliest image of Grahamātṛkā is painted on a 12th/13th-century wooden manuscript cover from Nepal (# 1, PLATE

[13] The most complete list of images of the goddess published so far has been compiled by Lokesh Chandra (2002: 1288-1292); it comprises nine entries.

[14] See e.g. Bhattacharyya 1924: 157; 1958: 224-225; Pal & Bhattacharyya 1969: 42-43, 71; Mallmann 1975: 178.

XVIII.A) where she appears as the first figure in a row of six goddesses, the other five comprising the Pañcarakṣā pentad. This combination points to a close association – already in early times – between Grahamātṛkā and the Pañcarakṣās, which is encountered in many of the later images (## 2, 4, 14-15, 18, 21-22, 31-32, 36, 39-43). The corresponding wooden cover has depictions of the Seven Mortal Buddhas.[15] The iconography of the Grahamātṛkā image corresponds to Type I; only the complexion is slightly yellowish rather than purely white, and the right face is dark green rather than blue.

The earliest known representations of Grahamātṛkā according to Type II are found in southern Central Tibet: the principal clay sculpture (# 30, FIGURE 13) and two wall paintings (## 12, 13, PLATE XX.A) in the Grahamātṛkā chapel (gZa'-yum lha-khang) of the Great Stūpa ('Kumbum') at Gyantse, dating from the second quarter of the 15th century. Type II is also applied to the small subsidiary figure of Grahamātṛkā in an Uṣṇīṣavijayā painting, which also includes subsidiary figures of the Pañcarakṣās (# 21), and to the principal figure of the goddess in a slightly later scroll painting (# 16, PLATE XX.B). The planetary deities (Navagraha) occur as subsidiary figures in at least one of the Gyantse murals (# 12) and in the latter thangka (# 16). The Navagrahas are shown twice – as is the goddess herself – in the 19th/20th-century Grahamātṛkā-*maṇḍala* from the 'Ngor Collection'. Interestingly, the principal image of the goddess (## 19, 23, FIGURES 4, 5, PLATE XXII), who has a figure of Sūrya placed upside down beneath her while the remaining *graha*s surround this central pair, corresponds to Type II whereas the peripheral image in the northwestern quarter (## 20, 24, FIGURE 5) seems to follow Type I; this, however, is not really certain due to the tiny size of the figure and insufficient printing quality of the published *maṇḍala*.

---

[15] Cf. Grönbold 1991: 26-28, no. 2, col.pl.; Mevissen 2004: Abb. 2. Perhaps the Seven Buddhas are meant to symbolize the first seven planets (Sun through Saturn) after whom the seven days of the week are named. On the possible connection between the Seven Buddhas and the seven planets see the thought-provoking discussion by Simson 1981.

That Type I was also depicted in southern Central Tibet in the 15th century is evident from two scroll paintings (## 14, 15, PLATE XXI) of which at least one was commissioned by Ngor-chen Kun-dga'-bzang-po and painted by Newari artists from the Kathmandu valley at Ngor monastery between 1429 and 1456. The thangka (# 14) is inscriptionally referred to as the fourteenth painting of a complete set of *maṇḍalas* based on Abhayākaragupta's *Vajrāvalī* cycle, with three additional *maṇḍalas* from Jagaddarpaṇa's *Kriyāsamuccaya* collection (cf. Jackson 1996: 78-82). One of the four sub-*maṇḍalas*, viz. the lower left one in the southeast of the whole composition, faithfully illustrates the Grahamātṛkā-*maṇḍala* described in the latter text. The goddess is seated eccentrically in the northwest of the central square which is dominated by the *maṇḍala* of the sun-god Sūrya surrounded by the other eight *grahas*. A two-fold link exists between this sub-*maṇḍala* and the Pañcarakṣā goddesses: on the one hand they occupy the southwestern sub-*maṇḍala* just above (the other two sub-*maṇḍalas* are dedicated to Vasudhārā and Uṣṇīṣavijayā), and on the other hand they dominate the overriding *maṇḍala*, thereby combining the four sub-*maṇḍalas* and forming an integrated whole (see PLATE XXI). This scheme is slightly modified in a modern painting (# 18) whereas another scroll reproduces only the Grahamātṛkā-sub-*maṇḍala* (# 17). We thus notice that Types I and II existed side by side and were used simultaneously in Tibet from the 15th century onwards (see Table 3).

Not only paintings but also three-dimensional images of Grahamātṛkā were produced in Tibet. Apart from the clay sculpture at Gyantse mentioned above (# 30, FIGURE 13), two metal sculptures of the goddess could be identified so far. Whereas the one listed under # 35 (PLATE XXIV.B) lost all its attributes, thus making it impossible to determine whether the iconography corresponds to Type I or II, the beautiful gilded bronze image listed under # 34 (PLATE XXIV.A) retains all its four attributes and may thus be classified under Type II, although the sitting posture deviates from the usual *vajrāsana*. The loose *vajra*, presently placed in her front right hand, has probably been moved there from its original position in the second right hand.

Century	Nepal			Tibet		Mongolia		China
	Type I	Type II	Type III	Type I	Type II	Type I	Type II	Type I
12th/13th	1	-	-	-	-	-	-	-
15th	-	-	-	14, (15)	12,13,16, 21,30,34	-	-	-
16th	33	-	31	-	-	-	-	-
17th	-	11, 22	32	-	-	-	-	-
18th	5, 26	2, 3, 4, 5	-	17	35	-	-	27
19th	-	6, 7, 8, 9, 10	-	20	19	29	28	-
20th	-	-	-	18, (24)	23	-	-	-

TABLE 3: Grahamātṛkā images (1-35) time-, type-, and regionwise

In Nepal the goddess manifested herself – after a long gap of several centuries – in two complex wooden roof-strut *maṇḍala*s in the courtyards of the monasteries Pinchẽ Bāhā and Chuṣya Bāhā in the city centre of Kathmandu (## 31, 32, FIGURES 14, 15). In both instances Grahamātṛkā is part of a group of seven *dhāraṇī*-deities known as Saptavāra (Seven Days of the Week),[16] among them Vasudhārā and Uṣṇīṣavijayā. The Pañcarakṣās are carved on neighbouring roof-struts.[17] Another group of rarely represented astral deities, the 27 Nakṣatras (lunar mansions) personified as two-armed seated goddesses in human form, appears on small relief panels at the bottom of the struts.[18]

[16] For the Saptavāra deities see Bühnemann (this volume): 32-37 and *passim*, and Grönbold 2001. For illustrations of the roof-strut figures see Kooij 1977: 60-66, figs. 30-36; Kooij 1978: 25-27, pls. XLVa-d, XLVIa-c (Mārīcī in XLVIb mirror-reversed). All illustrations are from the Chuṣya Bāhā; those of the Pinchẽ Bāhā are unpublished.

[17] Chuṣya Bāhā: Kooij 1977: 57-59, figs. 25-29; Mevissen 1989b: Kat. S.IV.A.1, Abb. 20a-c. Pinchẽ Bāhā: Chandra 2003: figs. on pp. 1955, 1976, 2001, 2011.

[18] Cf. Kooij 1977: 66-72, figs. 32, 34-37k; Kooij 1978: 27, pls. XLVa-d, XLVIa-c, XLVII.a (all from Chuṣya Bāhā). Two Nakṣatra goddesses are visible on our FIGURES 14 and 15. In the Pinchẽ Bāhā, some struts with Nakṣatras are missing and their original total number is unknown; except for our FIGURE 15, all are unpublished.

The two large wooden figures of Grahamātṛkā are peculiar in several respects: they are the only images that are shown standing, with only one head and two hands in *dharmacakramudrā*, the major identification mark of the goddess. This iconography, being derived by reduction from the standard three-headed and six-armed form of the goddess, may thus be classified as a separate type (Type III). Apparently this abbreviated form, for which no textual reference is known so far, was invented by those who conceived the struts. The same reduction strategy was also applied to the other usually multi-armed and multi-headed goddesses (e.g. Uṣṇīṣavijayā and Vasudhārā) represented on the struts. In the Chuṣya Bāhā even the Pañcarakṣās, including the twelve-armed Mahāmantrānusāriṇī and the eight-armed Mahāpratisarā, were reduced to single-headed and two-armed forms. – A unique feature of the Pinchẽ Bāhā is a second (tiny) image of Grahamātṛkā (Type I, # 33, FIGURE 16); paired with a relief of Uṣṇīṣavijayā it flanks the outer entrance.

In the 17th century the popularity of Grahamātṛkā began to rise considerably. In Nepal, especially during the 18th and 19th centuries, numerous Saptavāradhāraṇī manuscripts were produced,[19] often embellished with illustrations of the seven goddesses including Grahamātṛkā (## 2, 3, 5-11, FIGURES 1-3, PLATES XVIII.B, XIX.B).[20] In the Saptavāra system Grahamātṛkā is linked with the Saturday (Śanivāra), as visible on the leaf illustrated in PLATE I.B where we read "*sanicaravāla*" in the left margin. Generally the iconography of the goddess corresponds to Type II(b), though often there are deviations regarding the colour of the lateral heads (## 3, 5, 6, 7, 10) and the sitting posture (## 7, 9).

An enigmatic image, exceptionally found not in a Saptavāra but in a Pañcarakṣā manuscript (# 4, PLATE XIX.A), poses major identification problems as regards (i) the female nature of the goddess, which is not really explicit, (ii) the yellowish complexion, and (iii) the principal hands, which are crossed in front of the breast holding indistinguishable

---

[19] See Bühnemann (this volume): 32-37, 57, note 53, and Grönbold 2001: 370-371.

[20] It remains to be verified whether the Saptavāradhāraṇī manuscripts listed under ## 16-19 do (or did) contain images of Grahamātṛkā. The same applies to the wooden book covers listed under ## 43-45.

attributes rather than showing the usual preaching gesture. Further, although the colour of both lateral heads, the sitting stance, and three of the four attributes follow the iconography of Type II(a) images, the long-stemmed jewel(?) in the second right hand – instead of the *vajra* – is an attribute of Type I images. Therefore, the identification of this figure as Grahamāṭṛkā is not without doubt, even if the close association with the Pañcarakṣās may point in this direction.

Another presumably large number of Nepalese Grahamātṛkā images is hinted at by the Uṣṇīṣavijayā-*caitya* painting (# 22) in which the goddess – with Type II(b) iconography – appears in the socle of the *caitya* above a row depicting the Pañcarakṣā goddesses. In addition, the painting shows, among others, figures of the Navagrahas and Nakṣatras, arranged in a circle around the central *caitya*. The painting commemorates the *bhīmaratha* rite which is celebrated when a person reaches the age of 77 years, 7 months and 7 days (cf. Pal 1977; Vergati 1999). That Grahamātṛkā – together with Uṣṇīṣavijayā and Vasudhārā – plays an important role in this rite has first been noted by Tanaka (2001: 208).[21] A number of paintings has been listed under ## 36-41 in which a white, three-headed and six-armed goddess with her principal pair of hands joined in front of her breasts is depicted. Besides Uṣṇiṣavijayā-*caityas* the list comprises also *lakṣacaitya* paintings – commemorating a rite related to the *bhīmaratha* – and *paubhās* with Vasudhārā as the principal deity. Close scrutinization of these (and other) examples is necessary to build up a relevant corpus of representations of this so far little-known aspect of Grahamātṛkā, and it is hoped that further research will clarify questions regarding the function and religious significance of the goddess within the above mentioned rituals.

---

[21] Recent research carried out by Marianna Kropf on rituals dealing with Navagraha worship in the Newar communities of the Kathmandu valley seems to indicate that the Grahamātṛkā is not (only) linked with the *bhīmaratha* rite but (also) with the *mahāratha* rite, celebrated when a person reaches the age of 99 years, 9 months and 9 days (personal communication). In this connection it is interesting to note that the *grahamātṛkādhāraṇī* "insures longevity to ninety-nine years [and] prevents all evils resulting from adverse planets ..." (Mitra 1882: 92). The repeated occurrence of the number '9' may or may not be due to the relation of the goddess to the Navagrahas.

In the 18th and 19th centuries, also Type I images of Grahamātṛkā continue to be represented: they are found in two Nepalese sketch-books (## 25-26, FIGURES 6-7) and in two lamaistic pantheons from China (# 27, FIGURE 8) and Mongolia (## 28-29, FIGURES -12, PLATE XXIII).

DEVIATIONS FROM THE TEXTUAL DESCRIPTIONS

Only a rather small number of images corresponds to the respective textual iconography without deviations, e.g. ## 2 (PLATE XV), 12 (PLATE XX.A), 14, 15 (PLATE XXI), 16 (PLATE XX.B), 19 (PLATE XXII), 25 (FIGURE 6) and 26 (FIGURE 7). Most images, however, deviate in certain details from the prescribed iconography. The deviations encountered are of different nature. They concern (i) the complexion or colours of the lateral heads,[22] (ii) the hand attributes, and (iii) the stance of the goddess.

Ad (i): Three images show the goddess with a yellowish instead of a pure white complexion (# 1, PLATE XVIII.A; # 4, PLATE XIX.A; # 13), and also in # 7 (FIGURE 1) the complexion appears somehow darker than white. More often, the colours of the lateral heads have been altered: one image (# 22) shows exchanged colours of the lateral heads, while in five images (# 3, PLATE XVIII.B; ## 5, 6, 11, 21) the left face is blue instead of red. Since the latter five images correspond to Type II(b), this deviation can be explained as a partial intrusion of the colour scheme of Type II(a) into these II(b) images rather than as indicating a separate and otherwise unknown new *Type II(c).

Ad (ii): Alterations of certain attributes are manifold: in # 3 (PLATE XVIII.B) we see the upper right hand wielding a sword instead of a *vajra* (cf. # 36); in # 4 (PLATE XIX.A) the second right hand holds a long-stemmed jewel instead of a *vajra*; in ## 6 and 10 (FIGURE 3), and perhaps in # 11, there is a cluster of three jewels instead of a *vajra* in the second

[22] This feature can, of course, only be judged from the images that have been published in colour or have been thoroughly described.

right hand and three peacock feathers instead of a lotus in the second left hand; in # 17 the *pāśa* has been moved from a left to a right hand and the *ratnacchaṭā*, here rendered as a single *ratna*, from right to left.

The different forms of the gesture of the front hands, called *vyākhyānamudrā* or *dharmacakramudrā* in the textual sources, should also briefly be mentioned: we find (a) the 'classical' *dharmacakramudrā*, i.e. both hands or some fingers of both hands joined in front of the breast with the back of the left hand and the palm of the right hand facing towards the observer (FIGURES 1-3, 6-8, 16, PLATES XVIII.A-B, XX.A-B, XXII, XXIV.B); (b) a variation of this with the fingers of the left hand touching the wrist of the right hand (FIGURES 4, 13, PLATE XIX.B); (c) both hands held symmetrically with the palms facing the observer (FIGURES 9-12, PLATE XXIII.A-B); (d) the 'classical' *añjalimudrā* (FIGURE 14); (e) both arms crossed at the wrists with the backs of both hands facing the observer (PLATE XIX.A); and (f) both hands not joined but held apart from each other as if holding a large wheel (PLATE XXIV.A).

Ad (iii): Though all textual sources describe the goddess as being seated in *vajraparyaṅka* or *vajrāsana*, i.e. sitting with crossed legs while the feet rest on the opposite thighs, there are a number of images with deviating postures. Apart from the two standing wooden roof-strut figures (## 31-32, FIGURES 14-15), which also reduce other standard features (three heads, six arms) thus forming a separate type (*supra*), we find four images in which the goddess is seated in *ardhaparyaṅka*, i.e. sitting with one leg pendent or thrown to the front: in ## 7 (FIGURE 1) and 34 (PLATE XXIV.A) the left leg is moved, in ## 8 (PLATE XIX.B) and 9 (FIGURE 2) it is the right leg. Since five of these images (## 7-9, 31-32) are identified by label inscriptions or other written evidence as representations of Grahamātṛkā, it is clear that the iconography as laid down in the texts were not considered mandatory by the artists.

It should be noted that most of the deviations mentioned above occur in later images from Nepal, though also some images from Tibet, which generally keep close to the prescribed iconography, show distinct deviations (## 1[illegible], 17, 21, and especially 34, PLATE XXIV.A).

DEITIES ASSOCIATED WITH GRAHAMĀTṚKĀ

A number of different deities seem to be closely connected with Grahamātṛkā. The most important ones have been summarized in Table 4.

Already the earliest image of Grahamātṛkā from Nepal (# 1) shows her as the first figure in a row followed by the five Pañcarakṣā goddesses. The close association with the Pañcarakṣās is also prevalent right from the beginning of her occurrence in Tibet in the 15th century (## 14, 15) and remains valid up to modern times (# 18).

In Nepal, sometime in or before the 17th century, Grahamātṛkā became an integral part of the group of Saptavāra deities, though close relations to some goddesses of this group, especially Uṣṇīṣavijayā and Vasudhārā, are certainly older (## 14, 15, 21). Interestingly, five of the seven chapels on the first storey of the 'Kumbum' at Gyantse (Tibet), which correspond, by their position in the ground plan, to the chapel housing three Grahamātṛkā images (## 12, 13, 30), are dedicated to deities that (later) became members of the Nepalese Saptavāra group, viz. Vasudhārā, Dhvajāgrakeyūrā, Uṣṇīṣavijayā, Mārīcī and Parṇaśabarī, the two remaining chapels being dedicated to Sitātapatrā and Vaiśravaṇa.[23]

Being an astral goddess herself, it is not astonishing to find the images of Grahamātṛkā, the "Mother of the heavenly bodies", closely associated with representations of her "children", the nine planetary deities (Navagraha: ## 12-20, 22-24), and other astral deities such as the lunar mansions (Nakṣatra: ## 14-15, 17-18, 20, 22, 24, 31-32) and the zodiacal signs (Rāśi: ## 20, 24). From the 15th century onwards such images occur predominantly in Tibet, but also – especially in the 16th and 17th centuries – in Nepal (## 22, 31-32).

As is obvious from Table 4, the iconographic type of the goddess (Types I, II, III) is not relevant for her association with the above deities. Further research is necessary to deepen our understanding of the special relations between Grahamātṛkā and these deities.

---

[23] Cf. Ricca & Lo Bue 1993: 224 (Fig. A, ground plan), 227-228, 232-233, 237-238, 242-243.

TABLE 4:	Grahamātṛkā images (1-35): Associated Deities							
#	Uṣṇīṣ°	Vasu°	Pañca°	Nava°	Nakṣ°	Origin	Date	Type
1			●			Nepal	12th/13th	I
2	●	●	●			Nepal	ca. 18th	II
3	○	○				Nepal	ca. 18th	II
4			●			Nepal	1748	II
5	●	●				Nepal	ca. 19th	II
6	●	●				Nepal	ca. 19th	II
7	○	○				Nepal	1843	II
8	●	●				Nepal	ca. 19th	II
9	●	●				Nepal	ca. 19th	II
10	●	●				Nepal	ca. 19th	II
11	●	●				Nepal	1642/43	II
12	○	○		●		Tibet	15th	II
13	○	○		○		Tibet	15th	II
14	●	●	●	●	●	Tibet	1429-56	I
15	●	●	●	●	●	Tibet	ca. 15th(?)	I
16				●		Tibet	ca. 15th	II
17				●	●	Tibet(?)	ca. 18th(?)	I
18	●	●	●	●	●	Tibet	19th/20th	I(?)
19				●		Tibet	1870-92	II
20				●	●	Tibet	1870-92	I(?)
21	●	○	●			Tibet	ca. 15th	II
22	●		●	●	●	Nepal	ca. 17th	II
23				●		(Tibet)	20th	II
24				●	●	(Tibet)	20th	I(?)
25	●					Nepal	ca. 18th	I
26	●					Nepal	ca. 18th	I
27						China	ca. 1761	I
28						Mong.	after 1810	II
29	●	●				Mong.	after 1810	I
30	○	○		○		Tibet	15th	II
31	●	●	●		●	Nepal	late 16th	III
32	●	●	●		●	Nepal	ca. 17th	III
33	●	○	○		○	Nepal	late 16th	I
34						Tibet	ca. 15th	II
35						Tibet	ca. 18th	I/II

CATALOGUE OF GRAHAMĀTṚKĀ IMAGES

The following list has been compiled by surveying numerous publications. It is organized according to the material (painting, drawing, blockprint, sculpture) and provenance (Nepal, Tibet, China). Internally it roughly follows a chronological order.

The first section (## 1-35) comprises images that can with some certainty be identified as Grahamātṛkā, while the second section ("Further Images") lists fourteen entries (## 36-49) which need further scrutiny in order to verify the presence of the goddess and the specific type.

PAINTINGS / DRAWINGS / BLOCKPRINTS

NEPAL: Painting on wooden manuscript boards

1. Bayerische Staatsbibliothek, München (Cod. sanscr. 540), first image in the row followed by the Pañcarakṣās (cf. # 43); ca. 12th/13th century; Type I; deviations: complexion yellowish (cf. ## 4, 13), right face green instead of blue. Ref.: Grönbold 1991: 26-28, no. 2 (col.pl.); Mevissen 2004: Abb. 2, 3 (col.pls.). .... PLATE XVIII.A

NEPAL: Painting on paper manuscript leaves

2. The Gujarat Museum Society, N.C. Mehta Gallery, Ahmedabad (ms. 258), fol. 29b; ms. shows images of Pañcarakṣās on 5 fols.; ca. 18th century; Type II(b). Ref.: Bühnemann (this volume): 53-55, pl. XV. PLATE XV
3. Philadelphia Museum of Art (1959-93-90(2,a), gift of Mr and Mrs Lessing J. Rosenwald), folio of Saptavāradhāraṇī ms.; ca. 18th century; Type II(b), deviations: left face blue instead of red; right: sword instead of *vajra*. .... PLATE XVIII.B
4. Staatsbibliothek zu Berlin (Hs.or. 1934), Pañcarakṣā ms., fol. 111a (last image, following the Pañcarakṣās); dated NS 868 = 29 June 1748 AD; Type II(a); deviations: complexion yellow rather than white (cf. ## 1, 13), right: *ratnacchaṭā* (with repainting?) instead of *vajra*; front arms crossed. Ref.: Janert & Poti 1970: 109-111, Nos. 656-660; Mevissen 1989a: 370-371, no. 28, note 82 "possibly ... Mañjuvajra"; 1989b: Kat. M.II.A. 28(e) "Mañjuvajra", Tafel 19e (col.pl.). .... PLATE XIX.A

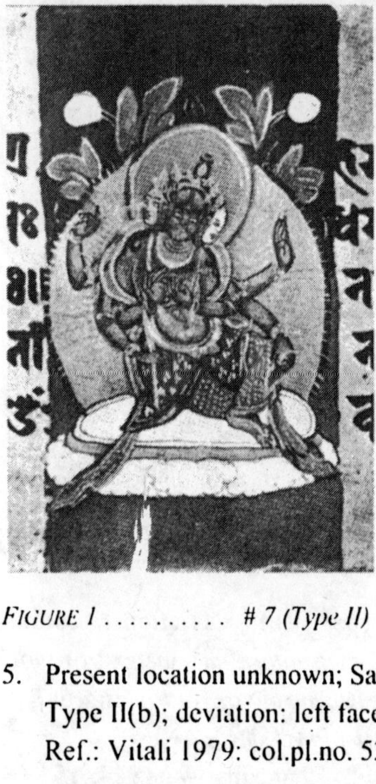

FIGURE 1 .... # 7 (Type II)

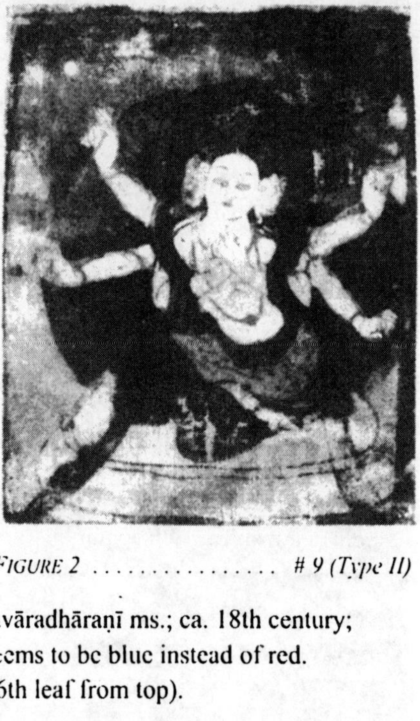

FIGURE 2 .... # 9 (Type II)

5. Present location unknown; Saptavāradhāraṇī ms.; ca. 18th century;
Type II(b); deviation: left face seems to be blue instead of red.
Ref.: Vitali 1979: col.pl.no. 52 (6th leaf from top).

6. Bibliothèque National Paris (Sanskrit 1814), Saptavāradhāraṇī ms., fol. 14v; ca. 19th century;
Type II(b); deviations: left face blue instead of red; right: *ratnacchaṭā* instead of *vajra*, left: *mayūrapiccha* instead of *kamala* (cf. # 10).
Ref.: Getty 1914: col.pl. LXI.*a* (erroneously labelled "*b*"; this error as well as Getty's wrong identification as "Bhṛikuṭī" have been pointed out by Bhattacharyya 1924: 59; in the revised edition [1928] and subsequent reprints [1962/1978] the error has been corrected); Bhattacharyya 1958: 225, n. 1 (not ill.); Mallmann 1975: 178 (n.i.); Chandra 2002: 1290 (n.i.).

7. Asiatic Society, Kolkata (Ms. B5 or G 10741 D; compare the labels of Pal & Bhattacharyya 1969: fig. 12, and Bhattacharyya 1978: fig. 9), Dhāraṇīsaṃgraha ms.; dated 1843 AD
Type II(a or b); deviations: colours, attributes, sitting posture *ardhaparyaṅka* (left leg) instead of *vajraparyaṅka* (cf. ## 8, 9, 34).
Ref.: Pal & Bhattacharyya 1969: 42, 58 n. 67, b/w fig. 16. (The Mārīcī painting in the same ms. deviates from the standard Mārīcī iconography in

showing the goddess single-headed without a lateral boar face, and her chariot drawn by only four pigs; cf. *ibid.*: fig. 12). .... FIGURE 1

8. Bayerische Staatsbibliothek, München (Cod. sanscr. 423), Saptavāradhāraṇī ms., fol. 26b; ca. 19th century;
Type II(b); deviation: sitting posture *ardhaparyaṅka* (left leg) instead of *vajraparyaṅka* (cf. ## 7, 9, 34).
Ref.: Grönbold 1978: 171, no. 190 (not ill.); Janert & Poti 1985: 947-948, no. 2865 (not ill.); Grönbold 2001: 374 (not ill.). ...... PLATE XIX.B

9. Lokesh Chandra Coll., New Delhi, Saptavāradhāraṇī ms.; ca. 19th cent.;
Type II(a/b); deviation: sitting posture *ardhaparyaṅka* (right leg) instead of *vajraparyaṅka* (cf. ## 7, 8, 34).
Ref.: Chandra 1981: 258, ill. in text-section of Vajravidhāra . FIGURE 2

10. Present location unknown, formerly Evans-Wentz Collection, Saptavāradhāraṇī ms.; ca. 19th century;
Type II(b); deviations: colours; right: *ratnacchaṭā* instead of *vajra*, left: *mayūrapiccha* instead of *kamala* (cf. # 6).
Ref.: Bhattacharyya 1924: 157 (erroneously referring to his pl. XLII. e), b/w pl. XLII.c; Bhattacharyya 1958: 225, 282 b/w fig. 165; Kirfel 1948: Tafel 22, fig. 66 (b/w); Mallmann 1975: 178 (not ill.). FIGURE 3

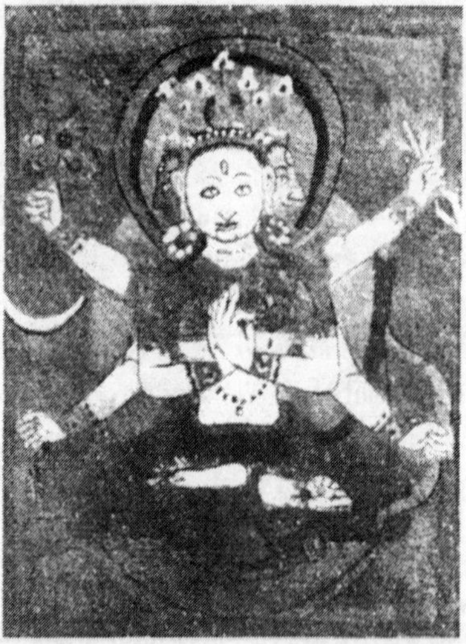

FIGURE 3 .... # 10 (Type II)

11. National Archives, Kathmandu (4-1483; NGMPP reel no. B 107/18); Saptavāradhāraṇī ms.; dated 1642/43 AD (cf. Bühnemann [this vol.]: 36);
Type II(b); deviations: left face blue instead of red; one right hand holding a lotus instead of *vajra*.
Ref.: Kooij 1977: 61, 65 (not ill.) informs that the goddess has 3 faces (yellow / white / blue) and 6 arms (2 in *dharmacakramudrā*, arrow / bow, lotus / bundle of flowers); he further mentions that the text of the manuscript describes the iconography of the goddess according to Type I.

TIBET: Wall painting

12. Gyantse, 'Kumbum', Grahamātṛkā Chapel, 1st Floor, North side, no. I.10/ 1Na' / N10 (cf. Lo Bue/Ricca 1990: 85, fig. 1), South wall facing North, to the left of principal clay figure of Grahamātṛkā (# 30), opposite of # 13; 1st half of 15th century;
Type II(a), with Navagraha-*maṇḍala*.
Ref.: Tucci 1941/1989, 1: 190-191; 2: 152; 3: b/w fig. 173; Béguin 1987: fig. 70 "Pañcarakṣā, *sKong-ma-lnga*" [!]; Lo Bue & Ricca 1990: 110 (not ill.); Ricca & Lo Bue 1993: 99, 238, col.pl. 83; Mevissen i.pr.: no. 61 (not ill.). .... PLATE XX.A

13. Gyantse, 'Kumbum', same chapel, North facing South, opposite of # 12, to the right of principal image (# 30), 1st half of 15th century;
Type II(a?); deviation: complexion yellow instead of white (cf. ## 1, 4);
Ref.: Tucci 1941/1989, 1: 192; 3: b/w fig. 181 (only detail); Ricca & Lo Bue 1993: 238, no. 4 describe the figure as "yellow, 3 heads, six arms" (not ill.).

TIBET: Scroll painting depicting Grahamātṛkā-*maṇḍalas*

14. Kimbell Art Museum, Fort Worth, Texas (AP 2000.01), formerly Zimmerman Family Collection, 89 x 73.7 cm, 1429-56 AD (cf. Jackson 1993: 122); quadruple *maṇḍala* structured and dominated by the Pañcarakṣās, centring on Mahāpratisarā;
Type I, with Navagraha-*maṇḍala* I; the other three *maṇḍalas* are dedicated to the Pañcarakṣās/Mahāpratisarā, Vasudhārā and Uṣṇīṣāvijayā (cf. ## 15, 17, 18).
Ref.: Rhie & Thurman 1991/1996: 226-229, col.pls. 73.1, 73.3; Lohia 1994 (col.pl. on front dust cover, painting not mentioned in the book); Fisher 1997: 164-165, fig. 139; Willson & Brauen 2000: 415, no. 505 (not ill.); *Archives of Asian Art* 52 (2000-01): 108, fig. 8; Mevissen i.pr.: no. 65, diagram C-I-6.

15. Present location unknown, quadruple *maṇḍala* centring on Pañcarakṣā/ Mahāpratisarā, 70.5 x 59.5 cm; ca. 15th century (?);
Type I, same programme and very similar to # 14; cf. ## 17, 18.
Ref.: Koller A 87/3, 25./26.6.1993: 2, Nr. 18, Tafel 6, Nr. 18 (col.pl.); Mevissen i.pr.: no. 66, diagram C-I-6, fig. 27. .... PLATE XXI

16. Present location unknown; single *maṇḍala*, 29 x 25 cm; late 15th century; Type II(a), with Navagrahas.
Ref.: Pal 1984: 214, no. 49 "Buddhist Goddess, Western Tibet (?), ca. 1500", col.pl. 49; Mevissen i.pr.: no. 62, diagram C-III. . . PLATE XX.B

17. Lionel Fournier Collection, Paris; single *maṇḍala*, ca. 18th century (?); Type I; deviations: *pāśa* on the right, *ratnacchaṭā* reduced to single *ratna* on the left; with Navagraha-*maṇḍala* I similar to ## 14, 15, 18.
Ref.: Jünemann 2002: Oktober (col.pl.); Mevissen i.pr.: no. 63, diagram C-I-6, fig. 25.

18. Present location unknown, 68 x 65 cm, quadruple *maṇḍala* with similar programme as ## 14, 15 but centring on Mahākāla; ca. 19th/20th century; Type I(?), with Navagraha-*maṇḍala* I; cf. ## 14, 15, 17.
Ref.: Koller A 53/3, 29.11.-1.12.1984: 2, Nr. 18, b/w Tafel 18, Nr. 18 (b/w); Mevissen i.pr.: no. 67, diagram C-I-6, fig. 28.

19. 'Ngor Collection' No. 6, present location unknown; Grahamātṛkā-*maṇḍala* in centre, 38.5 x 38.5 cm; painted between 1870 and 1892 in Eastern Tibet. Type II(b), with Navagraha-*maṇḍala* II (inner circle of # 20).
Ref.: bSod nams rgya mtsho 1983: col.pl. 6; 1989: pl. 6; 1991: 7-8, no. 6, diagram; Willson & Brauen 2000: 415, no. 505 (not ill.); Mevissen i.pr.: no. 64, diagram C-I-5. . . . . PLATE XXII

20. Same as # 19; Grahamātṛkā in surrounding circle in NW quarter, Navagrahas in NE quarter, Nakṣatras and Rāśis in SE quarter; 1870-92 AD. Type I(?), with linear Navagraha-*maṇḍala* to her left (outer circle of # 19).
Ref.: bSod nams rgya mtsho 1983: col.pl. 6; 1989: pl. 6; 1991: 7-8, no. 6, diagram; Willson & Brauen 2000: 415, no. 505 (not ill.); Mevissen i.pr.: no. 64, diagram C-IV.

TIBET: Scroll painting with Grahamātṛkā as subsidiary figure

21. Shelley and Donald Rubin Collection, Rubin Foundation, Uṣṇīṣaviyayā painting, 50.8 x 48.8 cm, Grahamātṛkā in vertical row on proper left margin (on the opposite side is a row of Pañcarakṣās); ca. 15th century; Type II(b); deviation: left face blue instead of red.
Ref.: Mullin & Watt 2003: 109, col.pl. (also http://www.himalayanart.org/image.cfm/663.html).

NEPAL: Scroll painting with Grahamātṛkā as subsidiary figure

22. Staatliches Museum für Völkerkunde, München (33-11-1), 88 x 60 cm, Uṣṇīṣavijayā painting, Grahamātṛkā in socle, Pañcarakṣās beneath socle; ca. 17th century;
Type II(b); deviation: exchange of colours of lateral heads (?).
Ref.: Lommel 1968: 31, 35, 124-125, No. 230, Abb. 15, 17; 1974a: 134, No. 513, Abb. 62, 63; 1974b: 93-94, 97, Farbtafel 55 (Grahamātṛkā always erroneously identified as a second Uṣṇīṣavijayā); Martin 1977: 166 (col.pl.); Grönbold 1984: 306, Tafel X.15 (b/w); Mevissen 1989b: Kat. M.IV.A.14, Tafel 35 (col.pl.); i.pr.: no. 77, diagram C-II-1.

TIBET: Line drawing

23. 'Ngor Collection' No. 6 (= drawing of ## 19, 20), Lokesh Chandra Collection, New Delhi; Grahamātṛkā-*maṇḍala* in centre; 20th century;
Type II(b); above Sūrya, with Navagraha-*maṇḍala* (inner circle of # 24).
Ref.: Vira & Chandra 1967: pl. 6; Dagyab 1991: 54-55, fig. F 6; Vira & Chandra 1995: 117, 146, no. 6; Chandra 2002: 1288-1290, ill.; Mevissen i.pr.: no. 64, diagram C-I-5, fig. 26. . . . . FIGURE 4

24. Same as # 23 (= drawing of ## 19, 20); Grahamātṛkā in surrounding circle in NW quarter, Navagrahas in NE quarter, Naksatras and Rāśis in SE quarter;

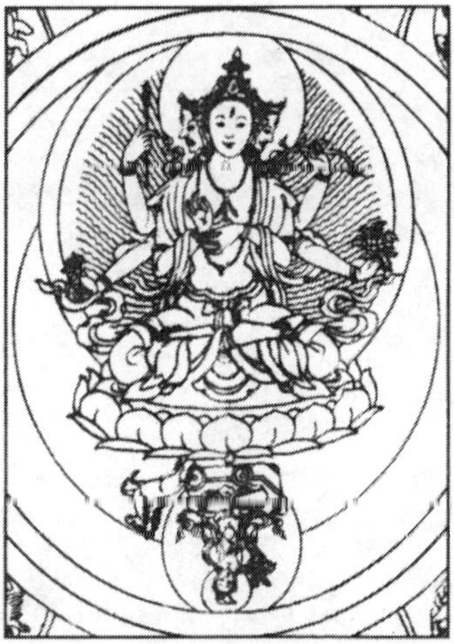

FIGURE 4 . . . . # 23 (Type II)

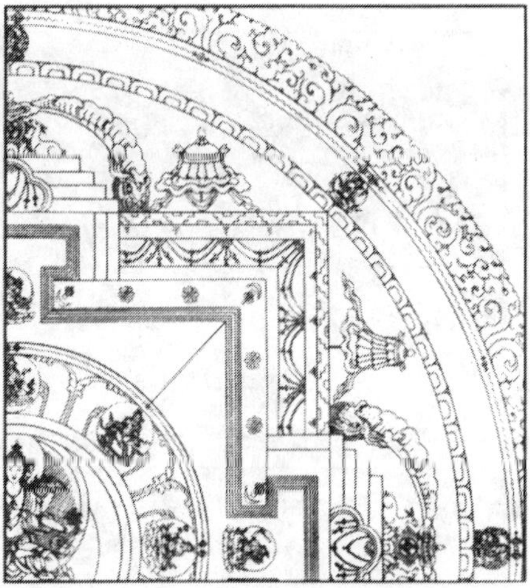

FIGURE 5 . . . . # 24 (Type I ?)

Type I (?); linear Navagraha-*maṇḍala* to her left (outer circle of # 23).
Ref.: Vira & Chandra 1967: pl. 6; Dagyab 1991: 54-55, fig. F 6; Mevissen i.pr.: no. 64, diagram C-IV. . . . . FIGURE 5

NEPAL: Line drawing

25. Lokesh Chandra Collection, 'Sketchbook No. 1', ca. 18th century;
Type I, colours indicated as *nī* (= *nīla*, dark), *te* (= *śveta*, white), *ra* (= *rakta*, red), cf. Bühnemann 2003: 13-14; followed by Uṣṇīṣavijayā and Cundā.
Ref.: Chandra 1984: 16, ill. (first row); 2002: 1290-1291, fig. (3); Bühnemann 2003: 90, 110, no. 134. . . . . FIGURE 6

26. Present location unknown, Sketchbook titled *Bauddhadevatācitrasaṃgraha (Rekhācitrātmaka)*, ca. 18th century;
Type I; labelled 'Grahamātṛkātārā', colours indicated as *ni* (= *nīla*, dark), *te* (= *śveta*, white), *ra* (= *rakta*, red), cf. Bühnemann 2003: 13-14; followed by Uṣṇīṣavijayā, Cundā and Parṇaśabarī.
Ref.: NGMPP reel no. E 1866/2, running no. E 35548; Bühnemann 2003: 36, 65, no. 104. . . . . FIGURE 7

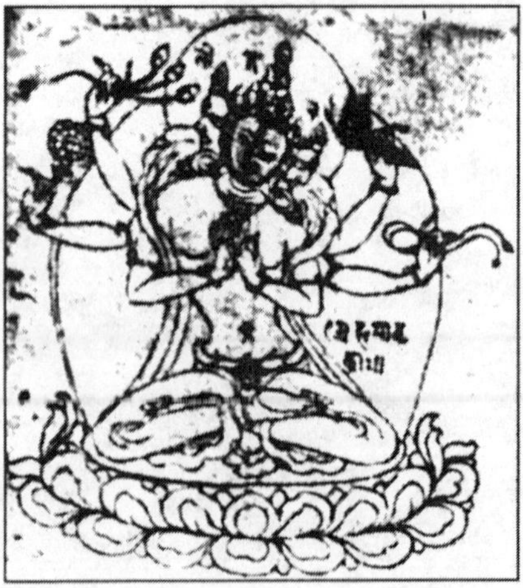

FIGURE 6 . . . . # 25 (Type I)

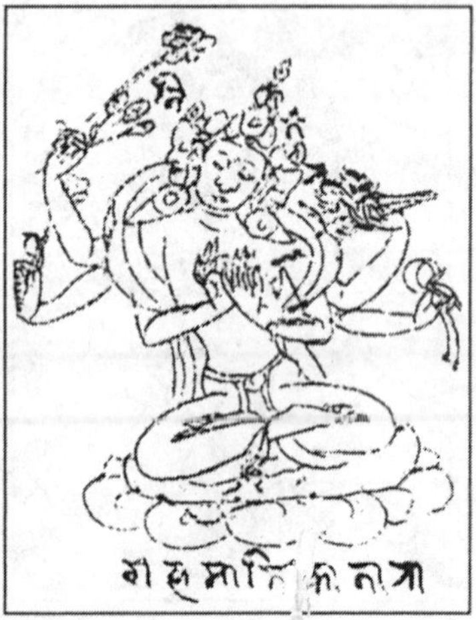

FIGURE 7 . . . . # 26 (Type I)

CHINA: Line drawing or blockprint

27. Present location unknown, *Chu Fo P'u-sa Shêng Hsiang Tsan* ms. ('360 Icons'), ca. 1761 AD;
Type I; labelled Tou-mu (Chin.), Amba usiha eme (Manchu), Grag-un eke (Mong.), gZa' yum (Tib.).
Ref.: Clark 1937, II: 292, no. 269/409; Chandra & Bunce 2002: 546-547, no. 269 (digitally enhanced); Chandra 2002: 1290-1291, fig. (4).
. . . . FIGURE 8

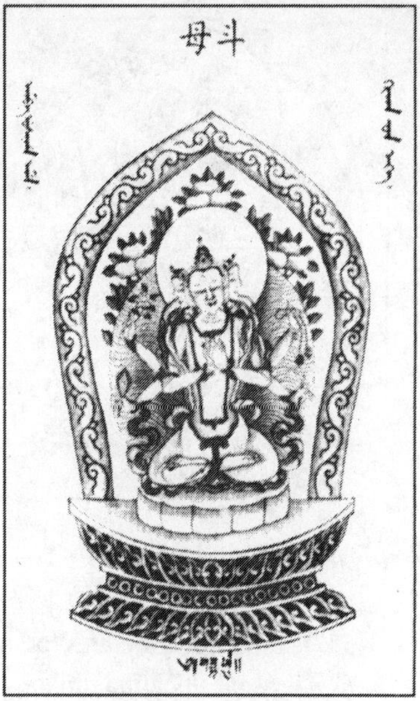

FIGURE 8 . . . . # 27 (Type I)

MONGOLIA: Blockprints

28. 'Icons Worthwile to See' (*Bris-sku mthoṅ-ba don-ldan*), also called 'Nar-thang Pantheon' or '500 Icons', Part I: *Rin-'byuṅ brgya-rtsa*, icon no. 223: *gZa' yum rig pa'i rgyal mo* (*Vidyārājñī Grahamātṛkā*); shortly after 1810; Type II(a).

Original blockprint sets in different collections:

1° Völkerkundemuseum der Universität Zürich (17942).
Ref.: Willson & Brauen 2000: 104-105, 300, fol. 74, no. 223 (col.pl.); painted possibly around 1850 AD (*ibid.*: 23). . . . . . PLATE XXIII.A

2° Institut für Kultur und Geschichte Indiens und Tibets, Universität Hamburg.
Ref.: Tachikawa et al. 1995: 266, no. 223 (R77a) 732.

3° Bayerische Staatsbibliothek, München (2° L. tibet. 6 q; formerly Albert Grünwedel Collection; cf. Grönbold 1989: 67, nos. 359-361; Eimer 1996: 243), icon no. 223. FIGURE 9

4° Bayerische Staatsbibliothek, München (2° L. tibet. 6 r; formerly Friedrich A. Peter Collection; cf. Grönbold 1989: 67-68, no. 362-363; Eimer 1996: 243), icon no. 223. FIGURE 10

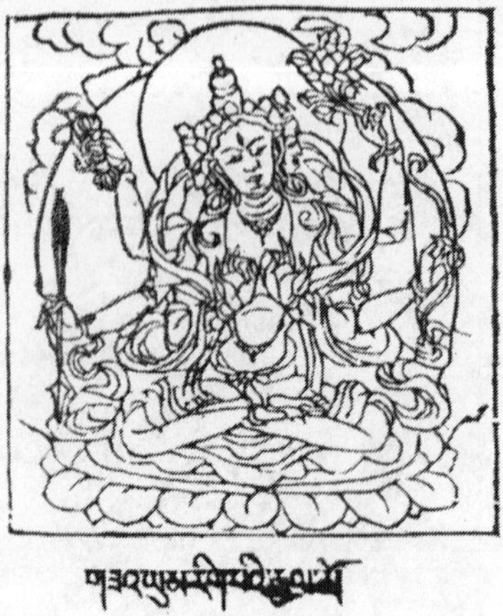

FIGURE 9 .... # 28.3° (Type II)

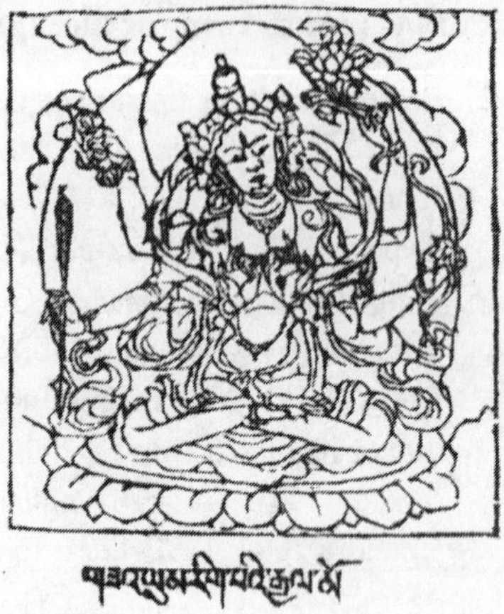

FIGURE 10 .... # 28.4° (Type II)

5° Library of Tibetan Works and Archives, Dharamsala; unpublished (?)

6° Present location unknown; formerly Field Museum, Chicago (ex Berthold Laufer Collection); unpublished (?).

7° Museum of the History of Religions, St. Petersburg (cf. Terentiev 1997: 166); unpublished (?).

8° Institute of Oriental Studies, St. Petersburg (call no. A 4162; cf. Terentiev 1997: 166); unpublished (?).

9° Ulan-Ude, Buryatia (cf. Terentiev 1997: 166); unpublished (?).

10° Lokesh Chandra Collection, New Delhi; one or more sets (cf. discussion in Willson & Brauen 2000: 8-11); unpublished (?).

Hand-drawn copies or tracings:

11° Lokesh Chandra Collection, New Delhi, version B;
Ref.: Chandra 1961: 2080 (right); 2002: 1288 (right).

12° Lokesh Chandra Collection, New Delhi, version A;
Ref.: Vira & Çhandra 1964: pl. 75; Chandra 1986/87/91: 279, no. 732.

13° Present location unknown; drawn by F.A. and Elisabeth Peter after # 28/4° (cf. Willson & Brauen 2000: 7, 23, note 12); unpublished (?).

29. Same blockprint set as # 28; Part III: *rDor-'phreṅ*, Skt. *Vajrāvalī*; icon no. 505: *gZa' yum rig pa chen mo* (*Grahamātṛkā Mahāvidyā*), preceded by Vasudhārā, followed by Uṣṇīṣavijayā; carved shortly after 1810 AD.

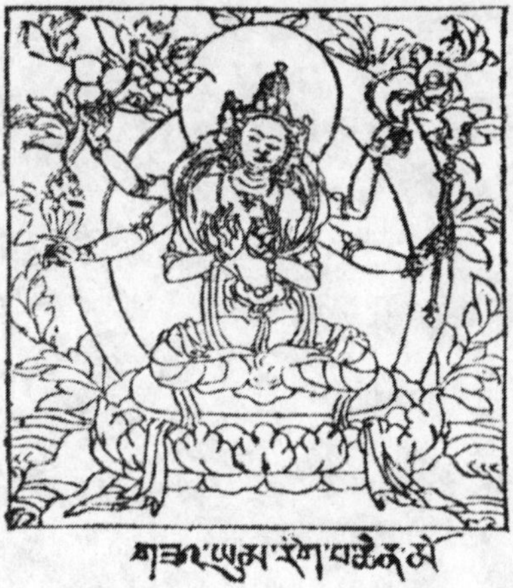

FIGURE 11 . . . . # 29.3° (Type I)

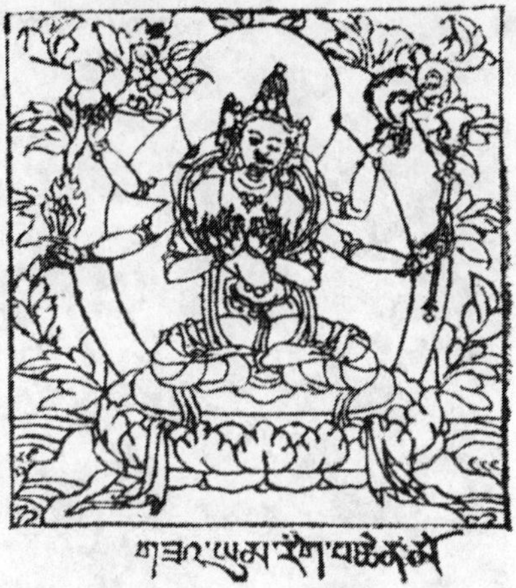

FIGURE 12 . . . . # 29.4° (Type I)

Type I.

Original blockprint sets in different collections:

1° Zürich, cf. # 28/1°. Ref.: Willson & Brauen 2000: 204-205, fol. 168, no 505 (col.pl.). . . . . PLATE XXIII.B
2° Hamburg, cf. # 28/2°.
Ref.: Tachikawa et al. 1995: 550, no. 501(D17a) 1007.
3° München, cf. # 28/3°. . . . . FIGURE 11
4° München, cf. # 28/4°. . . . . FIGURE 12
5° Dharamsala, cf. # 28/5°; unpublished (?).
6° Present location unknown, cf. # 28/6°; unpublished (?).
7° St. Petersburg, cf. # 28/7°; unpublished (?).
8° St. Petersburg, cf. # 28/8°; unpublished (?).
9° Ulan-Ude, cf. # 28/9°; unpublished (?).
10° New Delhi, cf. # 28/ 10°; unpublished (?).

Hand-drawn copies or tracings:

11° New Delhi, cf. # 28/ 11°, version B;
Ref.: Chandra 1961: 2080 (left); Chandra 2002: 1292 (left).
12° New Delhi, cf. # 28/12°, version A;
Ref.: Vira & Chandra 1964: pl. 171; Chandra 1986-91: 279, no. 1007.
13° Present location unknown, cf. # 28/13°; after # 29/4°; unpublished (?).

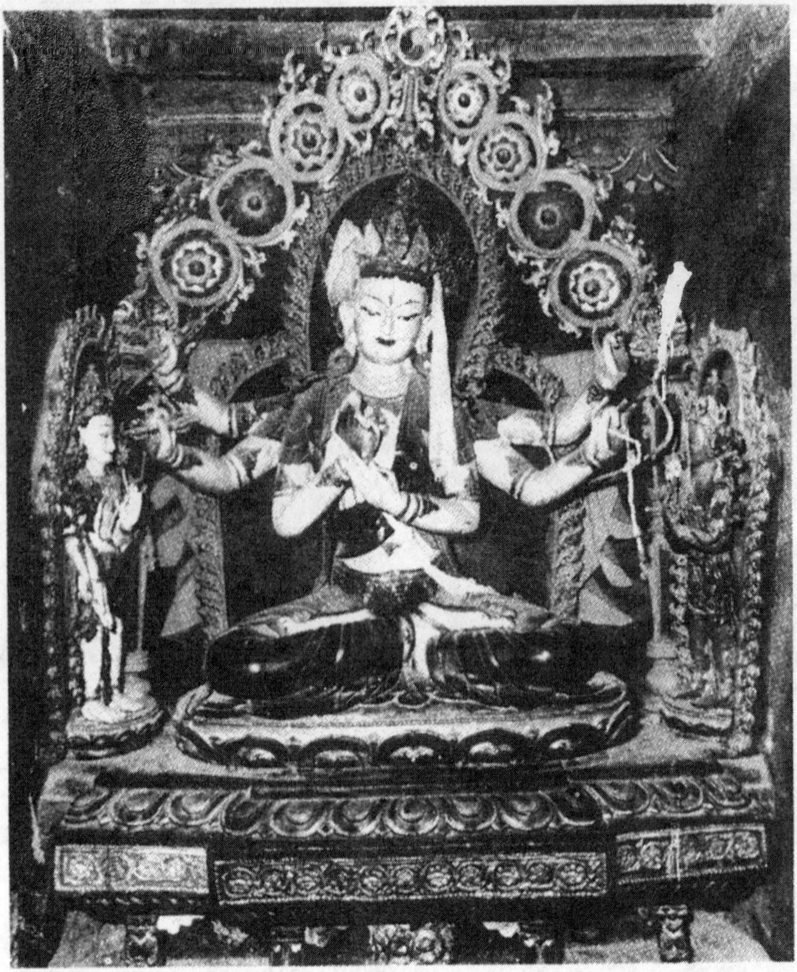

FIGURE 13 . . . . *# 30 (Type II)*

TIBET: Clay sculpture

30. Gyantse, Kumbum, Grahamātṛkā Chapel, 1st Floor, North side, no. I.10 / 1Na' / N10 (cf. Lo Bue & Ricca 1990: 85, fig. 1), East wall facing West, flanked by ## 12, 13; 1st half of 15th century;
Type II(a/b). Ref.: Tucci 1941/1989, 1: 190 (not ill.); Ricca & Lo Bue 1993: 238 (b/w fig.). . . . . FIGURE 13

NEPAL: Wood carving

31. Pinchẽ Bāhā (also Manijū Bāhā, Khuñ or Chun Bāhā, Jāmbūnadavana Vihāra), Wotu Tole, Kathmandu (for the location see Snellgrove 1961: 117, no. 25 on map); part of a sequence of struts depicting Saptavāra, Pañcarakṣā and other deities, Nakṣatra below; late 16th century (inscriptions dated 1591/92 and 1643/44 AD; cf. Locke 1985: 352-356); Type III, one head, two arms (left forearm missing), standing; label inscription reading '*grahamātrīka*'.
Ref.: Kooij 1977: 60 (not ill.); Bühnemann (this vol.): 32 (n. ill.); previously unpublished. FIGURE 14

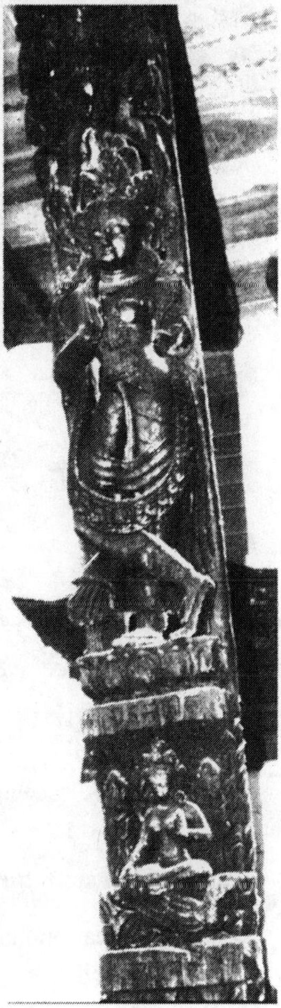

FIGURE 14 . # 31 (Type III)

32. Chuṣya Bāhā (Guṇākara Mahāvihāra), Jyatha Tole, Kathmandu (for the location see Snellgrove 1961: 117, no. 21 on map); part of a sequence of struts depicting Saptavāra, Pañcarakṣā and other deities, Nakṣatra below; ca. 17th century (inscriptions dated 1667/68, 1672/73 and 1675/76 AD; cf. Locke 1985: 272-274); Type III, one head, two arms, standing; label inscription reading '*grahamātṛkā*'.
Ref.: Kooij 1977: 65, fig. 36; Kooij 1978: 32, pl. XLVIc; Chandra 2002: 1292 (right). . . . . FIGURE 15

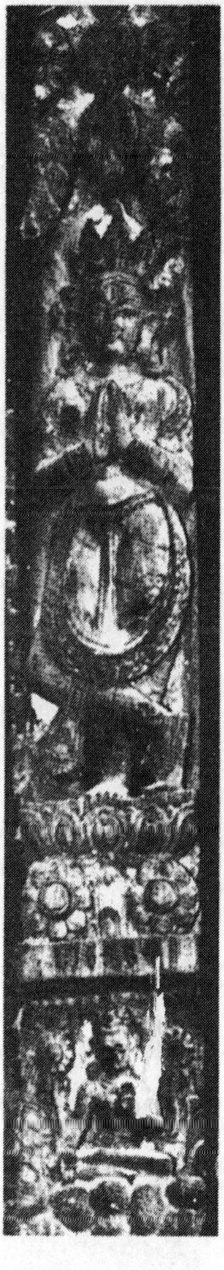

FIG. 15 . # 32 (III)

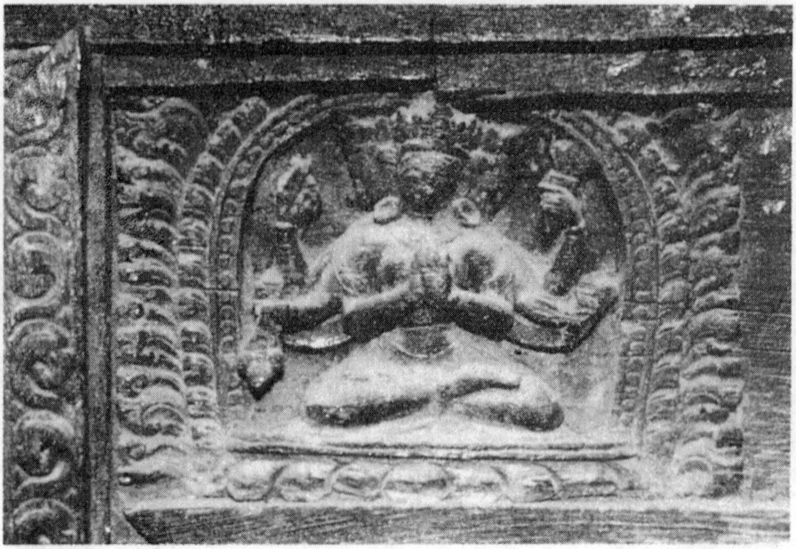

FIGURE 16 .... # 33 (Type I)

33. Pinchẽ Bāhā (cf. # 32), paired with Uṣṇīṣavijayā, flanking the eastern (main) entrance to the courtyard on the outside, proper left (i.e. North) of doorway;
Type I; second left hand damaged.
Ref.: previously unrecorded and unpublished .... FIGURE 16

TIBET: Metal sculpture

34. Present location unknown, height: 26.4 cm; ca. 15th century;
Type II; deviation: *vajra* held in right front hand, probably relocated from the second right hand; seated in *ardhaparyaṅka* (left leg) instead of *vajra-paryaṅka* (cf. ## 7, 8, 9).
Ref.: Sotheby's New York, 30.11.1994: no. 70 (col.pl.); Rossi & Rossi 1994: no. 22 (col.pl.). .... PLATE XXIV.A

35. Present location unkown, height: 18 cm; ca. 18th century.
Type I or II; all attributes missing.
Ref.: Koller A 61/3, 14.-15.11.1986: 6, Nr. 67, Tafel 11, Nr. 67 (col.pl.). .... PLATE XXIV.B

FURTHER IMAGES OF GRAHAMĀTṚKĀ (?)

The following fourteen entries list images of the goddess which

(i) have been tentatively identified by her major iconographic marks of identification, viz. her three heads, six arms, and the principal pair of hands joined in front of her breast. However, since the printing quality of most of the published images does not allow minute scrutiny, every entry must be studied in detail before reaching a final decision whether Grahamātṛkā is represented or not. Further, it is quite probable that there are many more paintings of Uṣṇīṣavijayā and Vasudhārā containing so far undetected figures of Grahamātṛkā.

(ii) Regarding the four additional manuscripts (## 46-49) it has to be verified whether they still contain images, and if so, whether the ones depicting Grahamātṛkā are preserved.

NEPAL: Scroll painting

Grahamātṛkā as subsidiary figure in Uṣṇīṣavijayācaitya paintings

36. Indian Museum, Kolkata (reg.no. AT/66/15), 88 x 64 cm; dated 1591 AD (N.S. 711);
    Grahamātṛkā(?) on the proper left of the *caitya*'s umbrellas;
    Type II(a); deviations: sword instead of *vajra* (right) and *vajra* instead of lotus (left); Pañcarakṣās in the bottom register.
    Ref.: Chakravarti 1969: 124-129, pls. I-IA, figs. 1-2, identifies the figure as Grahamātṛkā and describes it as follows (127-128): "The goddess seated in *vajrāsana* has three faces of white, blue and red ...; six arms – principal hands in *vyākhyāna mudrā* ... in two right hands the sword and an arrow and in two left hands *vajra* and the bow."

37. National Museum, New Delhi, 95.9 x 47.6 cm; 16th/17th century;
    Grahamātṛkā(?) in centre of the *caitya* instead of Uṣṇīṣavijayā.
    Ref.: Kramrisch 1964: 150, no. 93 "Ushnishavijaya", fig. 93.

38. Present location unknown, dated 1716 AD (N.S. 836);
    Grahamātṛkā(?) in *caitya* socle.
    Ref.: Pal 1977: fig. 13; Mevissen i.pr.: no. 78, diagram H-III.

Grahamātṛkā as subsidiary figure in (Lakṣa)caitya painting

39. Present location unknown; 75 x 77 cm; 17th/18th century; Grahamātṛkā(?) in centre of *caitya* socle; Pañcarakṣās in lower register. Ref.: Sotheby's London, 3.12.1979: lot 90 "Avalokitesvara"; Koller A 55/3, 20.-22.6.1985: Nr. 28 "Avalokiteshvara".

Grahamātṛkā as subsidiary figure in Vasudhārā paintings

40. David Salmon Collection, London, ht. 66.1cm, ca. 1375 AD; Grahamātṛkā(?) in the third square band containing Aṣṭadikpālas, Pañcarakṣās, Prajñāpāramitā and white Tārā(?); on the observer's right, between Kubera and Īśāna (i.e. in the northeast). Ref.: Pal 1978: fig. 74; Mevissen 1989b: Kat. M.IV.A.2, b/w Abb. 121.

41. Present location unknown, 90.8 x 77.5 cm, ca. late 14th century; Grahamātṛkā(?) in the corner to the observer's lower left (i.e. in the southeast) between Indra and Agni; Pañcarakṣās in lower register. Ref.: Sotheby's New York, 22.3.1989: lot 356.

42. Present location unknown, 104.5 x 83.5 cm, ca. 15th century; Grahamātṛkā(?) in the corner to the observer's lower left (i.e. in the southeast) between Indra and Agni; Pañcarakṣās in upper register. Ref.: Sotheby's New York, 25.3.1999: lot 31.

NEPAL: Painting on wooden manuscript boards

43. National Archives, Kathmandu (3-360 D), wooden cover containing 136 palm-leaves, 4.5 x 29.5 cm, dated 1374 AD (N.S. 494); Grahamātṛkā(?) as the last figure in a row following Pañcarakṣās (cf. # 1). Ref.: NGMPP reel no. B 31/4.

44. Cleveland Museum of Art, George P. Bickford Collection, inner side of cover of Dhāraṇī ms., 11.5 x 50.8 cm, ca. 18th century; Grahamātṛkā(?) as the second or fifth figure in a row of seven peaceful goddesses flanked by two wrathful goddesses. Ref.: Pal 1978: 52-53 "Pañcarakṣā goddesses", fig. 45; Pal & Meech-Pekarik 1988: 130, fig. 48.b.

45. Doris Wiener, Inc., New York; inner side of cover of Dhāraṇī ms., 14 x 55.3 cm, ca. 18th century;

Grahamātṛkā(?) as the second or fifth figure in a row of seven peaceful goddesses flanked by two wrathful goddesses.
Ref.: Pal 1978: 52-53 "Pañcarakṣā goddesses", fig. 46; Pal & Meech-Pekarik 1988: 130, fig. 49.a.

NEPAL: Painting on paper manuscript leaves

46. Asiatic Society of Bengal, Kolkata (10741), Saptavāradhāraṇī ms.;
Ref.: quoted by Bühnemann (this vol.): note 53 (cf. Shāstri 1917: 48-49).

47. Present location unknown, Saptavāradhāraṇī ms.;
Ref.: quoted by Bühnemann (this vol.): note 53 (cf. Takaoka 1981: CH 552).

48. Present location unknown, Saptavāradhāraṇī ms.;
Ref.: quoted by Bühnemann (this vol.): note 53 (cf. Takaoka 1981: CH 557).

49. Present location unknown, Saptavāradhāraṇī ms., dated 1635 AD;
Ref.: Vajracharya 2002: 56-57 illustrates two images (Vasudhārā and Gaṇapati) from a manuscript in the Watson Collection of Indian Miniatures at the Elvehjem Museum of Art (66.13.4), Madison, Wisconsin, which according to him is titled *Āryagrahamātṛkānāmadhāraṇī*. The text seems to be complete and contains miniatures of six goddesses. The leaf illustrating Grahamātṛkā is either missing or was never executed.

PHOTOGRAPHY CREDITS

The monochrome illustrations are reproduced from the following sources:

FIGURE 1: Pal & Bhattacharyya 1969: fig. 16;
FIGURE 2: Chandra 1981: 258;
FIGURE 3: Bhattacharyya 1924: pl. XLIIc;
FIGURES 4, 5: Vira & Chandra 1967: pl. 6;
FIGURE 6: Bühnemann 2003: 110, no. 134;
FIGURE 7: Bühnemann 2003: 65, no. 104;
FIGURE 8: Chandra & Bunce 2002: no. 269;
FIGURES 9-12: courtesy of Bayerische Staatsbibliothek, München;
FIGURE 13: Ricca & Lo Bue 1993: 238;
FIGURE 15: Kooij 1978: pl. XLVIc;
FIGURES 14, 16: photographs by the author, March 24, 2003.

The sources of the colour PLATES are given in the accompanying labels.

REFERENCES

BÉGUIN, Gilles 1987. *Les arts du Népal et du Tibet*. Paris.

BHATTACHARYYA, Benoytosh 1924. *The Indian Buddhist Iconography Mainly Based on The Sādhanamālā and Other Cognate Tāntric Texts of Rituals*. Oxford.

—— 1958. *The Indian Buddhist Iconography Mainly Based on The Sādhanamālā and Cognate Tāntric Texts of Rituals*. Second revised and enlarged edition, Calcutta.

BHATTACHARYYA, D.C. 1974. *Tantric Buddhist Iconography Sources*. New Delhi.

—— 1978. *Studies in Buddhist Iconography*. New Delhi.

BÜHNEMANN, Gudrun 1992. Some Remarks on the Date of Abhayākaragupta and the Chronology of His Works. *Zeitschrift der Deutschen Morgenländischen Gesellschaft* 142: 120-127.

—— 1992-93. Some Remarks on the Text of the Niṣpannayogāvalī as Found in Jagaddarpaṇa's Kriyāsamuccaya. *Zentralasiatische Studien* 23: 18-21.

—— 2003. *Buddhist Deities of Nepal: Iconography in Two Sketchbooks*. (Lumbini International Research Institute Occasional Papers, 4.) Lumbini.

—— (this volume) Tantric Deities in an Illustrated Dhāraṇī Manuscript from Nepal. In: A.J. Gail, G.J.R Mevissen & R. Salomon (eds.), *Papers of th 12th World Sanskrit Conference held in Helsinki, Finland, 13-18 July 2003. ol. 11.1*: 29-64, pls. IV-XVII. Delhi.

CHAKRAVARTI, Shyamalkanti 1969. Three Dated Nepalese Paṭas in the Indian Museum. *Indian Museum Bulletin* 4/2 (July): 124-133.

CHANDRA, Lokesh 1961. *Tibetan-Sanskrit Dictionary. Based on a close comparative study of Sanskrit originals and Tibetan translations of several texts*. Vol. 11. (Śata-Piṭaka Series, 3; Bhoṭa Piṭaka, 1.) New Delhi. Reprint Kyoto, 1971.

—— 1977. *Kriya-Samuccaya. A Sanskrit manuscript from Nepal containing a collection of tantric ritual by Jagaddarpaṇa, reproduced by Lokesh Chandra from the collection of Prof. Raghuvira*. 2 parts. (Śata-Piṭaka Series, 237.) New Delhi.

—— 1981. *Kāraṇḍavyūha and Other Texts. Sanskrit Manuscripts from Nepal reproduced from the Collection of Prof. Raghuvira*. New Delhi (Śata-Piṭaka Series, 268).

—— 1984. *Buddhist Iconography in Nepalese Sketch-Books*. (Śata-Piṭaka Series, 302.) New Delhi.

—— 1986/1987/1991. *Buddhist Iconography of Tibet*. 3 Vols. (Śata-Piṭaka Series, 341.) Kyoto, 1986. Newly revised and enlarged edition: *Buddhist Iconography*, 2 Vols. (Śata-Piṭaka Series, 342.) New Delhi, 1987. Reprinted in 1 volume. (Śata-Piṭaka Series, 342.) New Delhi, 1991.

—— 2002. *Dictionary of Buddhist Iconography. Vol. 4 (Dhyāna-pāramitā – Gzuṅs. las.byuṅ.baḥi lha.mo Nor.rgyun.ma)*. (Śata-Piṭaka Series, 604.) New Delhi.

—— 2003. *Dictionary of Buddhist Iconography. Volume 7 (Ma.bdud – Manjushiri).* (Śata-Piṭaka Series, 608.) New Delhi.

—— & Fredrick W. BUNCE 2002. *The Tibetan Iconography of Buddhas, Bodhisattvas and other Deities - A Unique Pantheon -.* New Delhi.

CLARK, Walter Eugene 1937. *Two Lamaistic Pantheons, edited with introduction and indexes from materials collected by the Late Baron A. von Staël-Holstein.* 2 Vols. Cambridge 1937. Reprint, bound in one volume, New York 1965.

DAGYAB, Loden Sherap 1991. *Die Sādhanas der Sammlung rGyud-sde kun-btus.* (Asiatische Forschungen, 115; Ikonographie und Symbolik des Tibetischen Buddhismus, Teil F.) Wiesbaden.

EIMER, H. 1996. Review of TACHIKAWA et al. 1995. *Zentralasiatische Studien* 26: 240-243.

FISHER, Robert E. 1997. *Art of Tibet.* London.

GETTY, Alice 1914. *The Gods of Northern Buddhism - Their History, Iconography and Progressive Evolution through the Northern Buddhist Countries.* Oxford. Rev. ed. 1928. Repr. Rutland, Vermont & Tokyo 1962, and New Delhi 1978.

GRÖNBOLD, Günter 1978. Saptavāra. In: *Bayerische Staatsbibliothek. Erwerbungen aus drei Jahrzehnten 1948-1978. Abendländische und orientalische Handschriften, Inkunabeln und seltene Drucke, Noten und Landkarten.* Ausstellung April - Juli 1978. Wiesbaden.

—— 1984. Die Mythologie des indischen Buddhismus. In: H.W. Haussig (ed.), *Götter und Mythen des indischen Subkontinents.* (Wörterbuch der Mythologie, I/V.) Stuttgart: 285-508, Tafeln I-XV.

—— 1989 *Die tibetischen Blockdrucke der Bayerischen Staatsbibliothek. Eine Titelliste.* Wiesbaden.

—— 1991. *Tibetische Buchdeckel.* (Bayerische Staatsbibliothek, Ausstellungskatalog 54.) München.

—— 2001. "Saptavāra". A Dhāraṇī Collection from Nepal. In: Raffaele Torella (ed.), *Le Parole e i Marmi. Studi in Onore di Raniero Gnoli nel Suo 70° Compleanno* (Serie Orientale Roma, XCII/1.): 369-375. Roma.

HARRISON, Paul 1996. Preliminary Notes on a *gZungs 'dus* Manuscript from Tabo. In: M. Hahn, J.-U. Hartmann, R. Steiner (eds.), *Suhṛllekhāḥ. Festgabe für Helmut Eimer* (Indica et Tibetica, 28.): 49-68. Swisttal-Odendorf.

JACKSON, David 1993. Apropos a Recent Tibetan Art Catalogue [Being a review of: RHIE/THURMAN 1991]. *Wiener Zeitschrift für die Kunde Südasiens* 37: 109-130.

—— 1996. *A History of Tibetan Painting. The Great Tibetan Painters and Their Traditions.* (Österreichische Akad. d. Wissenschaften., Philosophisch-Histor. Klasse, Denkschriften, 242; Beitr. z. Kultur- und Geistesgeschichte Asiens, 15.) Wien.

JANERT, Klaus L. & Ṅarayanan Narasimhan POTI 1970. *Indische Handschriften. Teil 2.* (Verzeichnis der Orientalischen Handschriften in Deutschland, II/2.) Wiesbaden.

—— 1985. *Indische Handschriften. Teil 7.* (Verzeichnis der Orientalischen Handschriften in Deutschland, II/7.) Stuttgart.

JÜNEMANN, Wolfgang (ed.) 2002. *Thangka Kalender 2003.* Text: An rea-Loseries-Leick. Durach.

KIRFEL, Willibald 1948. *Die dreiköpfige Gottheit. Archäologisch-ethnologischer Streifzug durch die Ikonographie der Religionen.* Bonn.

KOLLER. Galerie Koller Zürich. Auction Catalogues A 53/3, A 55/3, A 61/3, A 87/3; Cited according to date of sale (Day.Month.Year).

KOOIJ, Karel Rijk van 1977. The Iconography of the Buddhist Wood-carvings in a Newar Monastery in Kathmandu (Chuṣya-Bāhā). *Journal of the Nepal Research Centre* I: 39-82. Wiesbaden.

—— 1978. *Religion in Nepal.* (Iconography of Religions, XIII/15.) Leiden.

KRAMRISCH, Stella 1964. *The Art of Nepal.* Catalogue. New York: The Asia Society.

LO BUE, Erberto & Franco RICCA 1990. *Gyantse Revisited.* Firence/Torino.

LOCKE, John K., S.J. 1985. *Buddhist Monasteries of Nepal. A Survey of the Bāhās and Bahīs of the Kathmandu Valley.* Kathmandu: Sahayogi Press.

LOHIA, Sushama 1994. *Lalitavajra's Manual of Buddhist Iconography.* (Śata-Piṭaka Series, 379.) New Delhi.

LOMMEL, Andreas (Hg.) 1968. *Buddhistische Kunst. Katalog zur Ausstellung des Staatlichen Museums für Völkerkunde München.* München.

—— 1974a. *Buddhistische Kunst. Katalog zur Ausstellung des Staatlichen Museums für Völkerkunde München.* München.

—— 1974b. *Kunst des Buddhismus. Aus der Sammlung des Staatlichen Museums für Völkerkunde in München.* Zürich-Freiburg.

MALLMANN, Marie-Thérèse de 1975. *Introduction à l'iconographie du tântrisme Bouddhique.* (Bibliothèque du Centre de Recherches sur l'Asie Centrale et la Haute Asie, 1.) Paris.

MARTIN, Heinz E.R. 1977. *Die Kunst Tibets.* (Heyne Stilkunde, 11.) München.

MEVISSEN, Gerd J.R. 1989a. Studies in Pañcarakṣā Manuscript Painting. *Berliner Indologische Studien* 4/5: 339-374, figs. 0-10. Berlin.

—— 1989b *Ikonographie der Pañcarakṣā.s. Eine Studie über Ursprung und Verbreitung der bildlichen Darstellung der fünf weiblichen Schutzgottheiten im nördlichen Buddhismus.* M.A. thesis (unpubl.). Freie Universität Berlin.

—— 2004. Die früheste Darstellung der Grahamātṛkā. Buchmalerei in Nepal. *Indo-Asiatische Zeitschrift* 8: 47-62. Berlin.

—— in press. Images of Buddhist Goddesses Accompanied by Astral Deities. In: G. Bhattacharya et al. (eds.), *Kalhāra-mālikā. Adhyāpak Enamul Haque Abhinandan Grantha (Professor Enamul Haque Felicitation Volume)*. Delhi.

MITRA, Rājendralāla 1882. *The Sanskrit Buddhist Literature of Nepal*. Calcutta.

MULLIN, Glenn H. with Jeff J. Watt 2003. *Female Buddhas. Women of Enlightenment in Tibetan Mystical Art. Art from the Collection of the Shelley & Donald Rubin Foundation*. Santa Fe, New Mexico.

NEBESKY-WOJKOWITZ, René de 1956/1975. *Oracles and Demons of Tibet. The Cult and Iconography of the Tibetan Protective Deities*. S'Gravenhage 1956. Reprinted with an Introduction by Per Kværne, Graz 1975.

NGMPP. Nepal German Manuscript Preservation Project. Corpus and catalogue of micro-filmed manuscripts from Nepal kept in the Staatsbibliothek zu Berlin.

PAL, Pratapaditya 1977. The Bhīmaratha Rite and Nepali Art. *Oriental Art*, N.S. 23/2 (Summer): 176-189.

—— 1978. *The Arts of Nepal, Part II: Painting*. Leiden.

—— 1984. *Tibetan Paintings. A Study of Tibetan Thankas Eleventh to Nineteenth Centuries*. Basel.

—— & D.C. BHATTACHARYYA 1969. *The Astral Divinities of Nepal*. Varanasi.

—— & Julia MEECH-PEKARIK 1988. *Buddhist Book Illuminations*. New York, etc.

RHIE, Marylin M. & Robert A.F. THURMAN 1991. *Wisdom and Compassion. The Sacred Art of Tibet*. San Francisco-New York 1991. Expanded Edition, Bonn 1996.

RICCA, Franco & Erberto LO BUE 1993. *The Great Stupa of Gyantse - A Complete Tibetan Pantheon*. London.

ROSSI, Anna Maria & Fabio ROSSI 1994. *Selections 1994*. Catalogue, London.

SHĀSTRI, Hara Prasad 1917. *A Descriptive Catalogue of Sanscrit Manuscripts in the Government Collection. Under the Care of the Asiatic Society of Bengal: Vol. I. Buddhist Manuscripts*. Calcutta.

SIMSON, Georg von 1981. Die Buddhas der Vorzeit: Versuch einer astralmythologischen Deutung. *Studien zur Indologie und Iranistik* 7: 77-91.

SNELLGROVE, D.L. 1961. Shrines and Temples of Nepal. 2 parts. *Arts Asiatiques* VIII/1: [illegible]-10; VIII/2: 93-120.

BSOD NAMS [illegible]YA MTSHO [Hiroshi SONAMI] 1983. *Tibetan Maṇḍalas. The Ngor Collection*. Eds. Musashi Tachikawa & Malcolm P.L. Green. 2 Vols. Tokyo.

—— 1989. *The Ngor Mandalas of Tibet - Plates*. Ed. Musashi Tachikawa. (Bibliotheca Codicum Asiaticorum, 2.) Tokyo: Centre for East Asian Cultural Studies.

—— 1991. *The Ngor Mandalas of Tibet - Listings of the Mandala Deities*. Revised by Musashi Tachikawa et al. (Bibliotheca Codicum Asiaticorum, 4.) Tokyo: Centre for East Asian Cultural Studies.

SOTHEBY'S LONDON. Auction Catalogues. Cited according to date of sale (Day. Month. Year.).

SOTHEBY'S NEW YORK. Auction Catalogues. Cited according to date of sale (Day. Month. Year.).

TACHIKAWA, Musashi, Masahide MORI & Shinobu YAMAGUCHI (compilers) 1995. *Five Hundred Buddhist Deities*. (Senri Ethnological Reports, 2.) Osaka.

TAKAOKA, H. 1981. *A Microfilm Catalogue of the Buddhist Manuscripts in Nepal. Volume I*. Nagoya: Buddhist Library.

TANAKA, Kimiaki (ed.) 2001. *Art of Thangka From the Hahn Kwang-ho Collection*. Vol. 3. Seoul: The Hahn Cultural Foundation.

TERENTIEV, Andrey 1997. Review of TACHIKAWA et al. 1995. *Indo-Iranian Journal* 40/2 (April 1997): 165-166.

TUCCI, Giuseppe 1941/1989. *Gyantse and Its Monuments*. Part 1: *Inscriptions*; Part 2: *General Descriptions of the Temples*; Part 3: *Plates*. English translation of *Gyantse ed i suoi Monasteri*. (Indo-Tibetica, IV, Roma 1941.). Ed. Lokesh Chandra. (Śata-Piṭaka Series, 351-353.) New Delhi.

VAJRACHARYA, Gautama V. 2002. *Watson Collection of Indian Miniatures at the Elvehjem Museum of Art. A Detailed Study of Selected Works*. Madison.

VERGATI, Anne 1999. Image et rituel: À propos des peintures bouddhiques népalaises. *Arts Asiatiques* 54: 33-43.

VIRA, Raghu and Lokesh CHANDRA (eds.) 1964. *A New Tibeto-Mongol Pantheon*. Part 9. (Śata-Piṭaka Series, 21/9; Boṭha-Piṭaka, 8.) New Delhi.

—— 1967. *A New Tibeto-Mongol Pantheon*. Part 13. (Śata-Piṭaka Series, 21/13; Boṭha-Piṭaka, 8.) New Delhi.

—— 1995. *Tibetan Maṇḍalas (Vajrāvalī and Tantra-samuccaya)*. New Delhi: International Academy of Indian Culture (Śata-Piṭaka Series, 383).

VITALI, Roberto 1979. *Arte Himalayana, 28 Novembre — 22 Dicembre*. Milano: Eskenazi.

WILLSON, Martin and Martin BRAUEN (eds.) 2000. *Deities of Tibetan Buddhism. The Zürich Paintings of the Icons Worthwhile to See (Bris sku mthoṅ ba don ldan)*. Boston: Wisdom Publications.

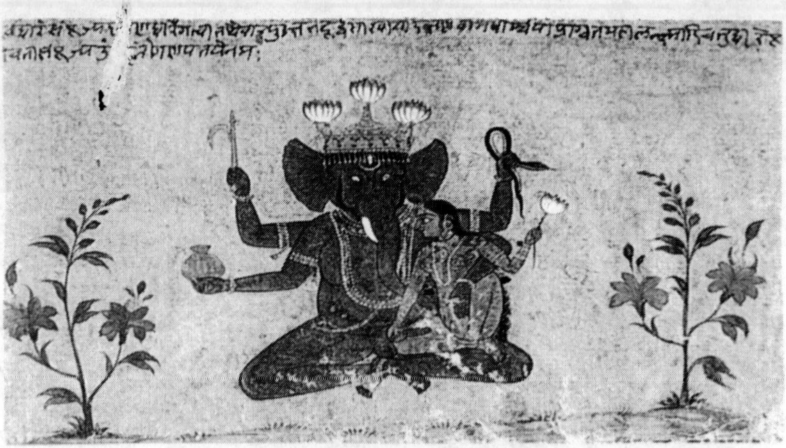

I.A. Miniature painting preserved in the Allahabad Museum; photograph by the author

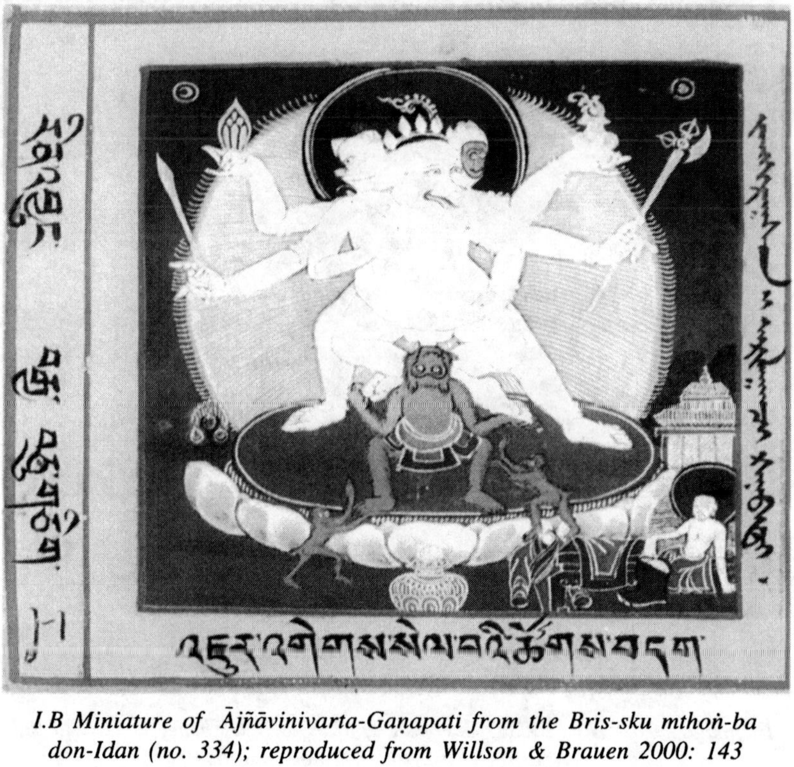

I.B Miniature of Ājñāvinivarta-Gaṇapati from the Bris-sku mthoṅ-ba don-Idan (no. 334); reproduced from Willson & Brauen 2000: 143

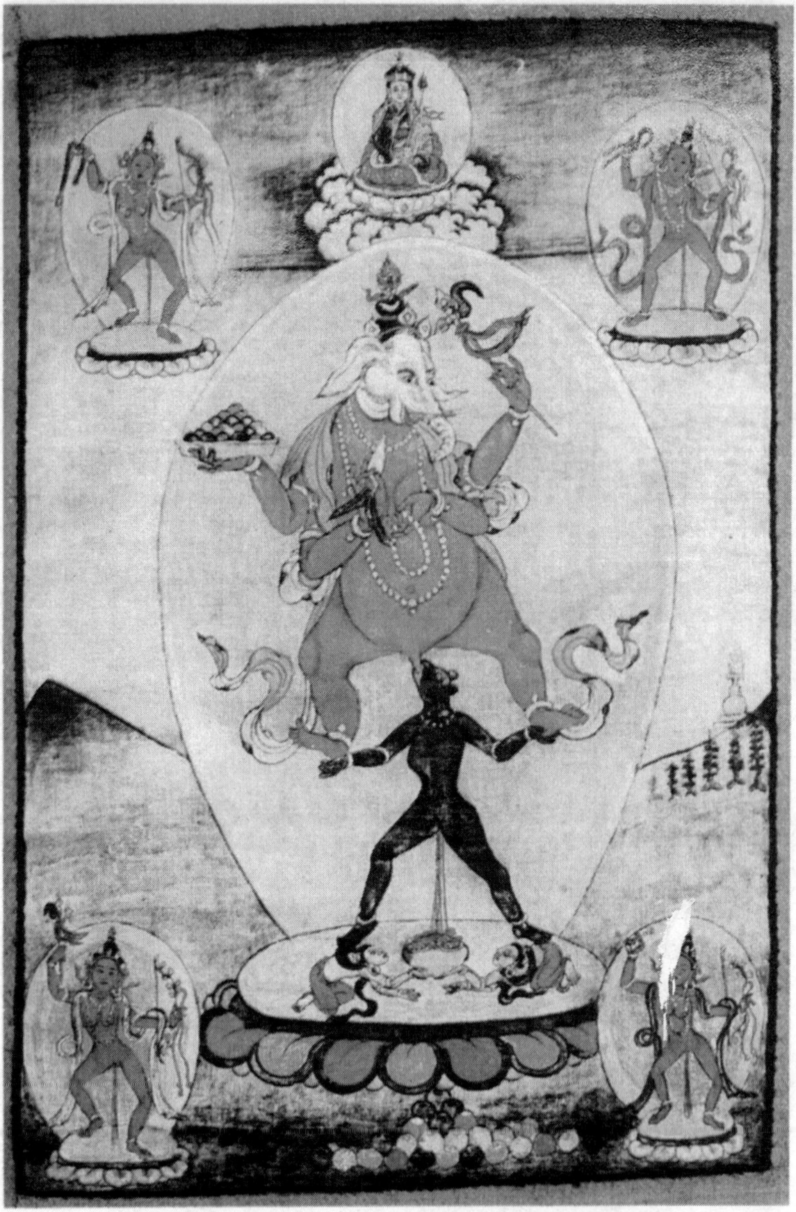

II Image # 207 - Red (rakta) Gaṇapati; courtesy of The Shelley & Donald Rubin Foundation (http://www.himalayanart.org)

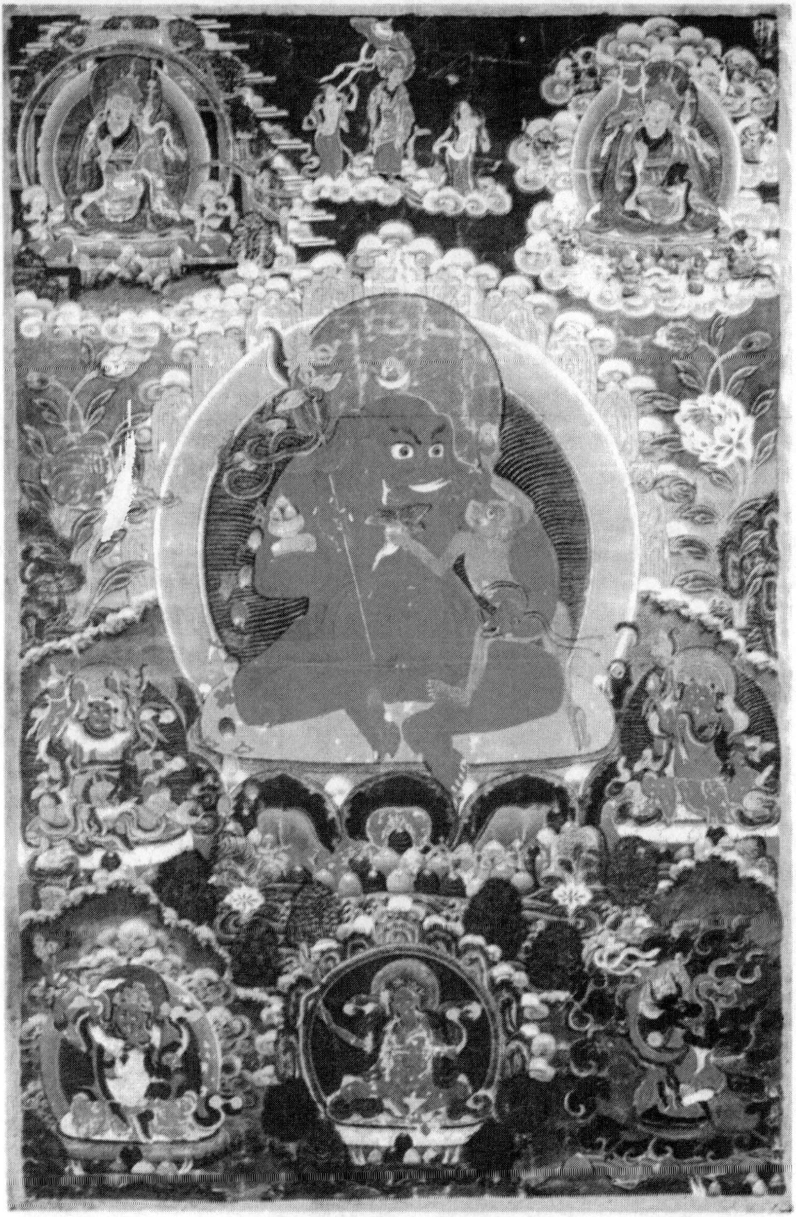

III Image # 500 - Gaṇapati; courtesy of The Shelley & Donald Rubin Foundation (http://www.himalayanart.org)

PLATES IV-XVII are reproduced from manuscript 258, preserved in the N.C. Mehta Gallery of the Gujarat Museum Society on the campus of the L.D. Institute of Indology, Ahmedabad

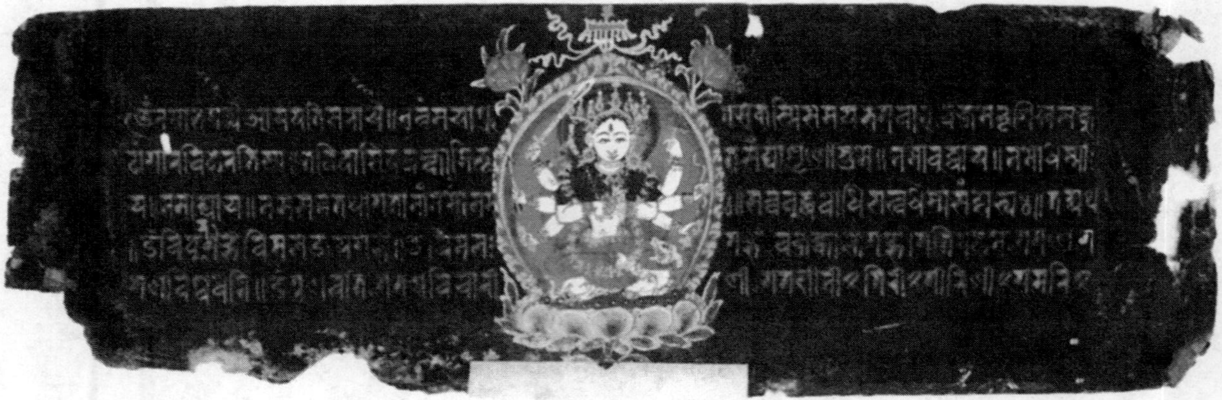

IV Mahāpratisarā, folio 1b

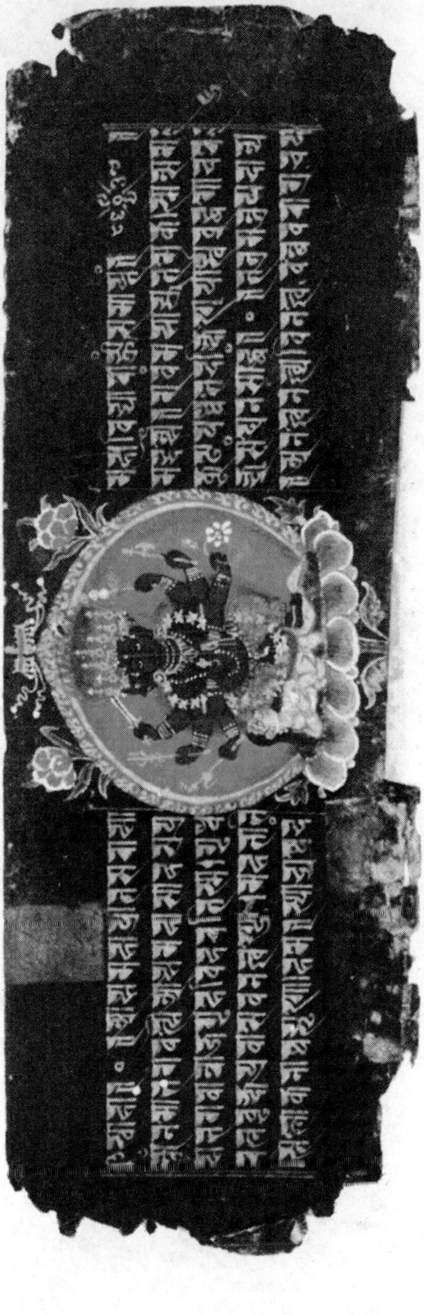

V *Mahāsāhasrapramardanī, folio 6b*

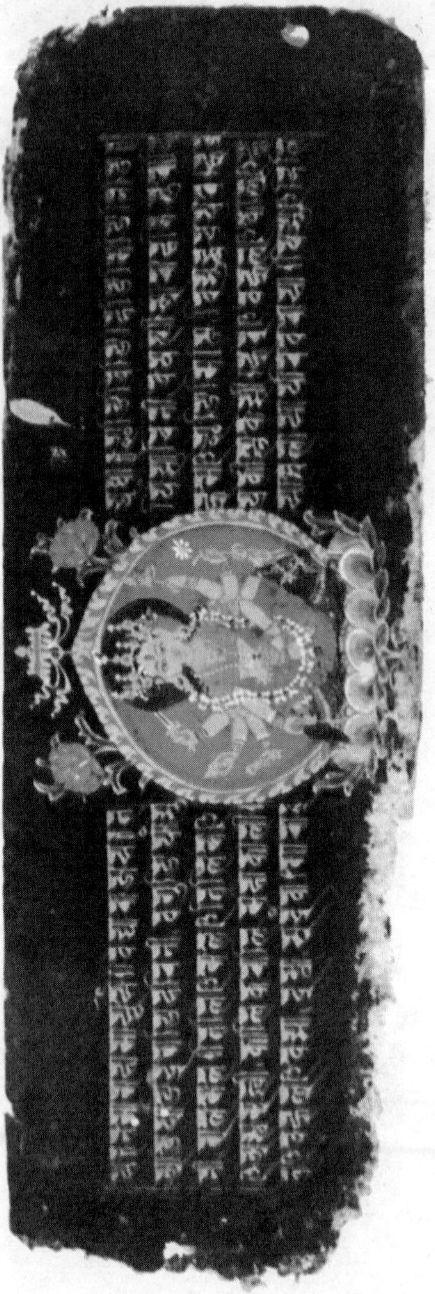

VI *Mahāmāyūrī*, folio 8b

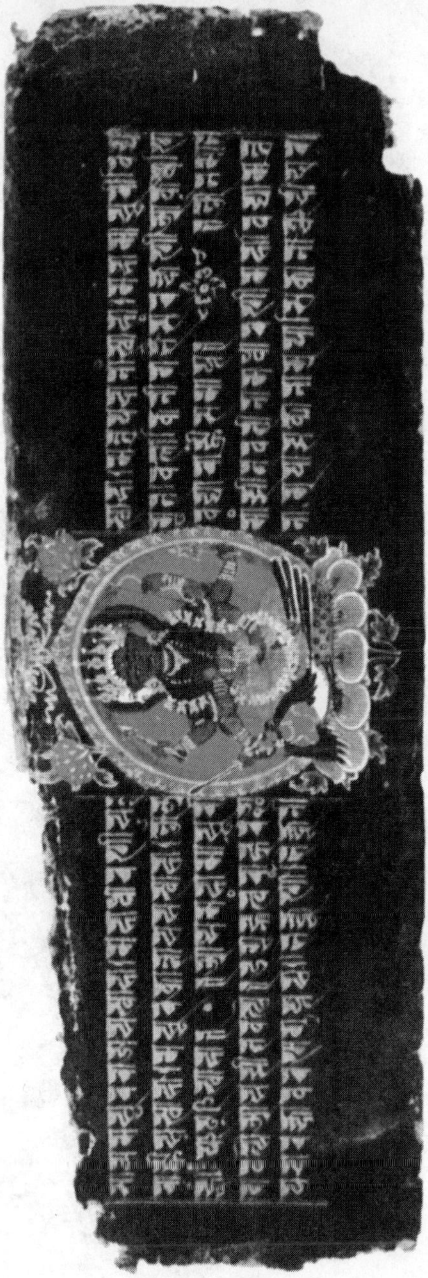

VII Mahāśītavatī, unnumbered folio

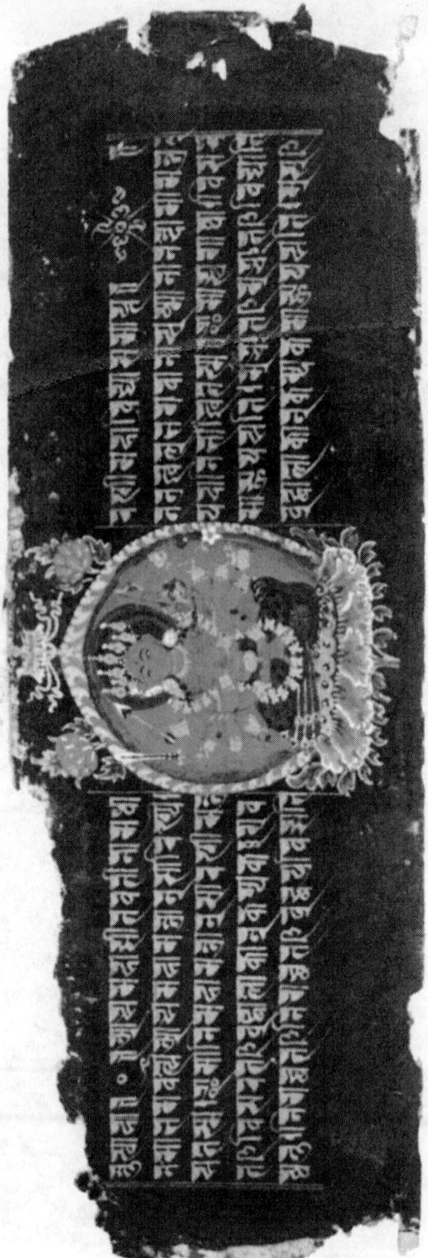

VIII Mahāmantrānusāriṇī, unnumbered folio

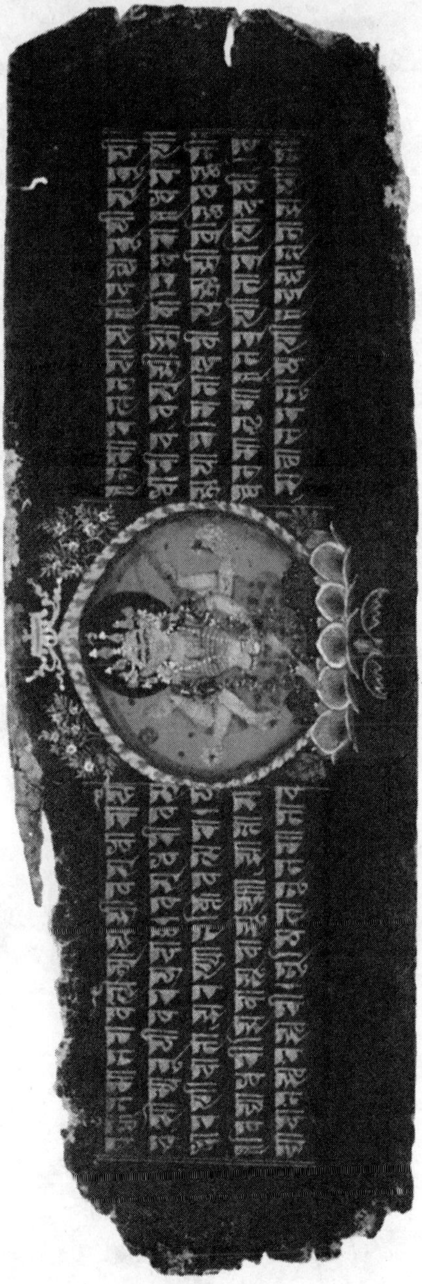

IX *Vasudhārā*, unnumbered folio

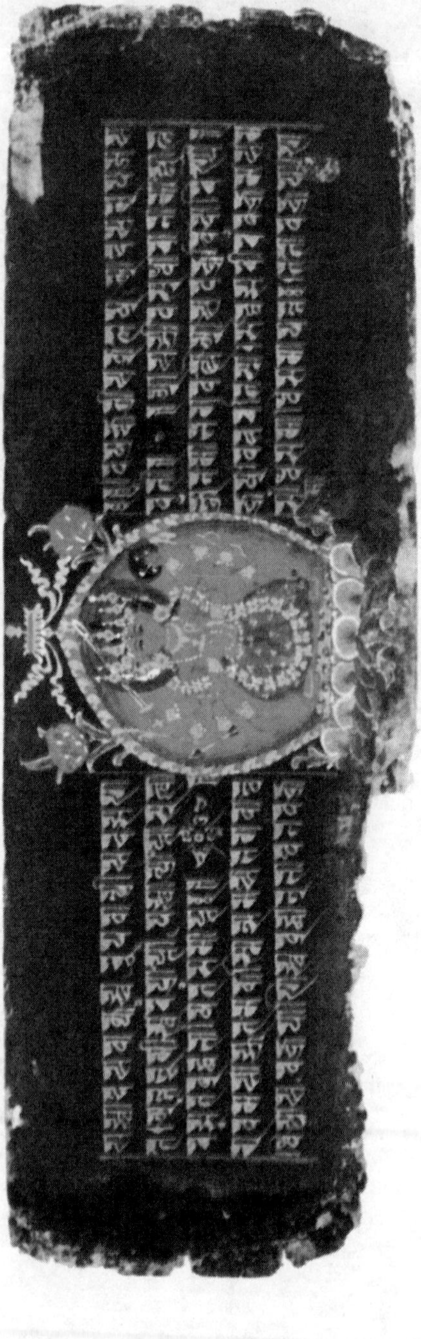

X [illegible]ravidāriṇī, unnumbered folio

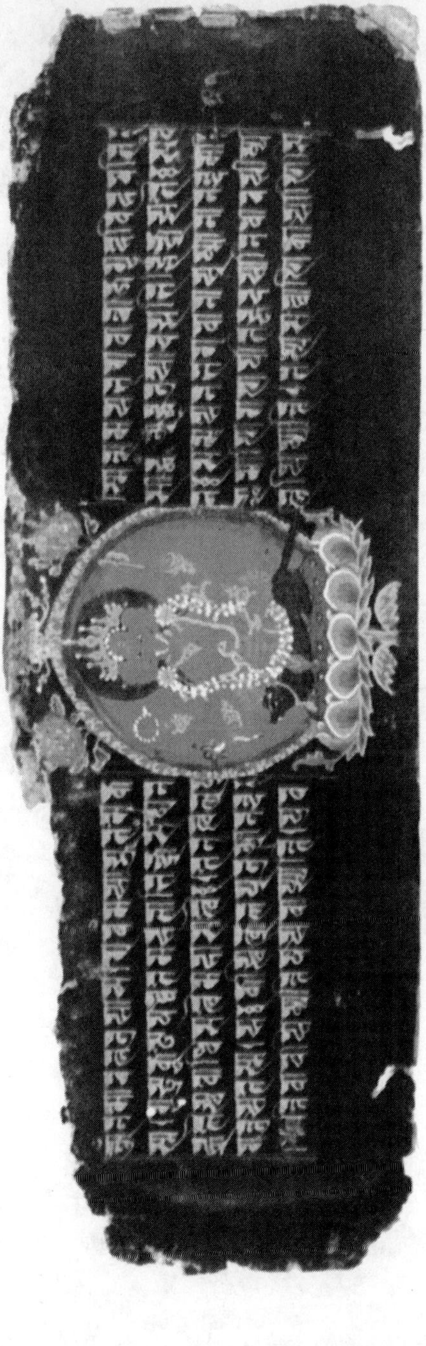

XI Gaṇapati (hṛdaya), folio 21b

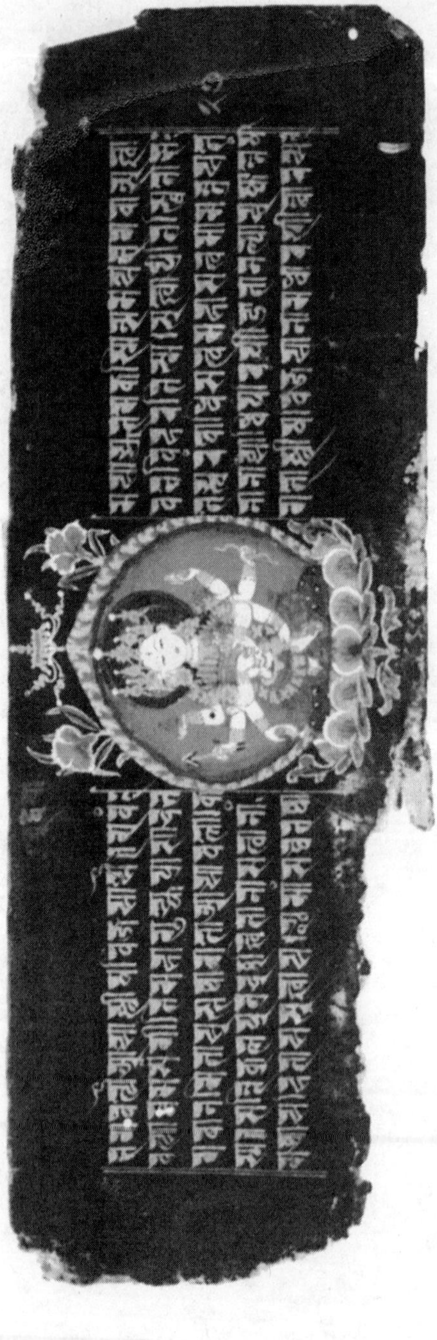

XII *Uṣṇīṣavijayā, folio 23b*

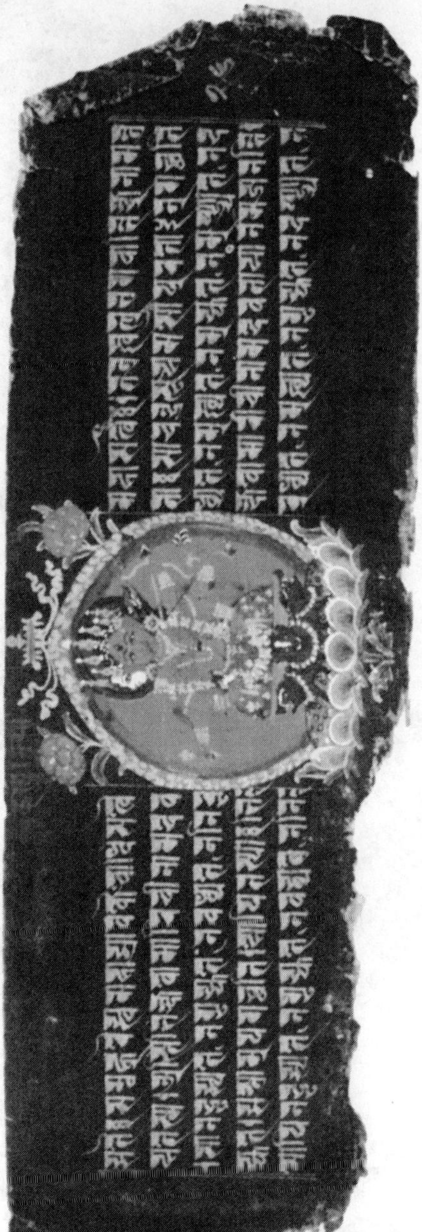

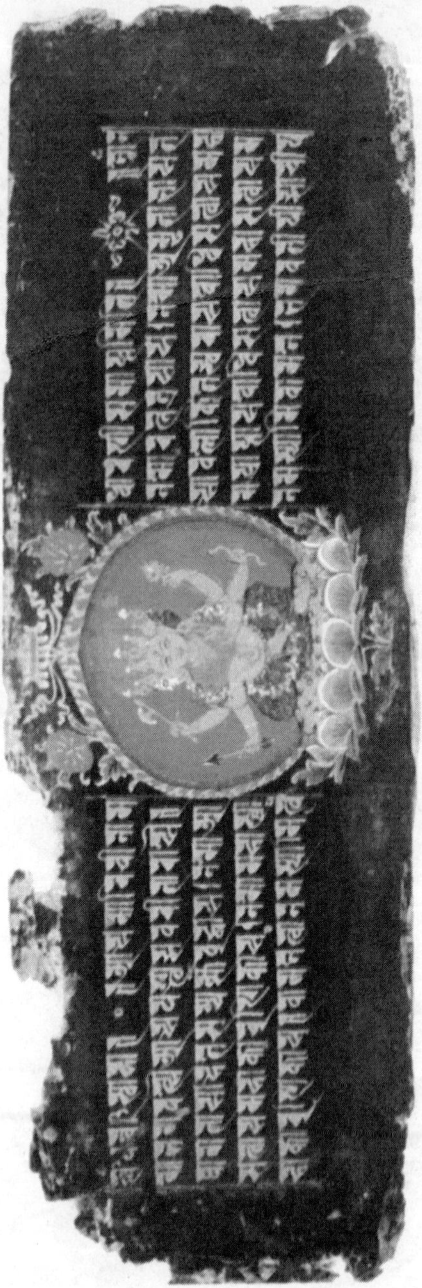

XIV *Parṇaśavarī, Unnumbered folio*

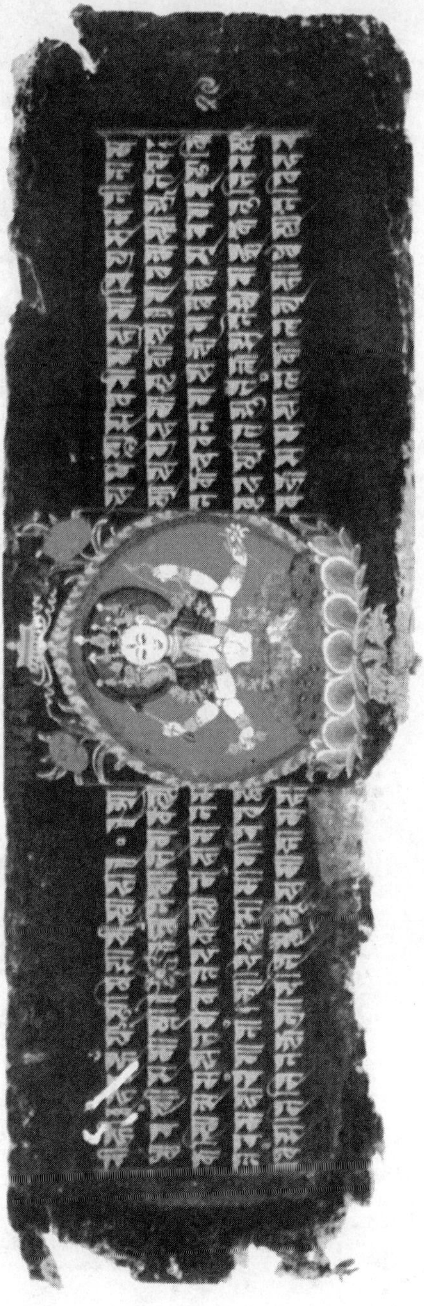

XV *Grahamātṛkā, folio 29b*

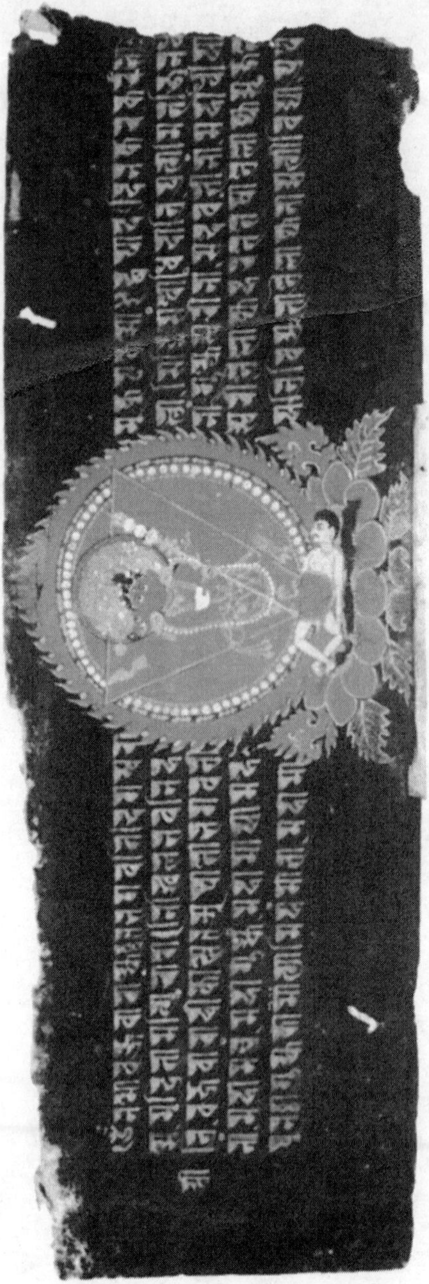

[illegible] broken off

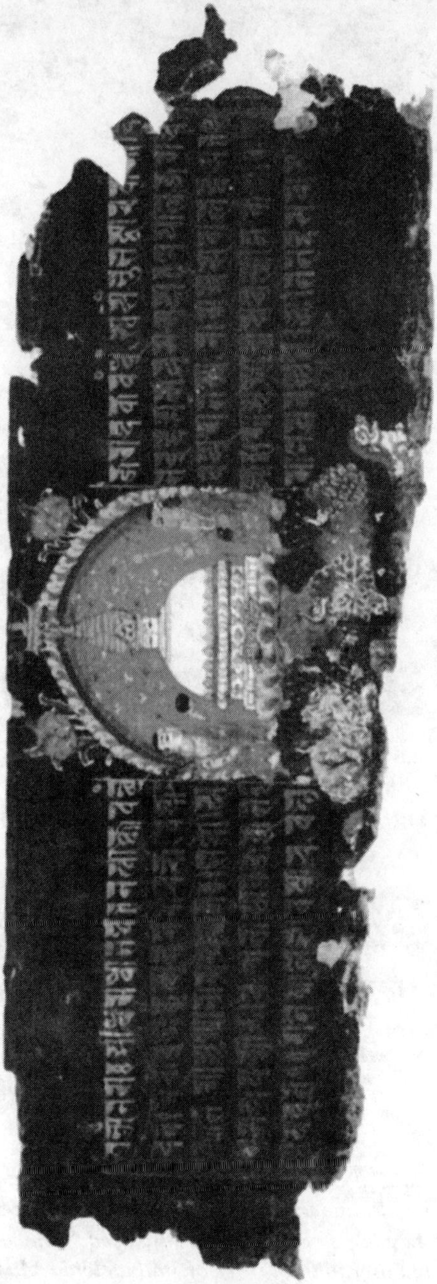

XVII *Svayambhūnāth Mahācaitya in Kathmandu, folio number broken off*

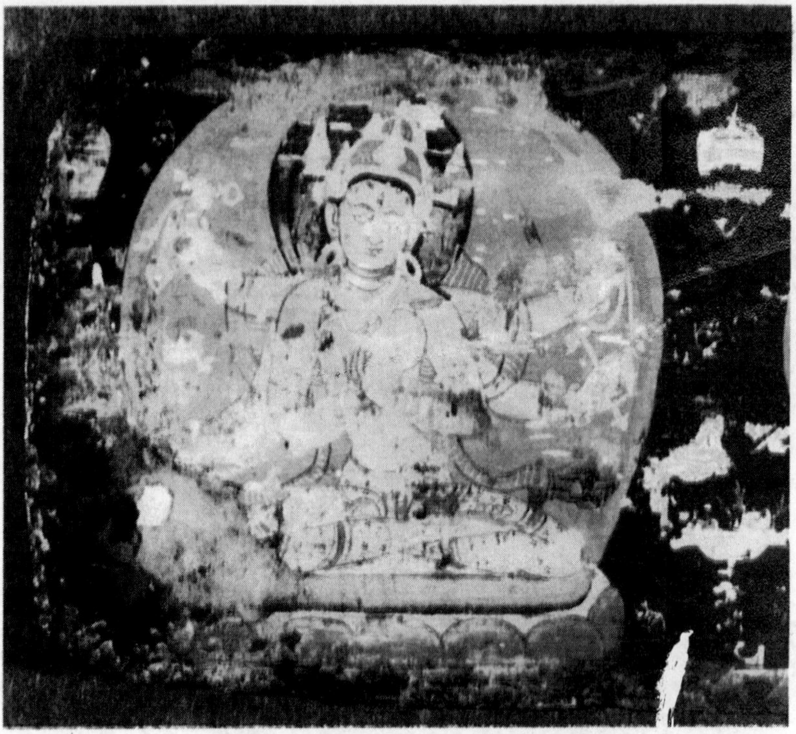

XVIII.A Grahamātṛkā # 1 (Type I), painting on wooden manuscript cover, Nepal, ca. 12th/13th century, Bayerische Staatsbibliothek, München (Cod. sanscr. 540); photograph courtesy of Bayerische Staatsbibliothek

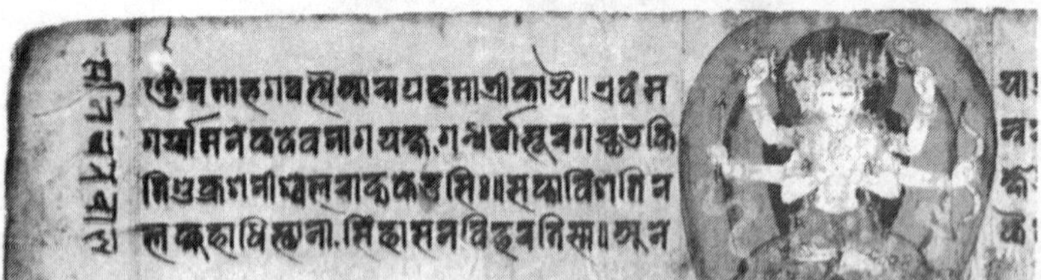

XVIII.B Grahamātṛkā # 3 (Type II), painting on paper manuscript leaf, Nepal, ca. 18th century, Philadelphia Museum of Art (1959-93-90(2,a), gift of Mr and Mrs Lessing J. Rosenwald), inscribed "sanicaravāla" on left margin; photograph courtesy of Philadelphia Museum of Art

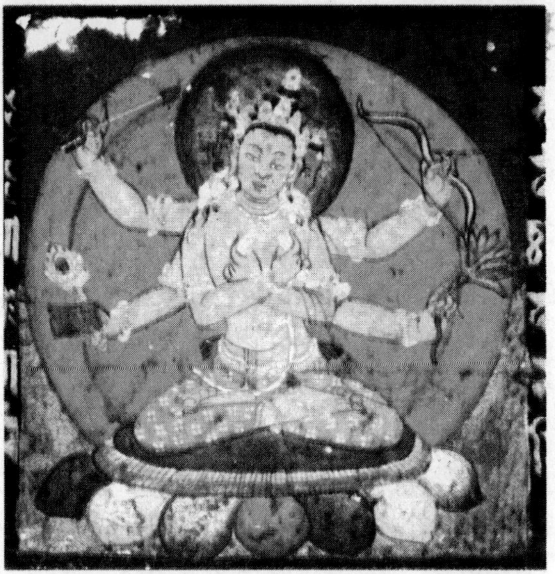

XIX.A
Grahamātṛkā(?) # 4 (Type II), painting on paper manuscript leaf, Nepal, dated 1748 AD, Staatsbibliothek zu Berlin (Hs.or. 1934) folio 111a; photograph courtesy of Staatsbibliothek zu Berlin

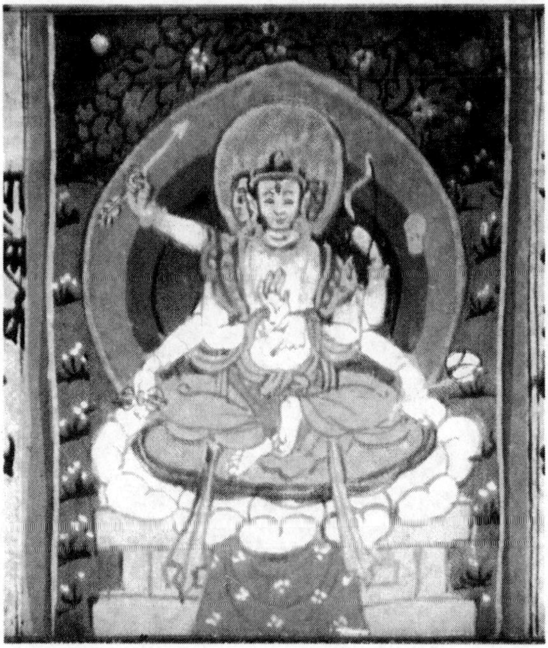

XIX.B
Grahamātṛkā # 8 (Type II), painting on paper manuscript leaf, Nepal, ca. 19th century, Bayerische Staatsbibliothek München (Cod. sanscr. 423) folio 26b; photograph courtesy of Bayerische Staatsbibliothek

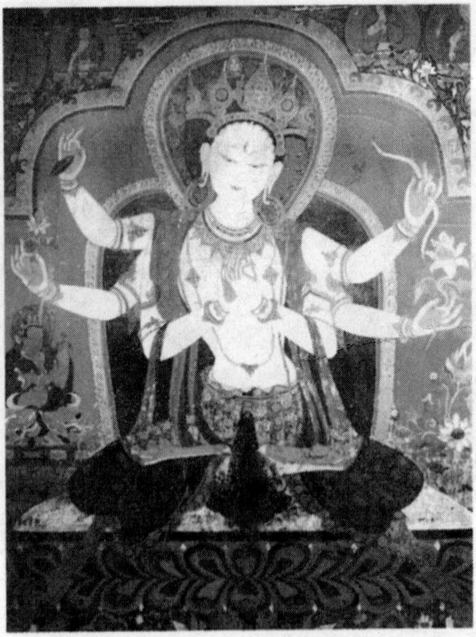

XX.A
Grahamātṛkā # 12
(Type II),
wall painting,
Tibet, Gyantse, 'Kumbum',
Grahamātṛkā Chapel,
1st half of 15th century;
after Ricca & Lo Bue 1993:
colour plate 83

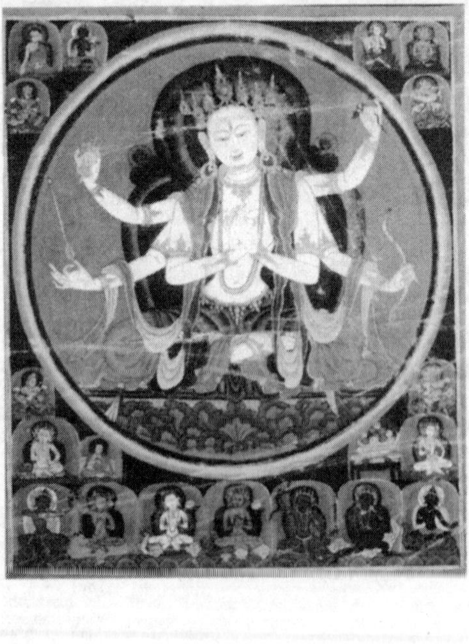

XX.B
Grahamātṛkā # 16
(Type II),
cloth painting,
Tibet, late 15th century;
after Pal 1984:
colour plate 49

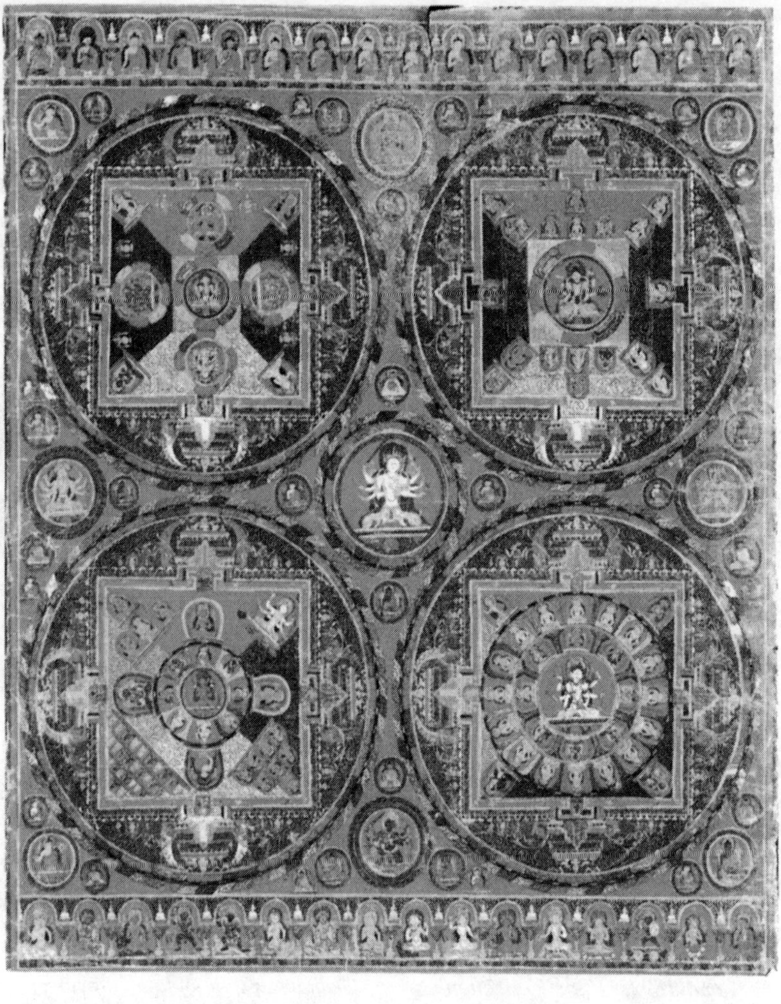

XXI Grahamātṛkā # 15 (Type I), cloth painting, Tibet, ca. 15th century(?), quadruple maṇḍala with Grahamātṛkā-maṇḍala on the lower left; after Koller A 87/3, 25./26.6.1993: Tafel 6, Nr. 18

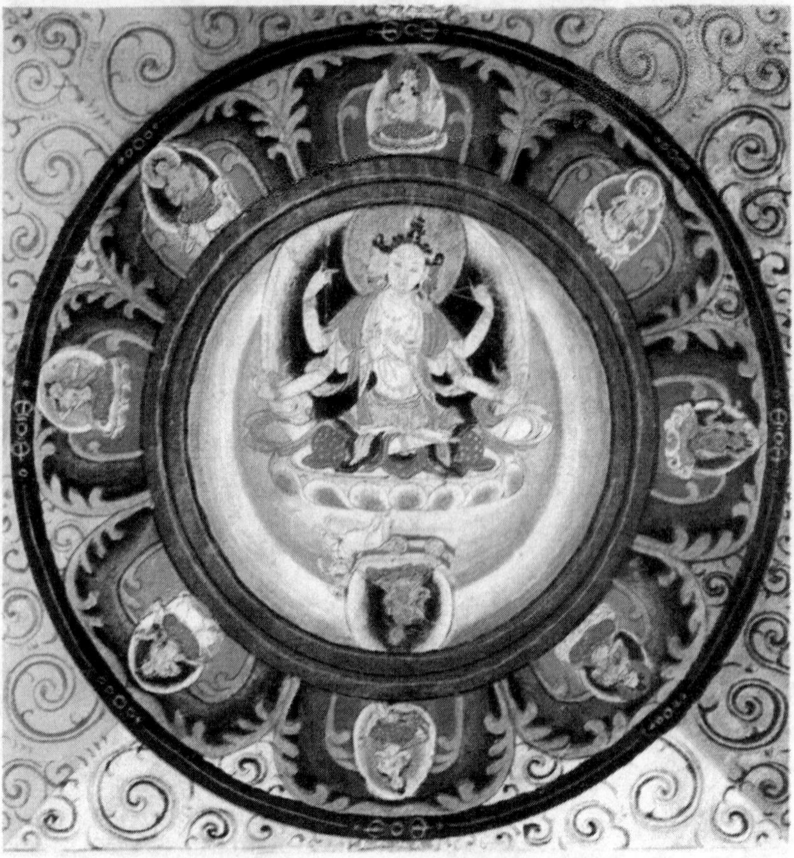

XXII Grahamātṛkā # 19 (Type II), cloth painting, Tibet, painted between 1870 and 1892, 'Ngor Collection' No. 6, Grahamātṛkā-maṇḍala in centre; after bSod nams rgya mtsho 1983: colour plate 6

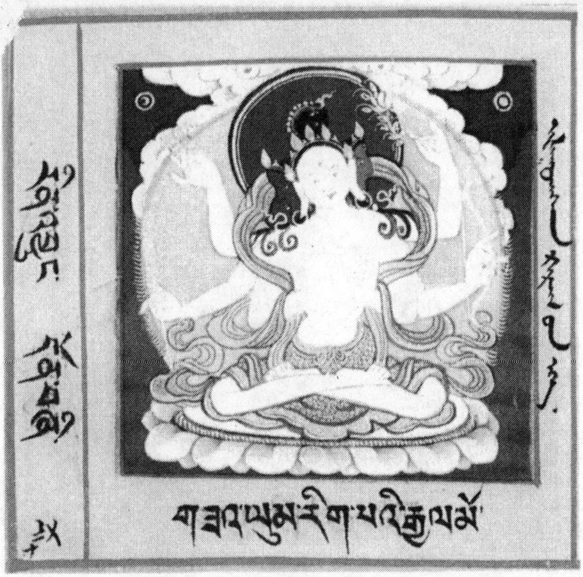

XXIII.B Grahamātṛkā # 28/1^{0} (Type II)

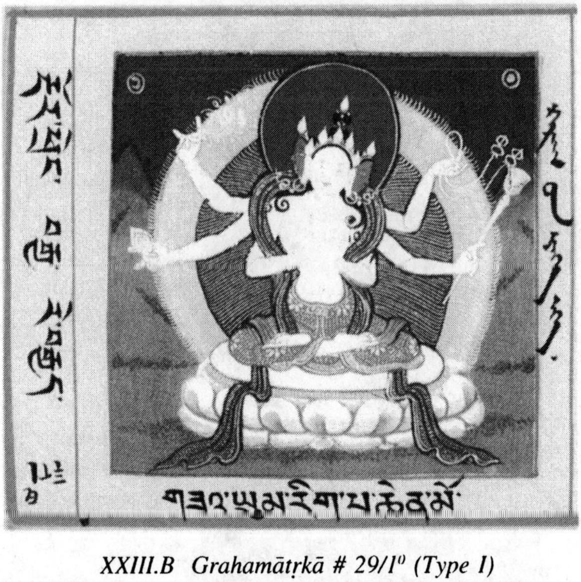

XXIII.B Grahamātṛkā # 29/1^{0} (Type I)
Painting on blockprinted paper, Mongolia, blocks carved shortly after 1810, painted around 1850; after Willson & Brauen 2000: no. 223 (XXIII.A) no. 505 (XXIII.B)

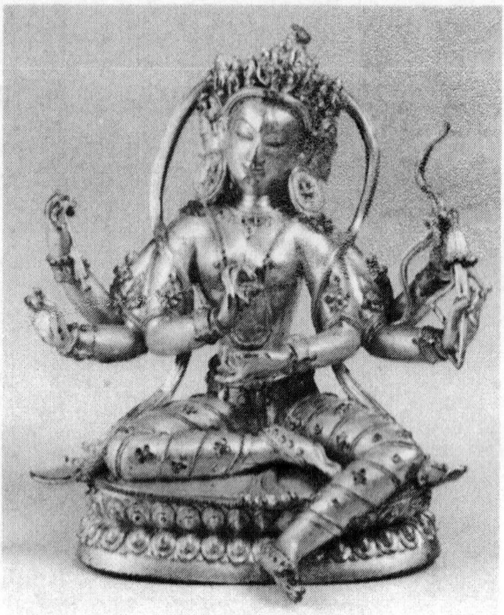

XXIV.A
Grahamātṛkā # 34 (Type II), gilt copper alloy, glass, and semi-precious gems, Central Tibet, ca. 15th century; after Rossi & Rossi 1994: no. 22

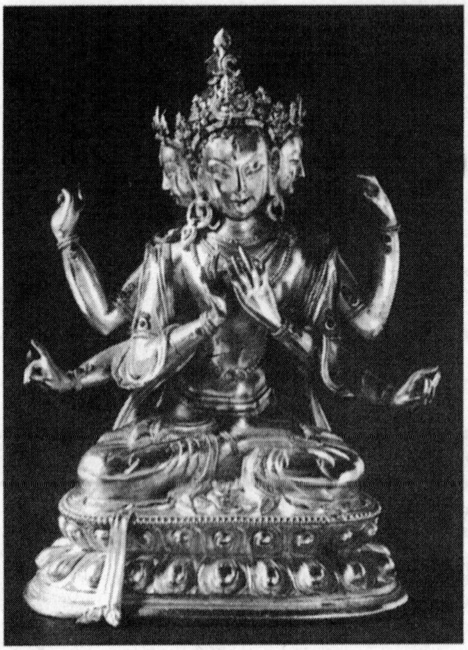

XXIV.B
Grahamātṛkā # 35, gilt copper alloy, and semi-precious gems, Tibet, ca. 18th century; after Koller A 61/3, 14.-15.11.1986: Tafel 11, Nr. 67

A Brief Introduction to *Saudhikāgama*, an Unpublished Sanskrit Text on Temple Architecture, Iconography and Town Planning from Orissa*

SADANANDA DAS

There are numerous texts in the whole of Sanskrit literature which deal with the subject of architecture and iconography but they are not as widely studied as other subjects such as literature, philosophy or grammar etc., and hence are not very well known. These texts include independent works classified under the heading of technical sciences or technical treatises (Śilpaśāstra or Vāstuśāstra). Though architecture and iconography are dealt with in a number of works, there are few specialized works of great importance in this field. Āgamas and Purāṇas often describe Śilpa and Vāstu or secular and sacred architecture, so that Śilpa, Vāstu and Āgama traditions are complementary or even sometimes overlapping. In this context the relevant texts include Purāṇas like the Agni, Matsya, Garuḍa, Nārada and Viṣṇudharmottara as well as Śaiva and Vaiṣṇava Āgamas like the Kāmikāgama, Ajitāgama, Rauravāgama, Aṃśumadvedāgama, and Pāñcarātrāgama (Sāttvata Saṃhitā, Pauṣkara Saṃhitā, Jayākhya Saṃhitā, and Hayaśīrṣa Pañcarātram). Other works such as the Mānasollāsa of Somadeva, Samarāṅgaṇasūtradhāra of Bhoja, Aparājitapṛcchā of Bhuvanadeva, Mānasāra, and Mayamatam are also important treatises for the subject in question here.[1]

---

* I am thankful to the Alice Boner Institute, Varanasi, for providing me working facilities while preparing this article.

[1] For a detailed bibliography see Acharya 1981: 749ff. and Dagens 1994: 906ff.

In this wide range of works on architecture and iconography, the Saudhikāgama (SĀ) occupies a distinct place. It is an unpublished Sanskrit text of encyclopaedic nature on Orissan temple architecture, town planning and iconography comprising about 4457 verses divided into nine chapters. Each chapter concludes with a colophon such as: "*iti śivavīrabhadraprasaṃgokte saudhikāgame prāsādamūrtilakṣaṇavarṇanaṃ nāma tṛtīyo 'dhyāyaḥ*", i.e. "thus ends chapter three, the description of the characteristics of temples and images in the dialogue between Śiva and Vīrabhadra in the Saudhikāgama".

The contents of the Saudhikāgama can be summarized as follows. The first chapter starts with a *maṅgalācaraṇa* to Śiva Candraśekhara. Then Mahādeva expounds the subject of Śilpa to Vīrabhadra in the form of a dialogue in which Mahādeva answers Vīrabhadra's questions. Mahādeva explains the definition of Āgama and the significance of the Saudhikāgama. Then he explains building sites and meditation on the Dikpālas and describes the Bhairavayantra and Yoginīyantra. Further he expounds on the various regional types of temples, the four types of towns, wells, tanks, villages and *śāśana* villages, and the characteristics of stones and woods for making images. At the end of the first chapter, he explains the doors and different types of *yantras*, *mukhaśālās*, etc.

In the second chapter Mahādeva praises Kaliṅga (modern Orissa) and expounds on the different types of Vāḍabhī temples, describing their parts in detail. Chapter three is devoted to the description of *liṅgas*, images and their measurements, ornaments and different types of *āsanas* etc. In the fourth chapter he expounds the *Gaṇapati-pratimā-lakṣaṇa*. Chapter five is devoted to the explanation of the *Śaivapratimā-lakṣaṇa*, *nṛtyamūrtis* and *Bhairavamūrtis*, chapter six to *Viṣṇupratimā-lakṣaṇa*, and chapter seven to *Sūryarahasya*. Chapter eight concerns the *Śaktirahasya* (i.e., the *Navadurgārahasya*, *Daśamahāvidyārahasya* and *Saptamātṛkārahasya*) and their *pañjaras*. The last chapter consists of a description of the *gaṇamūrtis*.

The term *saudha* refers to a great mansion or palace, a large house, a white washed mansion, or a stuccoed house. According to the Abhidhāna-cintāmaṇi (4.58) and Amarakoṣa (I.10) *saudha* denotes a palace.

As Prof. V.S. Agrawala points out in his preface to the *Śilpa Prakāśa*: "The word *Saudha* seems here to be taken in the sense of temple or shrine and the title *Saudhika* seems to correspond to the title *Salāṭa* in Saurāṣṭra, which means a stone worker".[2]

The Saudhikāgama is quoted for the first time in the Śilpa Prakāśa, a medieval text on Orissan Temple architecture. It is currently available only in two palm-leaf manuscripts in Oriya script, one from Purulia and the other from Dharakot. Dr. Alice Boner has collected these mss and partially translated the text in her article "Saudhikāgama on Pañjaras".[3]

The author of the Śilpa Prakāśa, Rāmacandra Mahāpātra Kaula Bhaṭṭāraka, who lived in a tantric village and was a follower of Kaulācāra doctrine, mentions Saudhikāgama frequently and explicitly as an authority and the main source of his knowledge. This text appears to have been in his time a generally acknowledged authority in the matters of tantric architecture and allied arts. It seems to refer to a tantric school of temple architecture of which little is known today, and this text gives valuable information about it. At the end of the first Prakāśa (vv. 559-560) of the Śilpa Prakāśa the author states: "This Sāstra follows the Kaulācāra tradition. The theory of art as understood by Kaulācāra doctrine is similar to that of the Aṃśukāgama. The two chapters of this book follow the composition of the Saudhikāgamā."

Now the question arises, "Why is this text called an Āgama?" The answer is that it is so called because it was revealed by Śiva or Mahādeva.[4] However, the Saudhikāgama is not found in the list of Āgamas,[5] so that it should perhaps be referred to as an Upāgama. This exposition is presented in a systematic way. Vīrabhadra asks, "O Lord! tell me the best knowledge to destroy sin: the discipline of Śilpa, the knowledge of building temples (*saudha*), the pure knowledge of architecture (*vāstu*),

---

[2] Bäumer/Das/Das 2004: x.

[3] Boner 1967-68.

[4] *saudhajñānaṃ saudhabhāgaṃ sthāpatyāṅgaṃ hi kauśalam,*
saudhāgamam iti khyātaṃ śaṅkareṇa subhāṣitam. (SĀ IX.242)

[5] See Bhatt 1961: "Table des Āgama et des Upāgama", facing page xix. See also Kaviraj 1972.

and the nature of images, especially of their *yantras* and diagrams (*pañjaras*). O Lord, please tell me the essence of art (*śilpa ttva*), that knowledge which is pure, eternal and certainly destroys a . sins" (SĀ I.8-10). Here Vīrabhadra specifically asks about temple architecture and iconography along with the relevant *yantras* and *pañjaras*.

After hearing his question Mahādeva says, "Very well, O great hero, you who are obedient towards me. To destroy your mental agonies, listen to the science of *Saudha* in detail" (SĀ I.11), and proceeds to elaborate on this subject through the rest of the text. Due to the length of the Saudhikāgama, it is not possible to discuss all of its topics in detail in this short paper; I will give here only a brief introduction to its contents.

The Saudhikāgama treats both secular and religious art and architecture. The first chapter starts with a salutation to Lord Mahādeva or Bhairava (Rudra). Later on in the discussion between Vīrabhadra and Mahādeva, the latter expounds the importance of Āgama and says that between the Āgamas and the Nigamas, the Nigamas confer only liberation, while the Āgamas bestow *siddhis* during one's lifetime and lead to liberation at the end (of life) (SĀ I.24). Therefore, between the Nigamas and Āgamas, the Āgamas are superior. They confer the four aims of existence, *dharma*, *artha*, *kāma* and *mokṣa* (SĀ IX.241). By sacrificial action alone neither liberation (*mukti*), nor accomplishment (*siddhi*), nor even human action (*pauruṣa*) (are obtained). All (these) are said to be completely fruitless and thus always censured in the Kaliyuga. Thus in this Kaliyuga the Āgamas are the best way, and they truly lead to the realization of reality (*tattvasiddhi*) (SĀ I.25-26).

Further Mahādeva says that there are many Āgamas which are adorned by the Śaiva doctrine and which contain the knowledge of reality (*tattvajñāna*), the supreme knowledge, the best and purest knowledge, which is the essential nature of Creation, the essential nature of Śiva and Śakti, which is truly great: the *yantra*, *mantra*, the *Vīratattva*, and the means of attaining it. He continues by explaining the supremacy of the *kaulācāra* path: "The *kaulācāra*, the *mahācāra*, the *vīrācāra* and the *trāṭaka* (yogic) method of concentration, together with (*khecara-*

mudrā) etc. are the pure knowledge of *yoga*" (SĀ I.28-29). He then continues describing the *vīrabhāmi*, *vīracakra* and *vīrasādhana*, the *sādhana* of *vīrāṅga* and *devīcakra*, the *sādhana* on the cremation ground, the *yoginī-sādhana*, the worship of various *pretas*, their praises, and so on. Then he says that he has already explained to Umā the *pūjā* of the earth, the different building sites and the worship of Bhairava etc. in the previous part (*pūrvabhāga*)[6], and tells Vīrabhadra to listen to this Āgama with its true nature (*tattvas*), which destroys sin. The knowledge of the Devī temple (*kaulagṛha*) and the like, and of *yantras*, he explains, is difficult to obtain (SĀ I.32-33).

The different kinds of temples, the erection of temples, and the characteristics of ponds, tanks, wells, forts, castles, villages, towns and donated (*śāsana*) villages are then described. If all these are made according to the *kaulācāra* rules, they will certainly confer all *siddhis* (SĀ I.34-35). Further, declares Mahādeva, "Listen to the different features of buildings and their parts, for the destruction of sin." He emphasizes the importance of knowing Śilpa and Vāstu and says that the knowledge of Śilpa is highly meritorious and the knowledge of *vāstu* always great. "For the sake of divine knowledge," he says, "I explain this Saudhikāgama together with the features of pure images with their *yantras* and *pañjaras*" (SĀ I.37-38). "O my son! listen carefully, this is not to be given to anybody. The doctrine of *kaulācāra* indeed is highly secret" (SĀ I.29)[7]. Afterwards he speaks of the merit of building a temple: "One who builds a temple with a pure mind dwells in heaven and saves his (ancestors for) seven generations. Thus is the fruit of building a temple." Next he describes the materials such as stone or

---

[6] This "previous part" has not been identified yet among the extant manuscripts of the text.

[7] See also *idaṃ yantraṃ tathā rekhānyāsaṃ gopyatamaṃ sadā,*
na deyaṃ guruputrebhyo vinā kaulātmakaṃ ḍhruvam.
yadi kaścit kada kimva yantranyasaṃ samacaret,
viphalā jāyate siddhir jvaraṃ bhavati dāruṇam.
vinā gurupadeśena na kuryāt yantrapañjaram,
vikale sukṛtaṃ sarvaṃ vinaśyati tathā dhruvam.
sarvagopyatamaṃ tattvaṃ kaulabījam iti smṛtam. (SĀ VIII.484-487a)

bricks for building *yantras* and shrines. Then he speaks of the preliminary rites to be performed before starting to build a temple. When beginning (to build) the temple, the preliminary rites should be done very carefully, as stated by Hayaśīrṣa, or prominently by (any) other Kaula tradition. (SĀ I.42).

After this introduction Mahādeva explains the building site and then says: "One should build a temple in a city, or on high places, or on the banks of rivers which flow with full current. Building in these places will certainly confer liberation" (SĀ I.43). Further he speaks about the ground which should be selected for building a temple. The soil of the building site should be dusty, slippery (*picchilā*), yellow or red in colour, smooth, and full of fragrance. Earth with these characteristics is best for building a temple. For the sake of a temple the best soil is soft and white, whereas for a pond a moistened and dark ground is enjoined (SĀ I.46). Red or silvery coloured sand is the best for a fort and brings victory. But by purifying according to the *kaula* rites, everything becomes auspicious." He goes on to explain the purification of the ground (SĀ I.48), mentioning in this connection the process of measuring the ground with a thread, which is called *sūtrakarma* or *sūtrapātanakarma*. After this one should draw a hexagram (*ṣaṭkoṇa*) at the side of the gnomon at the crossing of three roads in the village or in the town, and worship Kālikā (SĀ I.65).

Then one should offer *digbali* in all directions and worship the *kauṇapas*, *piśācas* and evil *yoginīs* (*duṣṭayoginī*) on different parts of the *yantra* which is established on the ground. After the ground is ploughed with recitation of *mantras*, a stone *yantra* is carefully established on it. Offering *arghya* (water, sesame, mustard, and *darbha* grass) on that *yantra*, one begins the *saudha* and invites the architects (*śilpināṃ varaṇaṃ caret*) (SĀ I.69). In connection with the building process, Mahādeva further explains the worship of the *bhairava-yantra* and the *yoginī-yantra,* which are meant for Śiva and Durgā temples respectively and which bestow *siddhis*. For the protection of the temple one should worship the groups of *yoginīs*. The best of the twice born, together with the architect, should offer prayers for protection (SĀ I.109).

After the worship of the *yantras*, Mahādeva explains the different types of temples. There are many types of temples, but among them only twel· e regional types are excellent. They are Madhyakrāntā, Virāṭa, V .ṇśaka, Māgadha, Pāñcāla, Maithila, Bhoṭa, Gurjara, Malla-kūrccaka, Kaliṅga, Madhya Saurāṣṭra and Drāviḍa. Then he explains each type with their different characteristics in brief, and describes the Vāḍabhī type in detail.

After explaining these twelve types of temples Mahādeva says that all of them always bestow merit and give a heavenly abode as well as liberation (SĀ I.194). By building a Rudra temple, a Viṣṇu temple, or a Śakti temple a person will attain the joy of the heavenly world. For building a temple, a town or a village is always best site. A temple which is not built on a proper place brings destruction and becomes fruitless (SĀ I.197-198). Therefore he next describes the characteristics of towns and villages.

Mahādeva then spoke: "Listen my son, I will tell you the characteristics of towns, their divisions and the plan of their layouts (*nyāsa-mārga*) as prescribed by the scriptures on architecture (*Vāstuśāstras*)". He describes four types of towns called Nandāvarta, Svastika, Tri-bhaṅga and Teruṇḍaka, which are of circular shape like a big lotus (SĀ I.199-200). He adds that among all these four towns Nandāvarta is the best, built according to the original *tantras*, and that the ground (*bhūmi*) should be of two (*yojanas*).[8] The Svastika and the Teruṇḍaka towns are to be established on one *yojana* of ground each, whereas the Tribhaṅga town should consist of 100 sections (*śatavarga*) and should be spread over a vast area on a river bank (SĀ I.202).

By the way of example, we may look at the description of the Nandāvarta town: "The ground for the Nandāvarta town should be extended in a square, a field equal in length and breadth (SĀ I.205). It should be divided into six parts in length and breadth. In each section a space should be designated for the road. A double space in the middle should be fixed for the central road or highway (*rājamārga*), running

[8] One *yojana* is equal to four *krośas* or eight to nine miles; see Apte 1985: 789.

from south to north for its full length. Then smaller paths are to be made. Some space should be left for making small roads and narrow lanes. The Nandāvarta town is always beautiful with its roads."

Next, it is stated that "In the north there is a path for the cows (*gopatha*), on the outside the way for the farmers (*kṛṣidaṇḍā*); in the west and south there is forest, and in the east a river. The cremation or the burning ground (*śmaśāna* and *dāhyabhūmi*) should be in the south, which should be surrounded by fields, and space should be left in the east for the cows and for agriculture. These are the outer parts of the town (*vāhyāvartāni*). Now, listen to the interior parts of the town. A hospital (*gadaśālā*) is to be made in the northeast direction as well as a place for teaching and poetry (*prabodhakāvya-mandiram*). In the north the citizens are to live along with the government servants and the army."

"At the border there is a beautiful park and a strong building for the treasury. On the roadside in front of that there is an assembly hall (*sabhya-nirvācanālaya*), and in the northwest (*vāyavya*), wells and tanks for low caste people. A pool (*jalādhāra*) should be made outside [the town] for the washermen. In the west, the court should be established in a strong building (SĀ I.212-217). At the roadside (*patha-prānta*) a carpentry workshop (*kāruśālā*) should be built, together with some houses for the citizens. In the west, in the central part should be placed a camp and the four-fold military force (*caturaṅgabala*). A prison and police station also should be located there. In the southwest (*nairṛta*) a tank and dwelling places (*vāsabhūmi*) are to be made along the road. At the side of the road, towards the north, should be a brothel (*veśyālaya*). To the north of it a beautiful dispensary (*ramya-bheṣaja-mandira*) should be established. A theatre is to be made between that place and the residential quarter. In the north a beautiful school should be set up. There one should establish hostels or monasteries (*maṭhas*)[9] and teachers' quarters (*gurugṛhas*). To the north of the school there should be place for the residences of the administrators and officers.

[9] See *maṭhaś chātrādinilayaḥ* in Mishra 1972, II.2.8.

In the south [dwell] fishermen, businessmen, and the community (*maṇḍala*) of actors and dancers. To the north of this there is a beautiful theatre."

"There are protectors and guardians of the city and craft shops (*śaṭha āpaṇāḥ*). On the side of the road there are shops of *rasa* (liquor) and houses of the lowly Śūdras. In the east, at the front, are the houses of the goldsmiths and in the southeast there are ironworkers and sculptors (*lauhakāras* and *śilākāras*). On both sides of the road there is a row of permanent shops. There is an excellent temple to the north of the road, in the front. Even if there are many (temples), one should build a temple somewhere in the west on the best place, following the practice of Śilpa. On the southeast side the ground is auspicious for the dwellings of *vipras* (*brāhmans*). On the south side, at the border, intelligent people should build the army quarters. People of the business class should be placed on the other side of the road" (SĀ I.225-230).

It is also said that a tank/pond should be built for the merchants, and that there must be a proper pipe for draining out the water. In this way the text describes in detail the other aspects of a city, and then continues with the description of the royal palaces, though I will not present these sections in detail here. There should be also parks and gardens (*vāṭikās* and *upavāṭikās*) in the city for the entertainment of the people. One should build the best city as it is described according to the rules (SĀ I.236).

Why, Mahādeva asks, is this town called Nandāvarta? Because it is protected by Śiva (Nandi being epithet of Śiva), it is called Nandāvarta (*Śivena rakṣitaṃ nagaraṃ nandāvarttaṃ tu nāmataḥ*). A town without temples of Śiva and Śakti is considered inferior. A town which is established according to the rules of architecture remains for four *yugas*.[10]

Then the text describes the method of building wells: one should build wells with bricks of round shape, of the size of ten *hastas*; this is the best type of well (SĀ I.271). Their depth should be 100 *hastas*, in

---

[10] An age of the world. The four *yugas* are the Satya, Tretā, Dvāpara and Kali, which last for 1,728,000, 1,296,000, 864,000 and 432,000 years respectively, for a total of 4,320,000 years. See Apte 1985: 786.

two rows. Further details are given regarding the selection of bricks: they should be of red colour, one *hasta* long, ten *aṅgulas* wide, and four *aṅgulas* high. They should contain neither rock nor stone, but should be made of pure clay, since this is the kind of brick that is fit for building wells (SĀ I.275). Further details are then given regarding the contents of wells and tanks.

Mahādeva then explains the techniques of digging a tank. There are different types of ponds for different towns and for temples. For a town, a large pond is best. Then Mahādeva describes the differences among *puṣkariṇī, taḍāga*, and *dīrghikā*, which are to be made with paths and steps according to the rules. The tank, *taḍāga*, is highly praised: Viṣṇu always dwells in the water, and Śiva is also pleased with water. In the water all the gods dwell; therefore one should worship Varuṇa. In this context, he further describes three types of tanks, which are best, medium and inferior according to their size and other characteristics. The one with twelve gates is considered the most excellent tank of all. It has a *maṇḍapa* in the centre, a shrine of Varuṇa, and a *pura* made of gems. This is the best tank, and it bestows glory and liberation.

Mahādeva then speaks about the *dhyāna* of Varuṇa, who is of peaceful form with two arms and decorated with jewels. He has a long noose in his right (hand) and a small water jar in his left (hand). His vehicle is Makara who is made excellent with fearful teeth. One should establish this image of Varuṇa on the *maṇḍapa*, on a divine pedestal. Having made a plate of gold and copper painted with mercury, a *yantra* is to be made and established secretly. After establishing this *yantra*, one should perform the *yantranyāsa* with *the Vaṃ-bīja*. Thereby one's glory becomes stable and the tank remains always full of water. On top of this *yantra* one should place the image of Varuṇa with all its diagrams (*pañjaras*)[11]. This is the *sātvikī* image. He further describes the building of steps, which will not be described here.

In conclusion, I may point out that the importance of this text lies in its unique value for the study of temple architecture, iconography and

[11] See Boner 1967-68.

town planning. It specifically describes the *yantras* or ground plans for building and protecting the temples, as well as the *pañjaras* or compositional diagrams for making images, explaining that one who worships an image with its *pañjara* and *dhyāna* obtains the highest abode, as it is essential to know the *yantra*, the *pañjara* and the *pratimālakṣaṇa*.[12] Though it gives a survey of different regional types of temples, it describes in detail only the Vāḍabhī type, which is meant for *śakti* temples since the text belongs to the *kaula* tradition of tantrism. Thus it describes the Vāḍabhī type of temple (*kaulagṛha*) with all its details, as well as the *kaula* ritual in connection with the description of the *śaktis* in the eighth chapter.

REFERENCES

ACHARYA, P.K. 1981. *A Dictionary of Hindu Architecture*. Delhi: Oriental Books Reprint Corporation (Mānasāra Series, vol. I).

APTE, V.S. 1985. *The Practical Sanskrit-English Dictionary*. Delhi: Motilal Banarsidass.

BÄUMER, B., DAS, R.P. and DAS, S. (eds.) 2004. *Śilpa Prakāśa. Medieval Orissan Sanskrit Text on Temple Architecture*, by Rāmacandra Mahāpātra Kaula Bhaṭṭāraka. Delhi: IGNCA and Motilal Banarsidass (originally published: Leiden: E.J. Brill. 1966).

BHATT, N.R. 1961. *Rauravāgama*. Pondichery: Institut Français d'Indologie.

BONER, Alice 1967-68. Saudhikāgama on Pañjaras. *The Adyar Library Bulletin* 31-32 (Dr. V. Raghavan Felicitation Volume): 113-124. Madras.

DAGENS, Bruno 1994. *Mayamatam. Treatise of Housing, Architecture and Iconography*, vol. II. Delhi: IGNCA and Motilal Banarsidass.

KAVIRAJ, Gopinath 1972. *Tantrik Sāhitya*. Lucknow: Hindi Samiti.

MISHRA, S. (ed.) 1972. *Amarakośa of Amarasiṃha*. Kuala Lumpur, Malaysia.

---

[12] *pañjarānusṛtāṃ devyā dhyānabhāgasamanvitām,*
mūrtiṃ ca ye pūjayanti yānti te cottamāṃ gatim. (SĀ IX.240)
yantraṃ ca pañjaraṃ caiva pratimālakṣaṇāni ca,
jñātavyeyaṃ sadā vatsa bhadrakālī bhayāvahā. (SĀ VIII.89)

Towards a Computer Encoding for Brāhmī[*]

STEFAN BAUMS

1. INTRODUCTION

This paper describes a project to develop a computer coding system for the Brāhmī script and to submit the result to the international standardisation body responsible for specifying the computer representation of the world's writing systems.[1] Official standardisation of the coding system will encourage its support across a wide range of computer systems, and is the best way to ensure its long-term survival.

---

[*] I would like to thank Lore Sander, who furnished advice on Khotanese and Tumshuqese Brāhmī; Gudrun Melzer, who provided an image of the rare *r̄ mātrā* from the Gupta period manuscripts that she studies; and Jost Gippert, Christiane Schaefer and Georges-Jean Pinault, who suggested improvements to the description of Tocharian Brāhmī. Andrew Glass carefully went through a draft of this paper and has been involved in the encoding project from the beginning. Any remaining inadequacies should be attributed to the present author. Contributions by specialists in particular forms of Brāhmī to the encoding project described here are not only highly welcome but strongly encouraged. It is important to ensure that the proposed encoding in fact meets the needs of the Indological community before it is submitted, accepted and implemented.

[1] The present paper is complementary in purpose to the formal proposal document (available at the URL http://depts.washington.edu/ebmp/brahmi-encoding/): the former aims to present the technical issues to the scholarly world, who are the future users of the technology, while the purpose of the latter is to represent our scholarly needs to a technical audience, who will implement the technology. The proposal document has now also been presented by my colleague Andrew Glass at the "International Symposium on Indic Scripts: Past and Future", 17 to 19 December 2003, convened by the research group "Grammatological Informatics Based on Corpora of Asian Scripts (GICAS)" at the Tokyo University of Foreign Studies, and it is being discussed on the Unicode Consortium's "indic" email list.

This will enable Indologists working with the Brāhmī script to fully use the generic text-processing functions of their software, such as searching and indexing. It will also ensure that Brāhmī data can be exchanged between different computer systems without the need for conversion, and that it will still be legible many years from now, even as general computer technology changes.

At the root of a computer coding system lies what is called a "coded character set". A coded character set is nothing more than a table that assigns to each character of a script a unique numerical value called its "code point". In the coded character set that is now commonly used throughout the world, the Latin character A, for instance, is assigned the code point 41, the Devanagari character क the code point 915, and the Chinese character 佛 the code point 4F5B[2]; such a mapping between characters and numerical code points is necessary because numbers are the only entities that computers can handle internally. In addition to defining a coded character set, a coding system will also specify other properties of a script, such as how characters combine with each other in a line of text, which of course is particularly important for writing systems of the Indian type.

Historically, there have been dozens of mutually incompatible coding systems. One used the code point C7 for the French character Ç, another used the very same code point for the Russian character Ч and a third one for the Greek character Η. This confusing situation, which seriously impeded the exchange of textual data across linguistic boundaries, was partly due to technical reasons that have since become irrelevant[3] and partly to lack of international coordination. In the late 1980s, however, an initiative was started to remedy the situation by

---

[2] It is customary to write code points not as decimal, but as hexadecimal numbers, that is, numbers using the base 16, with digits from 0 to 9 and then A to F. This is a matter of technical convenience (two hexadecimal digits will always represent one byte), but has no deeper significance. In the examples used above hexadecimal 41, 915 and 4F5B would correspond to decimal 65, 2325 and 20,315.

[3] Especially the use of only one byte for the representation of characters, imposing an upper limit of 256 on the number of characters that could be contained in the same coded character set.

developing one single coding system that would be capable of representing all the world's writing systems in a uniform and systematic fashion. This work was carried out jointly by the Unicode Consortium (representing the computing industry, academic institutions and government bodies[4]) and by the International Organization for Standardization[5]. The first version of this new coding system standard, known as the Unicode Standard or IS 10646, saw the light of the day in 1991, covering all the major modern scripts of the world with a total of 28,302 assigned characters. Since then it has been continually improved, and in its present version (2003) coverage has expanded significantly to include modern minority scripts and historical characters and scripts, with a total of 96,382 assigned characters (TUS, 1355f.).

2. THE COMPUTER ENCODING OF INDIAN SCRIPTS IN GENERAL

One of the defining principles of the Unicode Standard is that it encodes characters, the abstract units of a writing system, not glyphs, the graphical shapes that realise those units in writing. To take an example from the Indian sphere, क and ष are glyphs of the Devanagari writing system that represent one character each, namely U+0915 DEVANAGARI LETTER KA and U+0937 DEVANAGARI LETTER SSA[6] respectively, or *ka* and *ṣa* in Indological transliteration, whereas क्ष is a single glyph that represents a sequence of characters, namely <U+0915 DEVANAGARI LETTER KA, U+094D DEVANAGARI SIGN VIRAMA[7], U+0937 DEVANAGARI LETTER SSA>, or *kṣa* in Indological transliteration. It is clear that in the case of Indian writing systems, there is no one-to-one correspondence of characters and glyphs. The mapping

---

[4] Including the Governments of India, Pakistan and Tamil Nadu.

[5] More precisely, the working group ISO/IEC/JTC1/SC2/WG2.

[6] Here and in the following, code points are prefixed with "U+" to indicate that they refer to the Unicode coding system. Every character is also assigned an official name in the Unicode Standard, and such names are as here and in the following written in small caps. Sequences of Unicode characters are presented between angle brackets.

[7] See below for further discussion of the VIRAMA control character.

from a sequence of Unicode characters in a text file to a sequence of glyphs, for example on the display of a computer, is not a subject matter of the Unicode Standard, but rather is handled by complementary font technology such as the widespread OpenType format.[8] Nevertheless, it is the responsibility of Unicode to provide a coded character set that both represents the units of a real-world writing system as faithfully as possible and lays the foundations for a natural glyph rendering of that writing system at the font layer.

Akṣara writing systems such as Brāhmī and Kharoṣṭhī have two characteristic properties that a computer coding system needs to take account of: postconsonantal vowels are written in the form of diacritic elements added to the core of the akṣaras; and sequences of more than one consonant are written as consonant clusters, which are graphic combinations that often involve simplifications of their constituent elements. Unicode handles the first property by providing, in addition to the initial vowel characters (e.g. उ U+0909 DEVANAGARI LETTER U), a separate series of vowel diacritics (e.g. ु U+0941 DEVANAGARI VOWEL SIGN U) that have the property of being "combining characters", meaning that they cannot occur independently but are added to and to be interpreted in combination with the preceding character. Thus, the Devanagari akṣara कु will be encoded as a sequence of two Unicode characters, the independent U+0915 DEVANAGARI LETTER KA followed by the combining character U+0941 DEVANAGARI VOWEL SIGN U. It is an important principle of the Unicode Standard that characters always follow each other in the phonetic or logical order, disregarding the physical order of their glyphs when rendered. Therefore, the akṣara कि *ki* will be encoded exactly parallel to कु *ku*, even though the *i* diacritic precedes the *ka* core of the akṣara when rendered (<U+0915 DEVANAGARI LETTER KA, U+093F DEVANAGARI VOWEL SIGN I>); and the parallelism even holds in the case of those Indian scripts that have vowel diacritics consisting of more than one

[8] An open standard initially developed by Adobe Systems and Microsoft Corporation.

physical part, such as Bengali, কো *ko* being encoded as <U+0995 BENGALI LETTER KA, U+09CB BENGALI VOWEL SIGN O>.

Consonant clusters, the other characteristic feature of akṣara writing systems, are handled with the help of a special control character called VIRAMA which is placed between any two consonants that are to be joined. The consonant cluster न्ध *ndha*, for instance, will be encoded as <U+0928 DEVANAGARI LETTER NA, U+094D DEVANAGARI SIGN VIRAMA, U+0927 DEVANAGARI LETTER DHA>, and the same applies to longer consonant sequences such as न्ध्र *ndhra* <U+0928, U+094D, U+0927, U+094D, U+0930 DEVANAGARI LETTER RA>. The abstract virama control character is thus by no means necessarily displayed as a virāma glyph (्). In practice, a sequence of consonant characters joined by VIRAMA will be rendered as a proper conjunct wherever made possible by the font, and with a visible virāma mark only in those cases where the font lacks a conjunct glyph for the consonant sequence in question (e.g. ङ्म *ṅma* <U+0919 DEVANAGARI LETTER NGA, U+094D, U+092E DEVANAGARI LETTER MA>). It may be noted that this behaviour closely mirrors traditional typographic practice which resorted to aesthetically less pleasing (but semantically equivalent) virāma combinations where the metal type lacked a particular conjunct. Final consonants are similarly encoded with the VIRAMA control character (उपनिषत् *upaniṣat* <..., U+0924 DEVANAGARI LETTER TA, U+094D>).[9]

The Unicode Standard currently covers the following South Asian Brāhmī-derived scripts (2003, version 4.0): Devanagari, Bengali, Gurmukhi, Gujarati, Oriya, Tamil, Telugu, Kannada, Malayalam, Sinhala, Tibetan and Limbu (as well as the major Brāhmī-derived scripts of Southeast Asia). As the case of Limbu shows, efforts are now underway to add the modern minority scripts to the Unicode standard, and the same is true of historic writing systems: Ogham, Old Italic, Runic, Gothic, Ugaritic, Linear B, the Cypriot Syllabary and a very large number of premodern Han characters have recently been added to its

[9] For a more detailed and technical discussion of the modern Indian scripts in Unicode see TUS, 217-262.

repertoire. Thus, with the completion of the modern national scripts, the focus of the Unicode development effort is in effect shifting from the commercial and political to the scholarly.[10]

3. THE COMPUTER ENCODING OF KHAROṢṬHĪ AND BRĀHMĪ

On this background, Andrew Glass and the author of the present paper have recently co-authored a proposal for the addition of Kharoṣṭhī to the Unicode Standard,[11] in close and productive cooperation with members of the Unicode Technical Committee and other experts.[12] The Kharoṣṭhī proposal has now been accepted by the Unicode Consortium and is currently awaiting ratification by the International Association for Standardization; it is expected to be published as part of version 4.1 of the Unicode Standard.

Based on our positive experience with the Kharoṣṭhī proposal, it was felt that the more formidable task of developing an encoding for the variants of Brāhmī should now also be attempted. There have been several efforts in the past to formulate encodings for particular subvarieties of Brāhmī, but only one of these has advanced to the proposal stage.[13] In contrast to previous approaches, we are convinced of the importance of providing a unitary encoding for all subvarieties of Brāhmī: a single encoding that provides a character repertoire sufficient for the representation of all the forms of the script that occur in manuscripts and inscriptions from its beginnings in the 3rd century BCE until the emergence of the modern Indian scripts by around 1000

---

[10] Everson (2002) gives an overview of the historical and minority scripts that remain to be encoded, and refers to the Script Encoding Initiative that has been set up at the University of California at Berkeley to support and coordinate work on these scripts.

[11] Available at http://depts.washington.edu/ebmp/downloads/Kharoshthi.pdf.

[12] Especially Rick McGowan (Unicode Consortium), Kenneth Whistler (Sybase Inc.), Deborah Anderson (University of California at Berkeley) and Michael Everson (Everson Typography).

[13] Everson 1998, for Aśokan Brāhmī.

CE. Considering the strict separation in Unicode between an abstract character layer defined by the encoding and a concrete glyph layer produced by a computer's rendering system on the basis of specific fonts, it would be a duplication of effort and waste of architectural resources to reflect those palaeographic differences at the encoding layer that will already be reflected at the font layer:

Aśokan Brāhmī font	Kuṣāṇa Brāhmī font	Gupta Brāhmī font
Aśokan Brāhmī encoding	Kuṣāṇa Brahmī encoding	Gupta Brāhmī encoding

The varieties of premodern Brāhmī should instead be given a unitary encoding, their differences being expressed at the font level only:

<table>
<tr><td>Aśokan Brāhmī font</td><td>Kuṣāṇa Brāhmī font</td><td>Gupta Brāhmī font</td></tr>
<tr><td colspan="3">Brāhmī encoding</td></tr>
</table>

This architecture has the great advantage of reflecting not only the differences of the variants of Brāhmī at one level, but also their unity at another level. The fact that in this model there is one sense in which, for example, a *ka* is always a *ka*, whether it appears in Eastern Gupta Brāhmī or in Gilgit-Bamiyan type II Brāhmī, makes it possible to have the computer search for all *ka*s across script varieties, to index them and to group them together – an immense practical benefit for any sort of palaeographic work.[14]

[14] In the palaeographic treatment of the Buddhist manuscripts in the Schøyen Collection, for example, we have to do with a large number of varieties of the Brāhmī script (see Sander 2000 for a description of some of these) that nonetheless all were used in related textual traditions, had a well-defined user group, and evidently all found their way into the same monastic library. From a practical perspective, the advantage of a unitary encoding for those who constantly have to handle these script variants in parallel is readily apparent.

Moreover, the historical development and differentiation of Brāhmī was of such a gradual nature that any of the various suggested subclassifications inevitably involves a strong element of subjectivity (cf. Salomon 2003: 73f.), just as the ongoing discovery of significant new manuscript[15] and inscriptional[16] source material keeps changing our understanding of the historical processes involved. It has to be kept in mind in this connection that in order to ensure stability of the standard the Unicode Consortium has a strict policy never to remove a character or script once it has been encoded. Any particular subclassification of Brāhmī encoded now would therefore be set in stone for all time, and would inevitably lose congruity with our emerging understanding, even assuming that a suitable consensus on classification could be reached among Brāhmī scholars at the present time. For technical, scholarly and practical reasons, it is therefore strongly preferable to express the variety of Brāhmī at the font level, and to express its unity at the encoding level.

4. BRIEF OVERVIEW OVER THE HISTORY OF BRĀHMĪ

The earliest undisputed examples of writing from historical India are the edicts of Aśoka from the middle of the 3rd century BCE. While most of these inscriptions are in Brāhmī script, in the Indian Northwest Kharoṣṭhī, Aramaic and Greek were used as well. It would appear that the earliest known form of Brāhmī presupposes the existence of Kharoṣṭhī: Brāhmī follows the same system of vowel marking as Kharoṣṭhī, but has a greater number of distinct vowel signs that allow for a better representation of Indian languages, and Kharoṣṭhī has clear historical associations (with the Aramaic script) that Brāhmī lacks. It has been suggested that the Brāhmī script was specially invented for use in the royal inscriptions of Aśoka or similar documents, on the

[15] Such as the several thousand fragments of Buddhist manuscripts now in the Schøyen Collection, Oslo (Braarvig 2000).

[16] For example the Tamil Brāhmī inscriptions that have come to light in the course of the last century (Mahadevan 2003).

basis of an acquaintance with the Kharoṣṭhī and possibly also Aramaic and Greek scripts.[17]

The further development of Brāhmī script is characterised by very gradual changes in the forms of letters conditioned by cursivisation and modification of stroke order, and by changes in the writing utensils used. The characteristic headmarks of the modern Devanagari and Bengali scripts, for instance, have their origin in the mark left where a reed pen first touches the writing surface,[18] while the trend towards round letter forms in the southern varieties of Brāhmī is attributed to the South Indian technique of incising the letters into palm leaves, where straight lines would have tended to split the leaf.[19]

As a chronological framework, the system employed by Salomon 2003: 94-99 (based on Sircar 1970-1971: 113) is adopted here, distinguishing Old, Middle and Late Brāhmī, Transitional Scripts, and the modern Indian scripts. While spreading towards southern India in the Old Brāhmī period (3rd to 1st centuries BCE), the script underwent experimental and rather shortlived systemic innovations and saw the introduction of new characters in the Old Tamil and Bhattiprolu inscriptions (see below). In the Middle Brāhmī period (1st to 3rd centuries CE), regional variation increased; Dani distinguishes between East Indian, Northwest Indian, Northwest Deccan and South Indian styles.[20] Brāhmī was now for the first time being used to represent Sanskrit, and for this purpose five or six new characters were added to the script (*ṛ*, *ṝ*, *ḷa*, *au*, *ḥ* and maybe *ṅa*[21]). A special device was introduced for the marking of vowelless consonants, used both in Sanskrit, where it is called *virāma* and first occurs in manuscripts of the 1st century CE, and in Tamil, where it is called *puḷḷi* and attested in inscriptions from the 2nd century CE (Mahadevan 2003: 198). In the course of trade relations and cultural exchange, the Brāhmī script was

---

[17] Falk 1993: 109-112.

[18] Dani 1986: 79-81; Salomon 1998: 32, 34.

[19] Salomon 2003: 83.

[20] Dani 1986: 53.

[21] Unless the character *ṅa* was first introduced in Tamil Brāhmī; see section 6.

being exported to Central Asia and Southeast Asia. For several centuries, Indian forms of the script continued to be used in both these regions, primarily for the writing of Sanskrit texts. It was first during the Late Brāhmī period (4th to 7th centuries CE) that distinct Central Asian and Southeast Asian forms of Brāhmī developed, which then also began being used to write local languages. While the Central Asian tradition of Brāhmī came to an end with the Muslim invasions of the region at the end of the first millenium, the Southeast Asian forms of Brāhmī developed further into the modern Southeast Asian scripts. In the period of the Transitional Scripts (7th to 10th centuries CE), the Indian Northwest saw the emergence of the proto-Śāradā form of Brāhmī that became the precursor of Śāradā and other regional scripts such as Takri and Landa, which in turn inspired the development of the modern Gurmukhi script. In the rest of northern India, a style called Siddhamātṛkā predominated that gave rise to the modern Devanagari and Bengali scripts. In the Deccan, a proto-Kannada-Telugu script began to take form, while further south the Grantha script was developed for the writing of Sanskrit, and the Vaṭṭeḻuttu and Tamil scripts for the writing of Tamil.

5. THE ENCODING OF COMMON BRĀHMĪ SCRIPT FEATURES

The Brāhmī script shares many properties with Devanagari and its other descendants, and it should therefore as far as possible follow the encoding principles developed for the modern Indian scripts and described above. In almost all varieties of Brāhmī (except for Tamil and Bhattiprolu Brāhmī; see section 6), the basic consonantal graphemes denote the consonant in combination with an inherent *a* vowel. The presence of other vowels is indicated by adding vowel diacritics to the base consonant, as illustrated below from the Gilgit-Bamiyan type I variety of Brāhmī (6th/7th century CE, Northwestern India).[22] As with

[22] The font is drawn from a manuscript in the Schøyen Collection (edited in Baums 2002). Here and in the following, illustrations of Brāhmī letters are only used to identify the character under discussion, not to indicate any normative rendering of

the modern scripts, vowel diacritics are encoded as combining characters following the core of the akṣara. For the code points and character names used here and in the following, refer to the code charts and names list at the end of this paper.

ta	*tā*	*ti*	*tī*	*tu*	*tū*	*tṛ*
U+1101F	U+1101F, U+11035	U+1101F, U+11036	U+1101F, U+11037	U+1101F, U+11038	U+1101F, U+11039	U+1101F, U+1103A

te	*tai*	*to*	*tau*
U+1101F, U+1103E	U+1101F, U+1103F	U+1101F, U+11040	U+1101F, U+11041

A sequence of consonants without intervening vowels is written as a consonant cluster. In parallel with the other Indian scripts, these consonant clusters are to be encoded with the help of U+1104D BRAHMI SIGN VIRAMA. Consonant ligatures are written from top left to bottom right:

tma	*tsa*	*tkṣa*	*dgṛ*	*śma*	*sthā*
U+1101F, U+1104D, U+11028	U+1101F, U+1104D, U+1102F	U+1101F, U+1104D, U+11010, U+1104D, U+1102E	U+11021, U+1104D, U+11012, U+1103A	U+1102D, U+1104D, U+11028	U+1102F, U+1104D, U+11020, U+11035

---

them. As stressed throughout this paper, the visual display of Brāhmī characters will vary considerably according to the font or fonts used in actual applications. That being said, care has been taken to base the code tables at the end of this paper on a geographically and chronologically "central" font (from Sander 1968: Tafel 9 to 20, "Gupta-Alphabete der Gruppe B, h–k (Schrifttypus II)").

Pre- and postconsonantal *r* and postconsonantal *y* assume special reduced shapes in all but the earliest varieties of Brāhmī; the *kṣa* and *jña* ligatures, however, are in contrast to most modern Brāhmī-derived scripts usually transparent. Just like other consonant clusters, these are both to be encoded with the VIRAMA control character:

rtu	*tra*	*tya*	*rya*	*kṣa*	*jña*
U+1102A, U+1104D, U+1101F, U+11038	U+1101F, U+1104D, U+1102A	U+1101F, U+1104D, U+11029	U+1102A, U+1104D, U+11029	U+11010, U+1104D, U+1102E	U+11017, U+1104D, U+11019

When a consonant without inherent vowel cannot be written as non-final part of a ligature, such as when that consonant occurs at the end of a verse or paragraph, a visible virāma device is used. This device consists primarily of writing the vowelless consonant smaller and lower than other akṣaras, and often also of drawing a connecting line from the vowelless consonant to the preceding akṣara. Secondarily, a short horizontal line is frequently added above the vowelless consonant; it is this horizontal line that developed into the primary virāma marks of the modern Brāhmī-derived scripts.

cat	*jet*
U+11015, U+1101F, U+1104D	U+11017, U+1103E, U+1101F, U+1104D

The anusvāra sign (U+11045) is used to indicate that a vowel is nasalised (when the next syllable starts with a fricative) or that it is followed by a nasal segment (when the next syllable starts with a stop). The need for a separate encoding of candrabindu (indicating only nasalisation of a vowel) has not yet been demonstrated, but the code point following anusvāra has been left unassigned in case the need should arise.[23] The visarga sign (U+11047) is used to write syllable-final voiceless [h]. The velar and labial allophones of [h], preceding voiceless velar and labial stops respectively, are sometimes written with the separate signs jihvāmūlīya and upadhmānīya (U+11048 and U+11049); in contrast to visarga, these two signs are not combining diacritics, but behave like ordinary consonant signs, entering into ligatures with the following stop. (The third and fourth illustrations in the following table are from Gupta period manuscripts of the 4th/5th century CE.)

taṃ	*taḥ*	*ẖka*	*ḫpha*
U+1101F, U+11045	U+1101F, U+11047	U+11048, U+1104D, U+11010	U+11049, U+1104D, U+11025

The independent vowel signs *ṝ*, *ḷ* and *ḹ* and the dependent vowel signs *ḷ* and *ḹ* hardly ever occur in ordinary written texts, and therefore could not be illustrated in the code charts. The sounds they represent are, however, recognised by Indian systems of phonetics and therefore could in theory be written (cf. Dani 1986: 24f.).[24] This situation is exactly paralleled by that of the corresponding characters in Devanagari, with the exception that the encoding of the Devanagari characters had already been sanctioned by the pre-Unicode ISCII[25] standard and that they therefore had to be included in Unicode for compatibility reasons; in the case of Devanagari, illustrative glyphs were more readily available.

---

[23] Readers of this paper are encouraged to provide evidence for such a need, if indeed it exists, from manuscripts or inscriptions that employ a variant of Brāhmī that cannot be considered an early form of any particular one of the modern scripts.

[24] The contribution of illustrations of these characters from any relevant written source, including manuscript abecedaries, would be most welcome.

[25] Indian Script Code for Information Interchange, first published in 1988, and then in a revised form as IS (Indian Standard) 13194:1991 by the Bureau of Indian Standards in November 1991; see TUS, 2.9.

The Brāhmī script has separate number signs not only for the digits from 1 to 9, but also for the tens from 10 to 90, and for 100, 200, 300, 1000, 2000 and presumably 3000 (though the last has not yet been found attested). Numbers are written additively, with higher number signs preceding lower ones. Multiples of 100 above 300, and of 1000 above 3000, are expressed multiplicatively, with the multiplier following and forming a ligature with *100* or *1000*; I suggest that these ligatures be encoded with the control character ZERO WIDTH JOINER (U+200D).[26] (The first five illustrations in the following table are based on a Gupta period manuscript from the 4th/5th century CE;[27] the last two are from Western Kṣatrapa coin legends of the 1st to 4th centuries CE.[28])

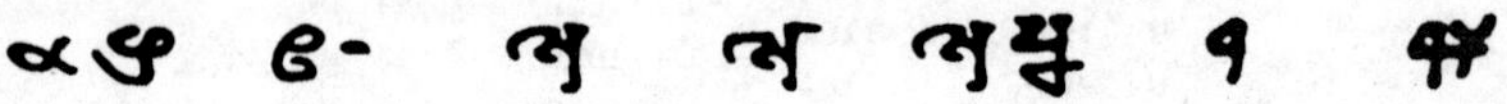

10 6 (= 16)	*50 1* (= 51)	100	200	*100 4* (= 104)	1000	*1000-4* (= 4000)
U+1105A, U+11056	U+1105E, U+11051	U+11063	U+11064	U+11063, U+11054	U+11064	U+11064, U+200D, U+22054

Later in the history of Brāhmī, a special sign for zero (U+11050) was invented, and the positional system came gradually into use.[29]

Seven punctuation marks should be encoded, namely single (·, U+11070) and double (॥, U+11071) daṇḍa, delimiting clauses and verses; dot (-, U+11072), double dot (=, U+11073) and horizontal line (~, U+11074), delimiting smaller textual units; and the crescent (϶, U+11075) and lotus (●, U+11076) marks, delimiting larger textual units.[30] The scribes of Brāhmī manuscripts use additional devices, such

---

[26] See TUS, 389-391 for a detailed description of the function of this control character.

[27] Sander 1968: Tafel 20, alphabet h.

[28] Salomon 1998: 58 (table 2.6, "Numerical Notation in Brāhmī and Kharoṣṭhī").

[29] Bühler 1904: 82f.; Salomon 1998: 61-63.

[30] The glyphs for the Brāhmī punctuation marks are taken from Kuṣāṇa- and Gupta-period manuscripts in the Schøyen Collection.

as horizontal wavy lines and larger floral designs, to structure their texts, but these are of very disparate appearance and often their shape and presence is determined by physical features of the manuscript. Therefore they should be considered graphic elements rather than punctuation proper, comparable to vignettes in European manuscripts and prints.

6. OLD TAMIL BRĀHMĪ

In the 2nd century BCE, as the Brāhmī script spread southwards, speakers of Old Tamil became acquainted with it and adapted it to write their own language. The Tamil form of Brāhmī is known to us from numerous stone inscriptions recording the donation of caves to Jaina monastic communities, mostly in southern Tamil Nadu; from pottery graffiti found at Arikamedu, Kodumanal and other ancient trading sites; and from coin legends and inscriptions on objects such as seals and rings. In contrast to the Middle Indo-Aryan dialects for which Brāhmī had been originally invented and used so far, the Tamil language has word-final consonants and non-homorganic consonant clusters that needed to be represented in the writing system. In its first phase of development, Early Tamil Brāhmī (2nd century BCE to 1st century CE), two competing modifications of Brāhmī orthography were used to achieve this aim. One system, Mahadevan's (2003) TB-I, does away with the inherent vowel of Brāhmī consonant signs, using the vowel mātrā *ā* to represent both short and long [a] / [aː]; in this orthography consonant signs without the *ā* mātrā always represent the bare consonant. In the second orthographic system, Mahadevan's TB-II, the *ā* mātrā always represents long [aː], whereas vowelless consonant signs can be read either with inherent short [a] or as bare consonants, depending on the context. The element of ambiguity in both these systems (of *ā* in TB-I and of bare consonant signs in TB-II), as well as pressure to conform with standard forms of Brāhmī that had been adopted in neighbouring regions, led to a further orthographic modification in Late Tamil Brāhmī (2nd to 4th centuries CE; Mahadevan's TB-III) with the adoption of the *puḷḷi* diacritic to unambiguously mark vowelless consonants. *Puḷḷi* takes the form of a dot above or within the upper part of the akṣara. In addition to this normal virāma function, *puḷḷi* is also used with the vowels *e* and *o* in order to mark them as short, since in contrast to Sanskrit and most Middle-Indo-Aryan dialects, the Dravidian languages have short as well as long *e* and *o* phonemes. Just as in other forms of Brāhmī, short [a] is always inherent in TB-III consonant signs, and *ā* always indicates long [a:].

The orthographic peculiarities of Old Tamil Brāhmī do not concern the elements of the writing system itself, but are a matter of the conventional phonetic interpretation of those elements. The encoding of Old Tamil Brāhmī should not reflect this phonetic interpretation, but should be based on what is actually written; bare akṣaras and akṣaras with *ā* mātrā should be encoded as such, just as with the other varieties of Brāhmī and the Brāhmī-derived scripts. This is in accordance with Mahadevan 2003, who in his edition of the Old Tamil inscriptions provides first a close transliteration (corresponding to the proposed computer encoding of Old Tamil Brāhmī) and then a phonetic transcription. The following example is the second line of inscription no. 1 in Mahadevan 2003: 315, illustrating the TB-I system:

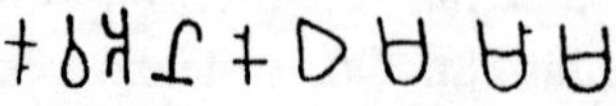

ku va a ṉa ke dha ma mā ma
kuv aṉkē dhammam

The same encoding principle obtains already in the case of Devanagari as used for Hindi and of Gurmukhi script used to write Panjabi, where by conventional phonetic interpretation morpheme-final unmarked consonant signs are pronounced without the *a* vowel, although this is not reflected at the encoding level. The two functions of Late Tamil Brāhmī *puḷḷi* can be subsumed under the heading of "vowel reduction" (short to zero, and long to short), and *puḷḷi* should be encoded as U+1104D BRAHMI SIGN VIRAMA; the Brāhmī VIRAMA character can thus follow both consonant characters and the vowel characters

E and O, in contrast to the modern scripts' VIRAMA characters, used only after consonant characters to mark the absence of a vowel.

For the representation of sounds peculiar to Dravidian, the makers of Old Tamil Brāhmī added four or five new consonant signs to the original repertoire of Brāhmī:[31] 𑀵 *ḻ*, 𑀴 *ḷ*, 𑀶 *ṟ*, 𑀷 *ṉ* and possibly 𑀗 *ṅ*.[32] The second of these, *ḷ*, is a retroflex lateral, phonetically identical to the *ḷa* that somewhat later appears in North Indian Brāhmī used for Sanskrit, and that also occurs in the Bhattiprolu inscriptions. Moreover, both the Tamil Brāhmī and the Bhattiprolu *ḷ* appear to be graphically derived from the regular letter *la*, the former by adding a hook to the lower right of *la*, the latter by modifying a horizontally mirrored *la*; this in contrast to the north-Indian *ḷa*, which is derived from the letter *ḍa*.[33] Old Tamil, Bhattiprolu and north-Indian *ḷa* should therefore all be encoded as U+11031. Additional code points are provided for *ḻ*, *ṟ* and *ṉ* in the positions U+11080 to U+11082.

7. BHATTIPROLU BRĀHMĪ

Nine short inscriptions in a Middle Indo-Aryan dialect, found in a stūpa at Bhattiprolu in Andhra Pradesh and dating probably from the 2nd century BCE, show an orthographic system that seems to be based on the Tamil Brāhmī system TB-I. Apparently in order to avoid the phonetic ambiguity of the latter's *ā* mātrā (standing for either [a] or [a:]), the Bhattiprolu inscriptions introduce a separate dedicated mātrā

---

[31] The Tamil Brāhmī glyphs are based on Mahadevan 2003: 217 (palaeographic chart 2, "The Tamil-Brāhmī Script").

[32] Falk (1993: 203) assumes that the first occurrence of *ṅa* in Tamil Brāhmī predates that in Kuṣāṇa Brāhmī, and takes this as an indication that the Sanskrit character *ṅa* was borrowed from South India. There are, however, only two possible occurrences of *ṅa* in the pre-Kuṣāṇa part of the Old Tamil corpus (Mahadevan 2003: 327, 348), both of them in what have been interpreted as proper names, and both of them originally read differently (as *ṇa* and *ṇu*, respectively).

[33] See Lüders 1912: 809f. In this case too, Falk (1993: 214) argues for a borrowing of the Kuṣāṇa sign from Tamil Brāhmī, not, however, from the letter 𑀴 *ḷ*, but rather from 𑀶 *ṟ*; I consider neither the phonetic nor the graphic similarity strong enough to adopt this suggestion.

for long [a:] by adding a vertical stroke to the end of the *ā* mātrā: ◌𑀸.[34] Thus in these inscriptions, *ā* unambiguously writes [a], and ◌𑀸 (here transliterated as *Ā*) writes [a:]. The following illustration is line 2 of inscription V in Bühler 1894, while the reading follows Lüders 1912:

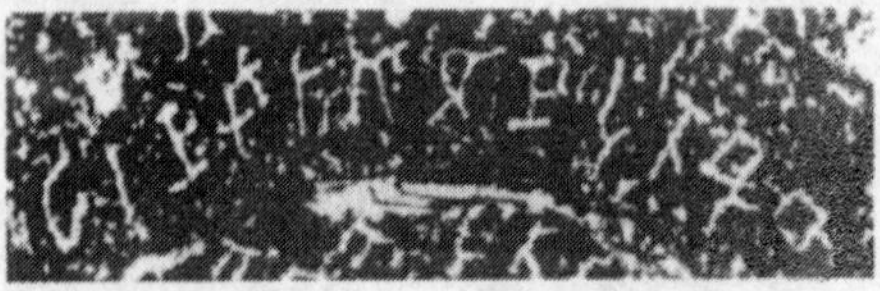

hi rā ṇā kĀ rā gĀ mā ṇī pu to bū bo

hiraṇakāra *gāmaṇīputo* *būbo*

Puzzlingly, the main reason for abandoning inherent [a] in Tamil Brāhmī, namely the ability to write word-final consonants and non-homorganic consonant clusters conveniently, does not apply in the case of the Bhattiprolu inscriptions, since Middle Indo-Aryan has neither of these phonetic features. This would seem to imply that the dedicated long *Ā* mātrā, too, was first introduced in a Tamil context, and that the resulting system was only later imitated in Bhattiprolu. But no such Tamil inscription has yet been discovered.

The shapes of five Bhattiprolu letters (*gha*, *ja*, *ma*, *la* and *sa*) differ to a certain degree from those seen in other varieties of Old Brāhmī; the *ma*, for instance, is upside-down. But only in the case of *gha*, which is graphically derived from the unaspirated *ga*, is there real innovation. Even *gha*, however, should be encoded as in the other varieties of Brāhmī, since its graphemic identity is not in doubt. The experimentation with letter shapes seen in Bhattiprolu and other forms of Old Brāhmī is entirely typical of early writing systems, such as the various Greek alphabets before the Athenian orthographic reform. The [ks] sound, for instance, was written X in the Western part of the Greek world (hence the Latin letter X) but Ξ in Greece itself, a situation not unlike that of the contrast between Bhattiprolu and standard Brāhmī *gha*.

---

[34] The Bhattiprolu ◌𑀸 glyph is based on the script table in Bühler 1894.

8. CENTRAL ASIAN BRĀHMĪ

The first Central Asian ethnic groups that modified Brāhmī for the writing of their own languages were the Khotanese on the Southern Silk Road and the Tocharians on the Northern (Hitch 1981; Sander 1986; Maue 1997).

The Khotanese writing system adds a diacritic double dot ◌̈ to the common Brāhmī repertoire, and shares with Uigur (on which below) the non-Indian orthographic practice of adding two vowel mātrās to a single akṣara to represent its set of falling diphthongs. Khotanese also developed an alternative analytic way of writing word-initial vowels, using initial *a* as a vowel carrier in combination with the various vowel mātrās, instead of separate initial signs for each vowel (Hitch 1981: 42-44).[35] In addition, Khotanese makes use of a hook-shaped diacritic sign placed below the akṣara, whose phonetic value is uncertain; this sign has not yet been included in the proposed encoding.

Tocharian (Pinault 1989: 33-36) added a set of ten new characters (the so-called *Fremdzeichen*, i.e., foreign or special signs) which differ from the corresponding regular Brāhmī characters in having as their inherent vowel not [a], but a different vowel transliterated as *ä* or by placing a line under the whole akṣara: *k̲a̲*, *t̲a̲*, *n̲a̲*, *p̲a̲*, *m̲a̲*, *r̲a̲*, *l̲a̲*, *ś̲a̲*, *ṣ̲a̲* and *s̲a̲*.[36] An alternative notation for the different vowel is the diacritic double dot seen already in Khotanese (◌̈, U+11095). In addition, the Tocharian script has an eleventh special sign *wa*.

The Uigur variant of Brāhmī (von Gabain 1950) adopted the Tocharian special signs (mostly using them word-finally with virāma), and also employs the double-dot diacritic ◌̈ to indicate high unrounded vowels. It added six further signs to write special consonants of the

---

[35] The same system had been employed by Kharoṣṭhī and is later also found (for some of the initial vowels) in the Devanagari, Gujarati and Tibetan scripts (Salomon 2003: 79f.).

[36] The glyphs for the Tocharian and Uigur special signs follow Sander 1968: Tafel 41, "Fremdzeichen".

Uigur language: *qa*, *γa*, *δa*, *dza*, *za* and *źa*.[37] The Uigur short vowels *ä*, *ü* and *ö* are spelled *-ya-*, *-yu-* and *-yo-* postconsonantally. The long vowels *ā̈*, *ṻ* and *ō̈* are written like the short ones, but with the addition of an *ā* mātrā (U+11035), so that in the case of *ṻ* and *ō̈* the akṣara carries not one but two vowel mātrās (<U+11038, U+11035> and <U+11040, U+11035> respectively). The initial vowels *ä*, *ü*, *ö* and *ō̈* are written by adding *-ya-*, *-yu-*, *-ya-* and *-yo-* respectively directly to the initial vowel signs *a* or *e*, *u*, *o* and *o*; therefore the resulting complexes *aya-* or *eya-*, *uyu-*, *oya-* and *oyo-* are single akṣaras that should be encoded with the control character U+200D ZERO WIDTH JOINER (cf. the discussion of Brāhmī umerals in section 5) between the initial vowel character and the *-y-*:[38]

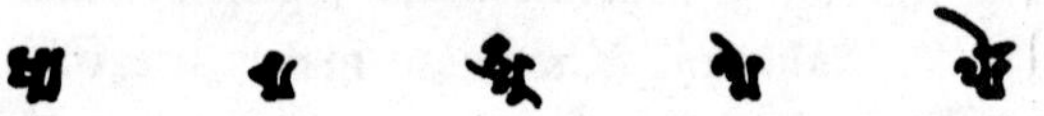

aya (= *ä*)	eya (= *ä*)	uyu (= *ü*)	oya (= *ö*)	oyo (= *ō̈*)
U+11000, U+200D, U+11029	U+1100A, U+200D, U+11029	U+11004, U+200D, U+11029, U+11038	U+1100C, U+200D, U+11029	U+1100C, U+200D, U+11029, U+11040

Tumshuqese, closely related to Khotanese, employs a large number of special signs; scholarly discussion of the precise inventory has focused on the following manuscript sign list, written on the verso of a Tocharian alphabet table (*dvādaśākṣarī*) and containing twelve entries (Konow 1935, 1947; Hitch 1981: 60-76; Maue 2004):

---

[37] Maue 1997: 3 argues that *dza* was actually pronounced [β], and the discussion in Maue 2004: 209 (on the Tumshuqese sign no. 4) seems to imply a retroflex articulation [ẓ] also for Uigur *źa*.

[38] Alternatively and on analogy with the postconsonantal vowels, these initial-vowel complexes could be encoded with U+104D BRAHMI SIGN VIRAMA; this would however be contrary to the usual "vowel reduction" function of the VIRAMA control character (cf. the discussion of Tamil Brāhmī *puḷḷi* above), as pointed out by Gautam Sengupta of Jadavpur University, Calcutta, at the GICAS symposium in Tokyo in December 2003.

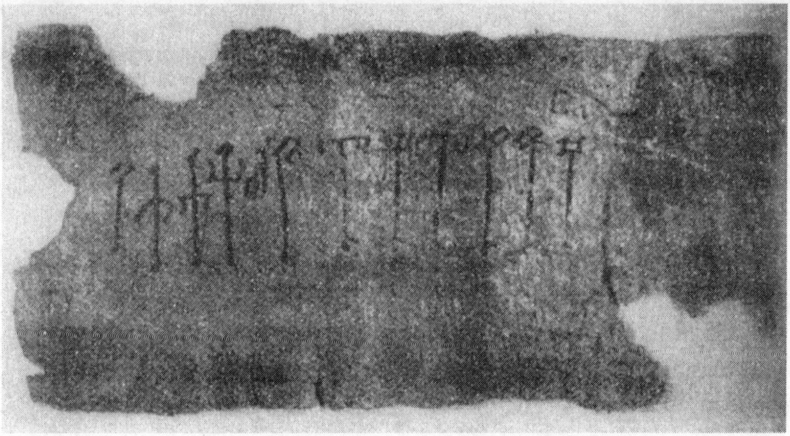

At least five of these signs (*za*, *γa*, *źa*, *ḏa* and *dza*) are shared with Uigur and therefore do not need to be encoded separately (their codepoints are U+1109D, U+1109A, U+1109E, U+1109B and U+1109C).[39] Three other signs (nos. 3, 8 and 9 from the left) would appear to be mere copies of signs no. 2, 4 and 7 (= *γa*, = *źa* and = *ḏa*), and are according to Konow not independently attested in Tumshuqese manuscripts.[40] The status of signs no. 5, 6 and 11 (, and) is disputed. Hitch 1981: 67-77 interpreted them as *la*, *khu* and *śu* instead of Konow's (1947) *żya*, *ẓa* and *gwa*; Hitch 1989 and Maue 2004 argue that no. 10 represents a voiced palatal fricative [ʝ]. Because of the remaining uncertainty, these signs are not yet included in the set of proposed Brāhmī characters. Sign no. 12 () is however generally agreed to be a genuine special character with the value *χša*, and accordingly is included at codepoint U+110A2.

The Central Asian varieties of Brāhmī share a ligature *rra* that does not occur in Indian Brāhmī. Although *rra* tends to be treated as a unit in Khotanese, probably representing a phoneme of that language distinct from the one written *ra*, it should be encoded as the ligature that orthographically it is

[39] The Tumshuqese glyphs used in the text of this paragraph are from the manuscript sign list published in Konow 1935 and reproduced above.

[40] See, however, Skjærvø 1987 and Maue 2004: 210.

9. NOTE ON VEDIC CHARACTERS

Accent marks and other characters peculiar to Vedic texts have been excluded from the proposal described here because they are no more closely associated with pre-modern Brāhmī than with the modern Brāhmī-derived scripts, and in fact the oldest extant Vedic manuscripts lack any accent marking. A code block for Vedic characters, combinable both with Brāhmī and with the modern scripts, should become the subject of a separate proposal by a specialist in Vedic codicology.

10. EXPECTED USE OF THE PROPOSED CHARACTER CODING

Is is anticipated that the main initial use of the proposed encoding of Brāhmī as part of the Unicode standard will be in the area of palaeographic work. Most of the fonts produced for the purpose of palaeographic discussion will aim to reproduce a particular manuscript hand or epigraphic ductus as closely as possible. Every akṣara occuring in the source is expected to be assigned a single comprehensive glyph in such fonts, and the use of glyphs for subparts of akṣaras will thus be minimal. The main operation to be performed at the rendering level will therefore be the mapping from a sequence of character code points to one particular akṣara glyph, not the relative positioning of subparts of akṣaras as is the case with most fonts for the modern Indian scripts. This greatly reduces the complexity of the rendering software that will need to be written for the display of Brāhmī.

Most fonts produced for specialised palaeographic purposes will not contain glyphs for every single Brāhmī codepoint, but only for those characters that are to be discussed or that occur in the manuscript hand to be described. Beyond such specialised fonts, however, the production and distribution of comprehensive fall-back fonts for the main subvarieties of Brāhmī is desirable. These fonts will contain normalised glyph shapes, and in their case the use of combining glyphs for subparts of akṣaras is feasible. The unitary nature of the proposed encoding, covering a range of visually distinctive forms of the script, has the consequence that a single fall-back font cannot be appropriate for every Brāhmī text.[41] Nonetheless, it is felt that the advantages of a unitary encoding, as outlined in section 3, far outweigh this one inconvenience.[42]

The strongest case for a separate encoding of a subvariety of Brāhmī would have been presented by Tamil Brāhmī, due to the systemic characteristics that distinguish it from other forms of Brāhmī (apart from the Bhattiprolu variant). In fact, however, it adds a strong theoretical argument in favour of a unitary encoding; as has been shown above, the only possible way to encode the three subvarieties of Tamil Brāhmī (TB-I, TB-II and TB-III) uniformly and naturally is to regard the Tamil Brāhmī orthographic system as a matter of phonetic interpretation, not of character coding. Any special encoding for this orthography would have separated TB-I and TB-II from TB-III, obscuring the historical development which after a period of experimentation reintegrated the Tamil variety into the mainstream of Brāhmī script history.

As a result of accepting a unitary encoding for premodern Brāhmī, there will inevitably arise borderline cases involving late documents from the transitional period between the varieties of Brāhmī that are covered by the present encoding proposal and the modern Indian scripts that are already encoded separately in the Unicode standard. In such cases it will be left to the users' discretion in each case whether their documents are most naturally encoded as Brāhmī or as a suitable modern Brāhmī-derived script; the question is analogous to the linguistic problem of when exactly to start regarding texts to be written in New Indo-Aryan instead of Middle Indo-Aryan. In practice, the set of characters provided by the Brāhmī range and by the modern-script ranges respectively will guide the user's decision. A medieval

---

[41] The display of, for instance, a 3rd-century Mahāyāna sūtra with an Aśokan Brāhmī font or of an Aśokan edict with a Gilgit-Bamiyan type II font would be visually quite jarring.

[42] The participants in the GICAS symosium in Tokyo shared this assessment and strongly approved of a unitary encoding.

Sri Lankan text, for instance, which uses the special Sinhalese vowel *ä* could not be encoded as Brāhmī, since the proposed encoding does not provide a code point for this vowel, and would have to be encoded as Sinhalese script using the Unicode Sinhala code range, which does provide a code point for *ä*.[43] It is worth pointing out yet again that this kind of decision-making problem would be far worse if the historical varieties of Brāhmī were encoded in a non-unitary manner.

REFERENCES

BAUMS, Stefan 2002. Jyotiṣkāvadāna. In: Jens Braarvig (ed.), *Buddhist Manuscripts, Vol. II* (Manuscripts in the Schøyen Collection): 287-302. Oslo: Hermes Publishing.

BRAARVIG, Jens (ed.) 2000. *Buddhist Manuscripts*. (Manuscripts in the Schøyen Collection.) Oslo: Hermes Publishing.

BÜHLER, G. 1894. The Bhattiprolu inscriptions. *Epigraphia Indica* 2: 323-329.

—— 1896. *Indische Palaeographie von circa 350 a. Chr. – circa 1300 p. Chr.* (Grundriss der indo-arischen Philologie und Altertumskunde, I. Band, 11. Heft.) Strassburg: Verlag von Karl J. Trübner.

—— 1904. *Indian Paleography*. Bombay: Bombay Education Society's Press, Byculla.[44]

DANI, Ahmad Hasan 1986. *Indian Palaeography*. Second edition. New Delhi: Munshiram Manoharlal Publishers.

EVERSON, Michael 1998. Proposal to encode Brahmi in Plane 1 of ISO/IEC 10646-2. http://std.dkuug.dk/JTC1/SC2/WG2/docs/n1685/n1685.htm.

—— 2002. Leaks in the Unicode pipeline: script script script... http://www.unicode.org/notes/tn4/.[45]

FALK, Harry 1993. *Schrift im alten Indien: ein Forschungsbericht mit Anmerkungen*. (ScriptOralia, 56.) Tübingen: Gunter Narr Verlag.

HITCH, Douglas A. 1981. *Central Asian Brahmi Palaeography: The Relationships Among the Tocharian, Khotanese, and Old Turkic Gupta scripts*. MA thesis, Department of Linguistics, University of Calgary.

—— 1989. Brāhmī. In: Ehsan Yarshater (ed.), *Encyclopædia Iranica, Vol. IV*: 432-433. London: Routledge & Kegan Paul.

---

[43] U+0D87 for the initial, U+0DD0 for the vowel diacritic.

[44] Translation of Bühler 1896, edited as an appendix to *Indian Antiquary* 33 by John Faithfull Fleet.

[45] This is Unicode Technical Note #4, presented at the 21st International Unicode Conference, May 2002, Dublin.

KONOW, Sten 1935. Ein neuer Saka-Dialekt. *Sitzungsberichte der Preußischen Akademie der Wissenschaften, philosophisch-historische Klasse*: 772-823.

—— 1947. The oldest dialect of Khotanese Saka. *Norsk Tidsskrift for Sprogvidenskap* 14: 156-190.

LÜDERS, Heinrich 1912. Epigraphische Beiträge. *Sitzungsberichte der Königlich Preußischen Akademie der Wissenschaften*: 806-831.

MAHADEVAN Iravatham 2003. *Early Tamil Epigraphy: From the Earliest Times to the Sixth Century A.D.* (Harvard Oriental Series, 62.) Chennai: Cre-A:.

MAUE, Dieter 1997. A tentative stemma of the varieties of Brāhmī script along the Northern Silk Road. In: Shirin Akiner and Nicholas Sims-Williams (eds.), *Languages and Scripts of Central Asia*: 1-15. London: School of Oriental and African Studies.

—— 2004. Konows Zeichen Nr. 10. In: Desmond Durkin-Meisterernst et al. (eds.), *Turfan Revisited – The First Century of Research into the Arts and Cultures of the Silk Road* (Monographien zur indischen Archäologie, Kunst und Philologie, 17): 208-212. Berlin: Dietrich Reimer Verlag.

PINAULT, Georges-Jean 1989. Introduction au tokharien. *LALIES : actes des sessions de linguistique et de littérature* 7: 5-224.

SALOMON, Richard 1998. *Indian Epigraphy: A Guide to the Study of Inscriptions in Sanskrit, Prakrit, and the Other Indo-Aryan Languages.* (South Asia Research.) New York: Oxford University Press.

—— 2003. Writing systems of the Indo-Aryan languages. In: George Cardona and Dhanesh Jain (eds.), *The Indo-Aryan Languages* (Routledge Language Family Series): 67-103. London: Routledge.

SANDER, Lore 1968. *Paläographisches zu den Sanskrithandschriften der Berliner Turfansammlung.* (Verzeichnis der orientalischen Handschriften in Deutschland, Supplementband 8.) Wiesbaden: Franz Steiner Verlag.

—— 1986. Brāhmī scripts on the Eastern Silk Roads. *Studien zur Indologie und Iranistik* 11/12: 159-192.

—— 2000. A brief palaeographical analysis of the Brāhmī manuscripts in volume I. In: Jens Braarvig (ed.), *Buddhist Manuscripts.* (Manuscripts in the Schøyen Collection): 285-300. Oslo: Hermes Publishing.

SIRCAR, D.C. 1970-1971. Introduction to Indian epigraphy and palaeography. *Journal of Ancient Indian History* 4: 72-136.

SKJÆRVØ, P.O. 1987. On the Tumshuqese karmavācanā text. *Journal of the Royal Asiatic Society*: 77-90.

TUS = *The Unicode Standard: version 4.0.* Edited by Joan Aliprand et al. Boston: Addison-Wesley, 2003.

VON GABAIN, A. 1950. *Alttürkische Grammatik: mit Bibliographie, Lesestücken und Wörterverzeichnis, auch Neutürkisch.* 2. verbesserte Auflage. (Porta linguarum Orientalium: Sammlung von Lehrbüchern für das Studium der orientalischen Sprachen, 23.) Leipzig: Otto Harrassowitz.

APPENDIX 1:
Proposed Unicode code charts for Brāhmī

	1100	1101	1102	1103	1104	1105	1106	1107
0	11000	11010	11020	11030	11040	11050	11060	11070
1	11001	11011	11021	11031	11041	11051	11061	11071
2	11002	11012	11022			11052	11062	11072
3	11003	11013	11023			11053	11063	11073
4	11004	11014	11024			11054	11064	11074
5	11005	11015	11025	11035	11045	11055	11065	11075
6	11006	11016	11026	11036		11056		11076
7	(r̄) 11007	11017	11027	11037	11047	11057	11067	
8	(l) 11008	11018	11028	11038	11048	11058	11068	
9	(l̄) 11009	11019	11029	11039	11049	11059		
A	1100A	1101A	1102A	1103A		1105A		
B	1100B	1101B	1102B	1103B		1105B		
C	1100C	1101C	1102C	(-l) 1103C		1105C		
D	1100D	1101D	1102D	(-l̄) 1103D	1104D	1105D		
E		1101E	1102E	1103E		1105E		
F		1101F	1102F	1103F		1105F		

	1108	1109	110A	110B	110C	110D	110E	110F
0	11080	11090						
1	11081	11091						
2	11082	11092	110A2					
3		11093						
4		11094						
5		11095						
6	11086							
7								
8								
9		11099						
A	1108A	1109A						
B	1108B	1109B						
C	1108C	1109C						
D	1108D	1109D						
E	1108E	1109E						
F	1108F							

APPENDIX 2:
Proposed Unicode character names list for Brāhmī

The format of the names list follows that used in TUS. The first column gives the proposed code point of the character, the second an illustrative glyph, the third the proposed Unicode name, and the fourth the usual Indological transliteration.

Independent vowel signs

11000	𑀅	BRAHMI LETTER A	*a*
11001	𑀆	BRAHMI LETTER AA	*ā*
11002	𑀇	BRAHMI LETTER I	*i*
11003	𑀈	BRAHMI LETTER II	*ī*
11004	𑀉	BRAHMI LETTER U	*u*
11005	𑀊	BRAHMI LETTER UU	*ū*
11006	𑀋	BRAHMI LETTER VOCALIC R	*ṛ*
11007	(*ṝ*)	BRAHMI LETTER VOCALIC RR	*ṝ*
11008	(*ḷ*)	BRAHMI LETTER VOCALIC L	*ḷ*
11009	(*ḹ*)	BRAHMI LETTER VOCALIC LL	*ḹ*
1100A	𑀏	BRAHMI LETTER E	*e*
1100B	𑀐	BRAHMI LETTER AI	*ai*
1100C	𑀑	BRAHMI LETTER O	*o*
1100D	𑀒	BRAHMI LETTER AU	*au*
1100E		<reserved>	
1100F		<reserved>	

Consonants

11010	𑀓	BRAHMI LETTER KA	*ka*
11011	𑀔	BRAHMI LETTER KHA	*kha*
11012	𑀕	BRAHMI LETTER GA	*ga*
11013	𑀖	BRAHMI LETTER GHA	*gha*
11014	𑀗	BRAHMI LETTER NGA	*ṅa*
11015	𑀘	BRAHMI LETTER CA	*ca*

11016	𑀙	BRAHMI LETTER CHA	*cha*
11017	𑀚	BRAHMI LETTER JA	*ja*
11018	𑀛	BRAHMI LETTER JHA	*jha*
11019	𑀜	BRAHMI LETTER NYA	*ña*
1101A	𑀝	BRAHMI LETTER TTA	*ṭa*
1101B	𑀞	BRAHMI LETTER TTHA	*ṭha*
1101C	𑀟	BRAHMI LETTER DDA	*ḍa*
1101D	𑀠	BRAHMI LETTER DDHA	*ḍha*
1101E	𑀡	BRAHMI LETTER NNA	*ṇa*
1101F	𑀢	BRAHMI LETTER TA	*ta*
11020	𑀣	BRAHMI LETTER THA	*tha*
11021	𑀤	BRAHMI LETTER DA	*da*
11022	𑀥	BRAHMI LETTER DHA	*dha*
11023	𑀦	BRAHMI LETTER NA	*na*
11024	𑀧	BRAHMI LETTER PA	*pa*
11025	𑀨	BRAHMI LETTER PHA	*pha*
11026	𑀩	BRAHMI LETTER BA	*ba*
11027	𑀪	BRAHMI LETTER BHA	*bha*
11028	𑀫	BRAHMI LETTER MA	*ma*
11029	𑀬	BRAHMI LETTER YA	*ya*
1102A	𑀭	BRAHMI LETTER RA	*ra*
1102B	𑀮	BRAHMI LETTER LA	*la*
1102C	𑀯	BRAHMI LETTER VA	*va*
1102D	𑀰	BRAHMI LETTER SHA	*śa*
1102E	𑀱	BRAHMI LETTER SSA	*ṣa*
1102F	𑀲	BRAHMI LETTER SA	*sa*
11030	𑀳	BRAHMI LETTER HA	*ha*
11031	𑀴	BRAHMI LETTER LLA	*ḷa*
11032		<reserved>	
11033		<reserved>	
11034		<reserved>	

Dependent vowel signs

11035	◌𑀸	BRAHMI VOWEL SIGN AA	*ā*
11036	◌𑀺	BRAHMI VOWEL SIGN I	*i*
11037	◌𑀻	BRAHMI VOWEL SIGN II	*ī*
11038	◌𑀼	BRAHMI VOWEL SIGN U	*u*
11039	◌𑀽	BRAHMI VOWEL SIGN UU	*ū*
1103A	◌𑀾	BRAHMI VOWEL SIGN VOCALIC R	*ṛ*
1103B	◌𑀿	BRAHMI VOWEL SIGN VOCALIC RR	*ṝ*
1103C	(-*ḷ*)	BRAHMI VOWEL SIGN VOCALIC L	*ḷ*
1103D	(-*ḹ*)	BRAHMI VOWEL SIGN VOCALIC LL	*ḹ*
1103E	◌𑁂	BRAHMI VOWEL SIGN E	*e*
1103F	◌𑁃	BRAHMI VOWEL SIGN AI	*ai*
11040	◌𑁄	BRAHMI VOWEL SIGN O	*o*
11041	◌𑁅	BRAHMI VOWEL SIGN AU	*au*
11042		<reserved>	
11043		<reserved>	
11044		<reserved>	

Various signs

11045	◌𑀁	BRAHMI SIGN ANUSVARA	*ṃ*
11047	◌𑀂	BRAHMI SIGN VISARGA	*ḥ*
11048	𑀃	BRAHMI LETTER JIHVAMULIYA	*ẖa*
11049	𑀄	BRAHMI LETTER UPADHMANIYA	*ḫa*
1104D	◌𑁆	BRAHMI SIGN VIRAMA	
1104E		<reserved>	
1104F		<reserved>	

Numbers

11050	𑁦	BRAHMI DIGIT ZERO	*0*
11051	𑁒	BRAHMI DIGIT ONE	*1*
11052	𑁓	BRAHMI DIGIT TWO	*2*
11053	𑁔	BRAHMI DIGIT THREE	*3*

11054	𑁕	BRAHMI DIGIT FOUR	*4*
11055	𑁖	BRAHMI DIGIT FIVE	*5*
11056	𑁗	BRAHMI DIGIT SIX	*6*
11057	𑁘	BRAHMI DIGIT SEVEN	*7*
11058	𑁙	BRAHMI DIGIT EIGHT	*8*
11059	𑁚	BRAHMI DIGIT NINE	*9*
1105A	𑁛	BRAHMI NUMBER TEN	*10*
1105B	𑁜	BRAHMI NUMBER TWENTY	*20*
1105C	𑁝	BRAHMI NUMBER THIRTY	*30*
1105D	𑁞	BRAHMI NUMBER FOURTY	*40*
1105E	𑁟	BRAHMI NUMBER FIFTY	*50*
1105F	𑁠	BRAHMI NUMBER SIXTY	*60*
11060	𑁡	BRAHMI NUMBER SEVENTY	*70*
11061	𑁢	BRAHMI NUMBER EIGHTY	*80*
11062	𑁣	BRAHMI NUMBER NINETY	*90*
11063	𑁤	BRAHMI NUMBER ONE HUNDRED	*100*
11064		BRAHMI NUMBER TWO HUNDRED	*200*
11065		BRAHMI NUMBER THREE HUNDRED	*300*
11066		<reserved>	
11067	𑁥	BRAHMI NUMBER ONE THOUSAND	*1000*
11068		BRAHMI NUMBER TWO THOUSAND	*2000*
11069		<reserved>	
1106A		<reserved>	
1106B		<reserved>	
1106C		<reserved>	
1106D		<reserved>	
1106E		<reserved>	
1106F		<reserved>	

Punctuation

11070	𑁇	BRAHMI DANDA	|
11071	𑁈	BRAHMI DOUBLE DANDA	||

11072		BRAHMI PUNCTUATION DOT	•
11073		BRAHMI PUNCTUATION DOUBLE DOT	:
11074		BRAHMI PUNCTUATION LINE	–
11075		BRAHMI PUNCTUATION CRESCENT BAR	Є
11076		BRAHMI PUNCTUATION LOTUS	❀
11077		<reserved>	
11078		<reserved>	
11079		<reserved>	
1107A		<reserved>	
1107B		<reserved>	
1107C		<reserved>	
1107D		<reserved>	
1107E		<reserved>	
1107F		<reserved>	

Tamil Brāhmī signs

11080		BRAHMI LETTER TAMIL LLLA	*la*
11081		BRAHMI LETTER TAMIL RRA	*ṟa*
11082		BRAHMI LETTER TAMIL NNA	*ṉa*
11083		<reserved>	
11084		<reserved>	
11085		<reserved>	

Bhattiprolu Brāhmī sign

11086		BRAHMI VOWEL SIGN BHATTIPROLU AAA	*Ā*
11087		<reserved>	
11088		<reserved>	
11089		<reserved>	

Central Asian Brāhmī signs

Code	Name	Transliteration
1108A	BRAHMI LETTER CENTRAL ASIAN KA	*ka̱*
1108B	BRAHMI LETTER CENTRAL ASIAN TA	*ta̱*
1108C	BRAHMI LETTER CENTRAL ASIAN NA	*na̱*
1108D	BRAHMI LETTER CENTRAL ASIAN PA	*pa̱*
1108E	BRAHMI LETTER CENTRAL ASIAN MA	*ma̱*
1108F	BRAHMI LETTER CENTRAL ASIAN RA	*ra̱*
11090	BRAHMI LETTER CENTRAL ASIAN LA	*la̱*
11091	BRAHMI LETTER CENTRAL ASIAN SHA	*śa̱*
11092	BRAHMI LETTER CENTRAL ASIAN SSA	*ṣa̱*
11093	BRAHMI LETTER CENTRAL ASIAN SA	*sa̱*
11094	BRAHMI LETTER CENTRAL ASIAN WA	*wa*
11095	BRAHMI SIGN CENTRAL ASIAN DOUBLE DOT	*ä*
11096	<reserved>	
11097	<reserved>	
11098	<reserved>	
11099	BRAHMI LETTER CENTRAL ASIAN QA	*qa*
1109A	BRAHMI LETTER CENTRAL ASIAN GA	*γa*
1109B	BRAHMI LETTER CENTRAL ASIAN DA	*δa/ḏa*
1109C	BRAHMI LETTER CENTRAL ASIAN DZA	*dza*
1109D	BRAHMI LETTER CENTRAL ASIAN ZA	*za*
1109E	BRAHMI LETTER CENTRAL ASIAN ZHA	*źa*
1109F	<reserved>	
110A0	<reserved>	
110A1	<reserved>	
110A2	BRAHMI LETTER CENTRAL ASIAN KHSHA	*χša*
110A3	<reserved>	
...		
110FF	<reserved>	

The Ceremony of *Tulāpuruṣa*: The Purāṇic Concept and the Epigraphical Evidence

ANNETTE SCHMIEDCHEN

The devotee who witnesses such a donative ceremony, thinks of it later, recounts it here in this world, or hears or reads about it attains, with a body like Indra's, a residence enjoyed by this god who is a destroyer of strongholds.[1]

INTRODUCTION

Some recent Indological studies have pointed to the necessity of analysing two categories of sources for the reconstruction of India's ancient and medieval history – literary texts and epigraphical records (e.g., Schc ·en 1991). This paper on the *tulāpuruṣa* ceremony seeks to demonstra ɜ how bodies of information derived from the two categories of sources complement each other and help to present a fuller description of the history of the ritual.

In the purāṇic literature, *tulāpuruṣa*, the ritual weighing of a king against gold and its distribution among brāhmaṇas, is called the first and best of the Great Gifts (MtP 274.6). The concept of the sixteen *mahādānas* has been expounded in the Matsyapurāṇa (chapters 274-289) and in the Liṅgapurāṇa (with some differences in the names; LiP II.28-44) in full detail (Kane 1974: 869-877). R.C. Hazra has fixed the

---

[1] MtP 274.78: *yo dīyamānam api paśyati bhaktiyuktaḥ kālāntare smarati vācayatīha loke / yo vā śṛṇoti paṭhatīndrasamānarūpaḥ prāpnoti dhāma sa puraṃdaradevajuṣṭam //.*

date of the composition of the chapters on Great Gifts in the Matsyapurāṇa between 550 and 650 A.D.; according to him, the chapters on *mahādāna* in the Liṅgapurāṇa were compiled roughly between 600 and 1000 A.D., most probably between 800 and 1000 (Hazra 1975: 176-180). The names of at least some of these Great Gifts are clearly earlier than the formulation of the purāṇic concept of the sixteen *mahādānas*. Some of the later sixteen Great Gifts have already been described in the Atharvavedapariśiṣṭas (AVPariś 9, 11, 13-16); for instance, *tulāpuruṣa* itself, *hiraṇyagarbha* (the donation of a golden vessel believed to represent Brahman), and *gosahasra* (the donation of a thousand cows). Descriptions of these sixteen *mahādānas* are also included in later digests specially devoted to the topic of *dāna*, for example, Hemādri's Dānakhaṇḍa of the Caturvargacintāmaṇi (CVC, pp. 175ff.) and Ballālasena's Dānasāgara (DS, pp. 70ff.). The Bengal king Ballālasena, who composed his works in the 12th century A.D., and Hemādri, who lived in Maharashtra in the 13th century under the Yādava dynasty (Kane 1975: 730-735, 749-755), quote long passages from the Purāṇas (mainly Matsyapurāṇa). Hemādri also gives citations from the Atharvavedapariśiṣṭas (there called Atharvaṇagopathabrāhmaṇa).

The Matsyapurāṇa (MtP 274.11-12) states that the *mahādānas* were performed by several ancient heroes and kings.[2] It gives general directions about the construction of the pavilion (*maṇḍapa*) required in making these Great Gifts and of the balance (*tulā*), which was to have two posts and a crossbeam of the same wood and was to be ornamented with gold. This is followed by the detailed description of the procedure of *tulāpuruṣa* itself. Eight brāhmaṇas versed in the Vedas (two for each of the four Vedas) should be made the priests (*ṛtvij*), and a man who is accomplished in the Vedānta and knows the Purāṇas and Śāstras should be made the preceptor (*guru*) (MtP 274.36-39). Then four *homas* were to be offered to the gods, and Vedic hymns were to

[2] See Koskikallio 2002: 325, n. 47 for a relatively late reference from the *Ānandarāmāyaṇa* that describes how Rāma had Sītā weighed "to define the eightfold amount of gold for Vasiṣṭha".

be recited. At the end of the *homa*, the *guru* should invoke the *lokapālas* with flowers, incense, and *mantras*. Afterwards the donor should have himself bathed by the brāhmaṇas and dressed in a white garment (MtP 274.58). Wearing garlands of white flowers, with flowers in his folded hands, he was to invoke and circumambulate the balance. After that he should step into one pan, and in the other pan brāhmaṇas should place pure gold (MtP 274.65-67). Then the earth should be invoked and thereafter the donor should leave the balance and give half of the gold to the *guru* and the other half to the brāhmaṇas; he may also make grants of villages to the *guru* and the other priests (MtP 274.68-72). Then he should honour brāhmaṇas, other respectable people, and the poor and helpless with gifts (MtP 274.73). The Liṅgapurāṇa (LiP II.28.85) says that the gold pieces on the balance should be dedicated to Śiva.[3]

THE EPIGRAPHICAL EVIDENCE

Most of the sixteen *mahādānas* are also mentioned in various Indian epigraphs, and the performance of the more important ones among them is registered in inscriptions as well. The *tulāpuruṣa* is very frequently spoken of in epigraphical records, both copper-plate grants and stone inscriptions. For several reasons, however, the inscriptional reports are not nearly as detailed as the purāṇic material. First, the purposes of these epigraphs differed considerably from those of the purāṇic literature. The respective inscriptions were not primarily designed to record or even describe the performance of *tulapuruṣa* ceremonies. Secondly, some knowledge of the main procedure was obviously taken for granted by the authors of the epigraphs, although there is hardly any direct inscriptional reference to the textual background of the *tulāpuruṣa* ritual. An early Vijayanagara epigraph does mention that certain donations were made according to the Hemādriśāstra, but these gifts are not explicitly linked to the *tulāpuruṣa* ceremony.[4] A verse about king Kṛṣṇarāya (1509-1529 A.D.)

---

[3] For the Bhaviṣyapurāṇa, see Hohenberger 1967: 124.

used in many later copper-plate grants and in a few stone inscriptions from Vijayanagara merely associates the weighing ritual with the "gifts described in the Āgamas":

> *Kāṃcīśrīśailaśoṇācalakanakasabhāveṃkaṭādripramukhyeṣv*
> *āvartyāvartya sarveṣv atanuta vidhivat bhūyase śreyase yaḥ /*
> *devasthāneṣu tīrtheṣv api kanakatulāpūruṣādīni nānā-*
> *dānāny evopadānair api samam akhilair āgamoktāni tāni //*[5]

> At Kāñcī, at Śrīśaila, at Śoṇācala, in the Golden Hall, at Veṅkaṭādri, etc.,[6] [i.e.] in all temples and also at all holy places, he over and over performed these various gifts described in the Āgamas, such as the golden *tulāpūruṣa*, together with all the minor gifts, according to the rules [and] for the supreme happiness.

For this paper, I have analysed some hundred epigraphical references to the weighing ritual. However, this collection of data does not claim to be in any way comprehensive; it has been basically assembled through a selective search in the volumes of *Indian Antiquary* (IA), *Epigraphia Indica* (EI), *Epigraphia Carnatica* (EC), *Epigraphia Zeylanica* (EZ), *South Indian Inscriptions* (SII), *Corpus Inscriptionum Indicarum* (CII), and other systematic compilations of inscriptions. The list could certainly be extended, although some dynastic corpora of epigraphs indicate there is no information about this ceremony for some medieval Indian dynasties.[7] Vijay Nath comments on the importance of the *mahādāna* rituals for newly rising and formerly unknown royal families:

> … most of the great gifts … are known to have been performed not by rulers whose power was already firmly established but by those political adventurers and founders of new dynasties who besides having prominent tribal antecedents were still seeking to augment their newly won political power. (Nath 2000: 437.)

---

[4] Cf. Shama Shastry & Lakshminarayan Rao 1941: 435ff. The undated inscription from southwestern Andhra Pradesh (Anantapur Dist.) probably belongs to the reign of Harihara II (1377-1404 A.D.).

[5] APPENDIX 3, nos. 80-83, 85, 87-88, 90-95, 98-101 (especially verse 23 or 24); modified in nos. 107-109.

[6] For the identification of these places, see APPENDIX 3, no. 80 = EI 1: 368, footnotes to the translation of verse 16.

[7] The evidence is negative for the early Kadambas, the early Western Cāḷukyas and the Western Gaṅgas.

Ronald Inden, on the other hand, strongly emphasizes the importance of the great donative ceremonies for the imperial claims of medieval Indian rulers in general (Inden 1979: 134).

The epigraphical material analysed for this paper extends over a period of ten centuries, from the 7th to the 16th centuries. That is not to say that there were no instances of the performance of the weighing ritual from later times nor records of it in other sources.[8] The chronological distribution of the data is rather irregular: for the 7th century I have found only one piece of evidence, and only a few references date from the 8th/9th centuries. It is not until the 10th/11th centuries that we see a marked increase in data on the *tulāpuruṣa* ritual as well as a wider geographical range for it. From the 12th/13th centuries, we still have large numbers of attestations, but with a certain concentration on just a few kings. For the period from the 14th to the 16th centuries, almost all the relevant evidence comes from Vijayanagara, where remains of the so-called king's balance are visible still today. However, after the 16th century we notice a tendency toward decline.

The geographical range of the epigraphical material includes the territories of the modern Indian states of Tamil Nadu, Karnataka, Maharashtra, Andhra Pradesh, Orissa, Madhya Pradesh, Uttar Pradesh, West Bengal and Assam[9] as well as of Sri Lanka, but once again not in similar numbers. The earliest inscriptional information about the weighing ritual comes from two southern regions: 7th/8th-century Tamil Nadu and 8th/9th-century Maharashtra and Karnataka. The

---

[8] For example, according to his own testimony Caṇḍeśvara, the well-known minister of the king of Mithilā and author of seven Dharmanibandhas or Ratnākaras, conquered Nepal and had a *tulāpūruṣa* (sic) performed in the Śaka year 1236 (= 1314 A.D.); see VR, pp. 670-671. (I owe this reference to Hans Bakker.) Until the 19th century, the princes of Travancore used to celebrate *tulābhāra* and *hiraṇyagarbha* rites in the territory of the modern state of Kerala immediately after their accession to the throne in order to legitimize their claim to power; cf. Bell 1915: 83-84. Marion Rastelli has kindly communicated that some of the Pāñcarātra texts, namely, the Paramasaṃhitā, the Pādmasaṃhitā, and the Pārameśvarasaṃhitā, also discuss the topic of the weighing ceremony in some detail.

[9] For Assam (Kāmarūpa), see APPENDIX 3, no. 47. The inscription was found in Bangladesh.

ceremony has been mentioned in 7th/8th-century inscriptions of the Pāṇḍyas, 9th-century epigraphs of the Pallavas and 10th/11th-century inscriptional records of the Coḷas, all from Tamil Nadu. According to several Sanskrit copper-plate grants from Maharashtra and some Kannaḍa stone inscriptions from northern Karnataka, at least five Rāṣṭrakūṭa monarchs performed the weighing ceremony between the 8th and 10th centuries. At least some military encounters between the early Pāṇḍyas and the Rāṣṭrakūṭas are recorded, so that we cannot exclude the possibility of the ritual tradition having travelled this way. Since the 11th century, the ceremony spread to other regions: from Maharashtra northwards to Madhya Pradesh, from Karnataka probably eastwards to Andhra Pradesh, and from Tamil Nadu further south to Sri Lanka. The influence of the famous digests compiled by writers as Ballālasena and Hemādri on the dissemination of the *tulāpuruṣa* tradition after the 12th and 13th centuries should not be underestimated either.[10]

TERMINOLOGY

The majority of the inscriptions mentioning the ritual weighing of kings and other nobles are written in Sanskrit, but some are in Tamil and Kannaḍa, and later also in Telugu. Different Sanskrit terms have been used more or less synonymously to denote this ceremony in epigraphy and literature. The compound most frequently employed is *tulāpuruṣa*, which in its masculine form[11] seems to refer to an implied word like *vidhi* ("rite"), meaning "[the rite when] a man/person [is sitting] on the scales". The longer neuter form is *tulāpuruṣa(mahā)dāna*, abbreviated as *tulādāna*. Another expression used for this ceremony in epigraphy as well as in literature is *tulābhāra*, "the weighing on the

[10] Queen Vilāsadevī, the wife of the Bengal king Vijayasena and mother of Ballālasena, is recorded to have celebrated a weighing ceremony in her husband's thirty-second regnal year. So far, however, no evidence is available for the performance of this ritual in the Yādava kingdom, where Hemādri lived.

[11] Monier-Williams 1899: 451. See no. 36 of the APPENDIX 3 for an epigraphical reference to the masculine form.

scales". Other technical terms like *tulāroha(ṇa)* and *tulādhiroha(ṇa)*, "the ascending of the balance", have been employed less frequently.

Early inscriptions from Tamil Nadu (Tamil and Sanskrit) and Sri Lanka (Sinhala and Tamil) use the compound *tulābhāra*, whereas in Sanskrit inscriptions from other regions and in Kannaḍa inscriptions *tulāpuruṣa*[12] and *tulāpuruṣa(mahā)dāna* are predominantly employed; these are also the forms most frequently used in the purāṇic literature. In Kannaḍa epigraphs the term *tuḷāpuruṣa* (neuter) also occurs, while in Sanskrit inscriptions after the 14th century *tulāpūruṣa* becomes increasingly common.[13] The terms *tulārohaṇa* and *tulādhiroha(vidhi)* appear in 13th-century inscriptions from Tamil Nadu.[14] – Atharvaveda-pariśiṣṭa 11 has been given the title *tulāpuruṣavidhi*,[15] and in the Matsyapurāṇa, the weighing ceremony is described by the word *tulā-puruṣa(dāna)*.[16] However, the Liṅgapurāṇa calls the ritual weighing of a person *tulāpuruṣa(dāna)*, *tulādhirohaṇa*, *tulāroha* or *tulābhāra*.[17] Hemādri proceeds in a similar manner – not only in his quotations from the Liṅgapurāṇa but also in his commentary on passages of the Matsyapurāṇa.[18]

---

[12] In Sanskrit copper-plate grants of the Rāṣṭrakūṭas, *tulāpuruṣa* mainly denotes the balance and not the weighing ceremony proper; cf. *tulāpuruṣasthite [mayi*]* (APPENDIX 3, no. 8), *tulāpuruṣam āruhya* (APPENDIX 3, nos. 11-15 & 19), *tulā-puruṣād anuttarataiva [mayā]* (APPENDIX 3, nos. 16, 18 & 19). See APPENDIX 3, no. 9 for an exception to this rule: *tulāpuruṣapradānaparvaṇi*.

[13] APPENDIX 3, nos. 72ff. (with exceptions). Evidently the form *tulāpūruṣa* has been used instead of *tulāpuruṣa* for metrical reasons in two Sragdharā verses in the copper-plate grants of Kṛṣṇarāya and Acyutarāya of Vijayanagara. See also note 8 and, for an earlier reference, APPENDIX 3, no. 32.

[14] APPENDIX 3, nos. 69-71. Sometimes no technical term for the ceremony has been employed, but the rite is paraphrased (e.g., with *tulā*); see, e.g., APPENDIX 3, nos. 41, 43 & 44.

[15] AVPariś 11.1.1 and colophon of AVPariś 11.

[16] MtP 274.6 & 274.19 and colophon of MtP 274.

[17] LiP II.28.15 (*tulādhirohaṇa*); II.28.78 (*tulābhara*); II.28.83 (*tulārohasuvarṇa*); colophon of LiP II.28 (*tulāpuruṣadānavidhi*).

[18] CVC, pp. 165, 175-176, 189, 191-193, 219 (*tulāpuruṣa*); 175, 194, 218, 219 (*tulāpuruṣadāna*); 216, 218 (*tulāpuruṣadānavidhi*); 216-217 (*tulādāna*); 190 (*tulādhirohaṇa*); 204, 206 (*tulārohaṇa*); 203 (*tulābhāra*).

Unlike the denominations of other *mahādānas* such as *hiraṇyagarbha* and *gosahasra*, the terms *tulābhāra* and *tulāpuruṣa* appear comparatively late in epigraphy, and often in combination with *hiraṇyagarbha* and *gosahasra*. The first epigraphical references to *hiraṇya-/hemagarbha* and *gosahasra* are much earlier than those to *tulāpuruṣa*; we already find them in Śālaṅkāyana and Viṣṇukuṇḍin inscriptions from the 4th to the 6th centuries A.D.

THE DONORS

Basically, we may distinguish two categories of evidence within the epigraphical material: first, contemporary reports on particular weighing ceremonies mostly written in prose and, secondly, general remarks on the ritual in the metrical genealogy sections of inscriptions and in eulogies (*praśasti*). As the genealogical accounts of certain kings and dynasties are highly stereotyped, identical verses occur in a number of royal grants, including verses referring to the *tulāpuruṣa*.[19] These metrical passages often mention *tulāpuruṣa* ceremonies of the donor's immediate predecessors. Some kings claimed that their very ancient ancestors had regularly performed this ritual. Particularly if events were recorded several centuries after they had allegedly taken place or if the frequency of the ceremonies held and the number of protagonists participating were gradually increased, one naturally feels inclined to question the authenticity of the information. But even from such at best semi-historical statements, it can be inferred how much political importance was attached to the *tulāpuruṣa* ritual.

Approximately one third of the references reports particular weighing ceremonies. We get information about probably historical *tulā-*

---

[19] We find repetitions of verses in the inscriptions of Śilāhāra Bhoja II (APPENDIX 3, nos. 33-35, verse 10); of Kalacuri Yaśaḥkarṇa (APPENDIX 3, nos. 37-39, verse 21); of the Gāhaḍavālas (APPENDIX 3, nos. 41, 43 & 44, verse 5; probably also in other grants, but this well-known passage has often been only partially edited or omitted entirely); of Gaṅga Anaṅgabhīma III and his successors (APPENDIX 3, nos. 48, 49 & 51, either verse 78 or 79; also in other grants); of the Vijayanagara kings (APPENDIX 3, nos. 80-83, 85, 87-88, 90-95, 98-101, 2 verses, and probably in other grants; for the first verse, see also APPENDIX 3, nos. 103-106, modified in no. 79).

puruṣa and *tulābhāra* ceremonies celebrated mainly by powerful kings but also by their queens,[20] crown princes[21] and other members[22] of the royal families, by vassal chiefs,[23] and by ministers[24]. The ritual could be performed either by individuals or by groups. The respective events were not always recorded by the protagonists themselves but sometimes also by persons closely related to, or dependent on, them.[25]

Although there is no epigraphical evidence for activities of donors who did not belong to the court, Vijay Nath believes that the weighing ritual was originally a popular custom which later developed into the royal ceremony:

> By incorporating a commonly held belief imbued with a strong magical overtone, namely, that a person could dispel evil influences by merely gifting some valuable substance which was in weight equal to his own, the author of the *Matsya Purāṇa* managed to impart to the *mahādāna* rite greater ritual efficacy and popular appeal. Moreover, his insistence upon gold being used as the chief precious metal at the *tulāpuruṣa mahādāna* transformed an ordinary folk practice into an impressive courtly ceremonial with all the attendant regalia. (Nath 2000: 424.)

---

[20] APPENDIX 3, nos. 4, 46, 55, 62, 68, 96-97.

[21] APPENDIX 3, nos. 55, 62, 68, 73, 96-97.

[22] APPENDIX 3, nos. 62 & 68 (general accounts).

[23] APPENDIX 3, nos. 21-22. According to no. 21, Cāḷukya Jayasiṃha III, the younger brother of king Vikramāditya VI, who is described as his vassal and as *yuvaraja*, performed the weighing ritual. No. 22 contains a more general reference: Kadamba Jayakeśin II, also a vassal of Cāḷukya Vikramāditya VI, reported in his genealogical account that his great-grandfather and grandfather had celebrated the weighing ceremony several times. The early evidence of the Hoysaḷa kings, who also acknowledged the supremacy of the Cāḷukyas, can be interpreted in the same way; see APPENDIX 3, nos. 23-31.

[24] APPENDIX 3, no. 50. This epigraph records that a minister of the Eastern Gaṅga king Anaṅgabhīma III celebrated the *tulāpuruṣa* ritual.

[25] APPENDIX 3, nos. 5 & 47. In no. 5 the Western Gaṅga vassal chief Pṛthivīpati II reports about the many *tulābhāra* ceremonies celebrated by his sovereign, the Coḷa emperor Parāntaka I. No. 47 mentions the performance of this ritual by a king of Assam. The Kannaḍa epigraphs that refer to the weighing ceremonies of some of the Hoysaḷa monarchs were recorded, not by the kings themselves, but by some of their subvassals and officials.

Particular weighing rituals have been recorded by inscriptions from the territories of the dynasties of the Rāṣṭrakūṭas, Pallavas, Coḷas, later Cāḷukyas, Gāhaḍavālas, Senas, Eastern Gaṅgas, and later Pāṇḍyas as well as from Vijayanagara.[26] Some Rāṣṭrakūṭa monarchs performed the ceremony in favour of, or in the presence of, their queens.[27] The Pallava and Coḷa royal ladies seem to have taken a more active part in the weighing ritual than their Rāṣṭrakūṭa counterparts. Vīramahādevī, for instance, the queen of Pallava Nṛpatuṅgavarman, celebrated her own *hiraṇyagarbha* and *tulāpuruṣa* ceremonies in the twenty-second year of her husband's reign (= 891 A.D.).[28] The famous Śivayoganātha temple inscription (Tiruviśalūr, Kumbakonam taluk, Thanjavur Dist.) registers certain grants by the Coḷa queen Lokamahādevī in favour of the god Mahādeva on the occasion of the performance of *tulābhāra* by king Rājarāja I and of *hema-/hiraṇyagarbha* by herself in the temple in the twenty-ninth year of the king (= 1013 A.D.).[29] Queens also took an active part in *tulāpuruṣa* in other regions and periods. Vilāsadevī, the queen of the Sena king Vijayasena of Bengal and mother of Ballālasena, the author of the Dānasāgara, performed *tulāpuruṣa* in the thirty-second year of her husband's reign.[30] Several *tulāpuruṣa* ceremonies held by the Vijayanagara ruler Kṛṣṇarāya have been recorded in his inscriptions. At least in one case, the epigraphical report says that he celebrated the weighing ritual and had the *mahādānas* of *ratnadhenu* and *saptasāgara* performed by his two queens.[31] A Tamil inscription of king Acyuta of Vijayanagara states that on the occasion of the monarch's celebrating a *tulābhāra* ceremony, one of his *rājamahiṣīs* composed two Sanskrit verses and had them engraved in several holy places, so that "the descendants of the prince might rule as emperors".[32]

---

[26] APPENDIX 3, nos. 4, 7, 8-20, 21, 25-26, 42, 45, 46, 47, 69-71, 72-73, 75, 78, 84, 86, 89, 96-97 & 102.

[27] APPENDIX 3, nos. 9 & 16.

[28] APPENDIX 3, no. 4.

[29] APPENDIX 3, no. 7.

[30] APPENDIX 3, no. 46.

[31] APPENDIX 3, no. 86.

In the Purāṇas, for example, the Matsyapurāṇa, the persons who are advised to perform the *tulāpuruṣa* ceremony are not always definitely specified, although the ritual is especially recommended for kings. The description in Atharvavedapariśiṣṭa 11 first refers to the performers in general as *yajamāna* and *dātṛ*, and only thereafter, in specific contexts, to the "poor" (*niḥsvapakṣa*) and the king (*narādhipa*).

THE DONATIVE OBJECTS AND THE DONEES

The precious material that is recommended for royal *tulāpuruṣa* ceremonies in the purāṇic literature, and that according to the inscriptions was actually used in most cases was, of course, gold (*kanaka*, *kāñcana*, *suvarṇa*, *hiraṇya*, *hema*).[33] The respective texts prescribe that the king should be wearing all royal insignia, and his sword, shield, coat of mail and helmet, when ascending the scales.[34] Some Vijayanagara inscriptions, however, explicitly refer to *kanakamaṇitulāpūruṣa* and *muktātulāpūruṣa*, the weighing against gold and jewels

---

[32] Inscriptions in Kannaḍa, Telugu and Tamil at a temple in Kāñcī (APPENDIX 3, no. 96) report that king Acyuta performed a *tulāpuruṣa* ceremony together with the senior queen and the crown prince Veṅkaṭādri in the Śaka year 1454 (= 1532 A.D.). The three Sanskrit verses of another stone epigraph, only a few months younger, which was found in the Chittoor Dist. of Andhra Pradesh (APPENDIX 3, no. 97), also refer to a weighing ritual celebrated by Acyuta, the senior queen and the heir apparent in Kāñcī. The Tamil introduction of an inscription at the Raṅganātha temple at Śrīraṅga (APPENDIX 3, no. 102) dated in Śaka 1461 (= 1539 A.D.) mentions that a second queen of Acyuta composed two Sanskrit verses on the occasion of a royal *tulābhāra* ritual and had them engraved at several holy places, so that "the descendants of the prince Veṅkaṭādri might rule as emperors". The two Sanskrit verses, however, refer to a different ceremony, which took place at Vijayanagara (Hampi). The final passage is again written in Tamil. Various versions of these two verses, engraved in different scripts and with diverse introductory and final passages, exist at several places in Karnataka, Andhra Pradesh, and Tamil Nadu; see APPENDIX 3, no. 102 = EI 24: 287, n. 8.

[33] A Rāṣṭrakūṭa copper-plate grant says that the balance (*tulāpuruṣa*) was "filled with heaps of very lustrous gold" (*prabhūtoj[j*]valakanakarāśiparipūrita*) (APPENDIX 3, no. 14 = EI 38: 19, line 51; see also no. 15).

[34] AVPariś 11.2.1: *sakhaḍgaḥ saśirastrāṇaḥ sarvābharaṇabhūṣitaḥ / ... narādhipaḥ //*; MtP 274.65cd: *sakhaḍgacarmakavacaḥ sarvābharaṇabhūṣitaḥ //*.

or against pearls.[35] In Atharvavedapariśiṣṭa 11, theoretical permission is given for a poor man to make up the weight with less valuable substances, that is, other metals, garments, liquids, or grain (such as rice).[36] This passage presumably allowed potential donors to defray the costs of the weighing ceremony partly or even completely with substitutes.

Epigraphical information about the recipients of the gold or other precious material is rather scanty. In some inscriptions, brāhmaṇas and temples are explicitly mentioned as beneficiaries. The 9th-century temple inscription from the reign of Pallava Nṛpatuṅgavarman mentioned above reports that the queen presented fifty *kaḻañcu* of gold from the ritual to the temple of Mahādeva, where the ceremony had been probably held and where a Coḷa copy of this epigraph was engraved after the renovation of the temple.[37] In some stone inscriptions from 13th-century south India it is stressed that the kings had the *vimānas* of some temples in Tamil Nadu (for example, at Cidambaram, Śrīraṅga, and Veṅkaṭagiri) covered with the gold against which they had weighed themselves.[38]

The immediate purpose of the copper-plate inscriptions that mention *tulāpuruṣa* ceremonies is not to record that these rites were performed, but to register the gifts of land that were made after they had been celebrated. On the occasion of such ceremonies, kings of the Rāṣṭrakūṭa, Hoysaḷa, Gāhaḍavāla and Sena dynasties as well as of the Vijayanagara lineages granted villages not only to learned brāhmaṇas – sometimes as sacrificial fee (*dakṣiṇā*) for individuals or for the regular feeding (*sattra*) of large groups in the royal capital – but also to astrologers and brāhmaṇa generals (*daṇḍanāyaka*), to Hindu tem-

---

[35] APPENDIX 3, no. 97 (*muktātulāpūruṣa*) and no. 109 (*kanakamaṇitulāpūruṣa*). A variety of precious substances is mentioned in the inscriptions from Sri Lanka, too: not only gold, but also silver, coins, jewels, pearls, ornaments, and clothes; see APPENDIX 3, no. 56 = EZ 2: 129, line 3; no. 63 = EZ 1: 130-131, lines 5-6.

[36] AVPariś 11.1.15: *atha cen niḥsvapakṣeṇa yathā saṃpadyate dhanam / dhātubhiḥ saha taulyaṃ tu vāsobhiś ca rasais tathā / vrīhyādisaptadhān ir vā yathā saṃpadyate gṛhe //.*

[37] APPENDIX 3, no. 4; for *kaḻañcu/kaḻañju*, see Sircar 1966: 139.

[38] APPENDIX 3, nos. 69-71.

ples and to Jain monasteries. Besides having made new donations, some Rāṣṭrakūṭa monarchs claimed to have restored *devabhoga* and *agrahāra* villages that had been confiscated by earlier kings, "before getting down from the pan".

Very often it remains unclear whether the respective recipients had participated in the ceremony proper. A 12th-century copper-plate grant of Gāhaḍavāla Jayacandra of Kanauj records that after having bathed in the Gaṅgā at Kāśī and made the Great Gift of *tulāpuruṣa* in the presence of god Kṛttivāsas (Śiva), the king granted a village to nine brāhmaṇas in such a manner that half of it became the property of his spiritual instructor (*ācārya-purohita*), while the other half was shared by eight priests.[39] This reminds one of the regulations in the Matsya-purāṇa (MtP 274.71-72) mentioned above. At the end of the 11th century, Vijayasena of Bengal granted a piece of land as *dakṣiṇā* for the *homa* performed by a brāhmaṇa during the golden *tulāpuruṣa* ceremony celebrated by his queen Vilāsadevī on the occasion of a lunar eclipse.[40]

The texts on *tulāpuruṣa* focus on the proper distribution of the gold, whereas the donation of land, though also recommended, was apparently regarded as being of minor importance. Yet, the language of the copper-plate records gives the impression that in the practice of *tulāpuruṣa*, grants of whole villages and portions of land played a far more important role than the distribution of gold. This phenomenon could be due to the specific character of the epigraphical medium of copper-plate inscriptions, which were developed in order to register royal land grants in favour of religious recipients, predominantly brāhmaṇas. On the other hand, the donative practices of the kings may have modified the ideal *tulāpuruṣa* described in the texts, especially with regard to the gift items that were actually distributed. In early medieval India, royal grants of villages and land were, after all, a wide-spread instrument for guaranteeing power and legitimacy, far

---

[39] APPENDIX 3, no. 45 = EI 4: 126, lines 22-24: ... *ācāryyapurohitaśrīpraha-rājasya grāmārddhaṃ ... ṛtvigjana 8 grāmasyārddhaṃ ...*

[40] APPENDIX 3, no. 46.

beyond the context of *mahādāna*. Besides, it is the epigraphy in particular which indicates that after the 9th and 10th centuries, villages donated to religious benificiaries were no longer considered to be a source of income only in kind but also in cash. It appears that the taxes increasingly tended to be calculated on a monetary basis.[41] This interpretation of the epigraphic material in general seems to be supported by the information about a *tulāpuruṣa* ritual performed by a king of Assam in the 11th century. King Jayapāladeva of Kāmarūpa is reported to have offered "nine hundred pieces of gold … and a title-deed granting an income of one thousand [pieces of gold]" (*hemnāṃ śatāni nava ... daśaśatodayaśāsanaṃ ca*).[42]

OCCASIONS AND LOCATIONS FOR THE WEIGHING RITUAL

According to Atharvavedapariśiṣṭa 11 and Matsyapurāṇa 274, *tulāpuruṣa* was to be performed on certain occasions: at eclipses, solstices, equinoxes, *saṃkrāntis*, on auspicious or inauspicious astrological constellations, on the occasion of sacrifices, festivities, and marriages, on getting wealth, etc.[43] Many of these dates are not very specific and were recommended and used for all kinds of donations. I dated in-

---

[41] APPENDIX 3, nos. 11-15 & 19. These copper-plate grant record that Rāṣṭrakūṭa Indra III and Govinda IV donated some villages "together with" (*saha*) a certain amount of silver (and gold) coins (*dramma* and *suvarṇa*) It remains uncertain whether the land grants were indeed accompanied by gifts of money or whether the amounts of cash mentioned in the respective passages rather represented the income expected from the villages; for this problem, see also Schmiedchen 2001: 80-82.

[42] APPENDIX 3, no. 47 = EI 13: 292, lines 19-20, verse 22. In the middle of the 15th century, Saṅgama Mallikārjuna of Vijayanagara granted a village "together with" (*yukta*) money (348 *niṣka*); see APPENDIX 3, no. 75 = EC 3: 109, line 46 (Gu. 147).

[43] AVPariś 11.1.2: *tad udagayana āpūryamāṇapakṣe puṇye nakṣatre ... grahaṇakāle vā ...* See also MtP 274.19-22: *tulāpuruṣayogo 'yam yeṣām ādau vidhīyate / ayane viṣuve puṇye vyatīpāte dinakṣaye // 19 // yugādiṣūparāgeṣu tathā manvantarādiṣu / saṃkrāntau vaidhṛtidine caturdaśyaṣṭamīṣu ca // 20 // sitapañcadaśīparvadvādaśīṣv aṣṭakāsu ca / yajñotsavavivāheṣu duḥsvapnādbhutadarśane // 21 // dravyabrāhmaṇalābhe vā śraddhā vā yatra jāyate / tīrthe vāyatane goṣṭhe kūpārāmasaritsu ca // 22 //.*

scriptions mentioning *tulāpuruṣa*, weighing ceremonies are recorded to have actually been held on the occasion of solar and lunar eclipses, other new-moon and full-moon days, solstices, etc.[44]

In the 10th-century Rāṣṭrakūṭa land-grant records, the *tulāpuruṣa* is often connected with the ritual of coronation of the king or *paṭṭabandha* (binding of the turban).[45] The Rāṣṭrakūṭa kings left their residence in order to celebrate their coronation with a ritual weighing at holy places such as the banks of the river Godāvarī.[46] The epigraphical material does not entirely elucidate the question of the chronological relationship between the *rājyābhiṣeka* or consecration of the king on the one hand, and the *paṭṭabandha* and *tulāpuruṣa* ceremonies on the other. Only two of the relevant references describe these three rituals, which were connected with fresh donations of villages as well as with the confirmation of earlier grants, as taking place all at the same time.[47] It appears, however, that the combined performance of the *paṭṭabandha* and the *tulāpuruṣa* rituals was confined to the Rāṣṭrakūṭas. On the other hand, the combination of *abhiṣeka* with *tulāpuruṣa* is recorded for a king of the Eastern Gaṅga dynasty.[48]

From the relevant inscriptions, we can also derive information about the places where *tulāpuruṣa* ceremonies were held. Some of the royal weighing rituals seem to have taken place in the royal residences.[49] Vilāsadevī, the queen of king Vijayasena, performed *tulā-*

---

[44] For solar eclipses, see APPENDIX 3, nos. 9 & 10; for lunar eclipses, APPENDIX 3, nos. 17, 18, 21, 27, 46 & 72; for winter solstices, APPENDIX 3, nos. 16, 26 & 28.

[45] Five Rāṣṭrakūṭa copper-plate grants date from one and the same day in the Śaka year 836, which probably fell on 24th February 915 A.D. This was obviously the date when the coronation (*paṭṭabandha*) of Indra III took place, which was combined with a weighing ceremony (APPENDIX 3, nos. 11-15). Rāṣṭrakūṭa Govinda IV seems to have celebrated *tulāpuruṣa* rituals on the occasion of his own and his queen's coronation festivals; see APPENDIX 3, nos. 16 and 19, and Schmiedchen 2001: 82.

[46] APPENDIX 3, no. 19 = EI 7: 40, line 46.

[47] APPENDIX 3, no. 14 = EI 38: 18, lines 46-47; also no. 15.

[48] APPENDIX 3, nos. 48-49 (verse 79) and 51 (verse 78).

[49] APPENDIX 3, nos. 9, 17, 18 & 46. At least some of the *tulābhāra* ceremonies performed in Sri Lanka and the weighing ritual celebrated by king Mallikārjuna of

puruṣa in the palace of Vikramapura.[50] More often, however, it was celebrated at holy places (*tīrtha*) and temples (*devasthāna, devāyatana*), as prescribed by the Purāṇas.[51] To judge from the inscriptions, the rivers Gaṅgā, Godāvarī, Tuṅgabhadrā, and Kṛṣṇaveṇī and some of their confluences were regarded as most suitable for *tulāpuruṣa*.[52] Several weighing ceremonies recorded in inscriptions took place in temples of Śiva and Viṣṇu.[53] For instance, in 1100 A.D., Gāhaḍavāla Candradeva bathed in the confluence of the Gaṅgā and Var'.ṇā in Kāśī at the Ādikeśavaghaṭṭa, and performed the *tulāpuruṣa* rit al in presence of an image of Ādikeśava (Viṣṇu).[54] In 1175 A.D., Gāhaḍavāla Jayacandra, an adherent of Viṣṇu, also celebrated the we.ghing ceremony after a ritual bath in the Gaṅgā at Benares – but in the presence of Kṛttivāsas (Śiva).[55] Purī, Kāñcī, Śrīraṅga, and Rāmeśvara were other epigraphically documented sacred places for the performance of *tulāpuruṣa*.[56]

Rāṣṭrakūṭa Govinda III seems to have performed this ritual in his residence at Mayūrakhaṇḍī.[57] In contrast, Rāṣṭrakūṭa Indra III left his

---

Vijayanagara in 1448 A.D. (APPENDIX 3, no. 75) also took place in their respective capitals.

[50] APPENDIX 3, no. 46 = EI 15: 284, lines 39-40.

[51] MtP 274.22-23. Accordingly, pilgrimage sites (*tīrtha*), sacred places (*āyatana*), cowsheds (*goṣṭha*), wells (*kūpa*), groves (*ārāma*), rivers (*sarit*), houses (*gṛha*), and ponds (*taḍāga*) were regarded as suitable places. In AVPariś 11, however, no places are mentioned.

[52] For the Gaṅgā, see APPENDIX 3, nos. 42 & 45; for the Godāvarī, APPENDIX 3, nos. 19 & 73 (also called Gautamī); for the Kṛṣṇaveṇī, APPENDIX 3, nos. 84 & 86; for the Tuṅgabhadrā, APPENDIX 3, nos. 72 & 74; for the Varadā, APPENDIX 3, no. 27.

[53] For Śiva as Mahādeva, see APPENDIX 3, nos. 4 & 7; as Govindeśvara, APPENDIX 3, no. 16; as Kṛttivāsas, APPENDIX 3, no. 45; as Kāḷeśvara, APPENDIX 3, no. 73; as Virūpākṣa, APPENDIX 3, no. 74; as Śūlapāṇi/Amareśa, APPENDIX 3, nos. 84 & 86. For Viṣṇu as Ādikeśava, see APPENDIX 3, no. 42; as Hari, APPENDIX 3, no. 97.

[54] APPENDIX 3, no. 42 = EI 14: 197, line 1; 198, line 16.

[55] APPENDIX 3, no. 45 = EI 4: 125-126, lines 20-22.

[56] For Purī, see APPENDIX 3, no. 50; for Kāñcī, e.g., APPENDIX 3, nos. 96 & 102; for Śrīraṅga, e.g., APPENDIX 3, nos. 69 & 109; for Rāmeśvara, APPENDIX 3, nos. 62-67.

[57] APPENDIX 3, no. 9.

capital at Mānyakheṭa for the village of Kurundaka in order to celebrate his coronation (*paṭṭabandha*) together with a *tulāpuruṣa* ritual there.[58] Rāṣṭrakūṭa Govinda IV held his first attested weighing ceremony (for his queen) in the "courtyard of Govindeśvara", that is, probably in a Śiva temple.[59] This shrine was possibly situated in the town of Mānyakheṭa, where only a few weeks later Govinda IV had a second *tulāpuruṣa* ritual performed which is referred to in at least two inscriptions from northern Karnataka.[60] A grant written some months later reports that Govinda IV had left his capital Mānyakheṭa in order to celebrate his coronation combined with a weighing ritual.[61] It is still a matter of controversy whether this festival was actually the late coronation of the ruler or rather the first anniversary of that event.[62]

THE PURPOSE OF *TULĀPURUṢA*

Atharvavedapariśiṣṭa 11.2.2-5 and Matsyapurāṇa 274.5 recommend that those who want to achieve religious merit, a long life, and good health should perform *tulāpuruṣa*. Through the weighing ceremony all kinds of sins could be wiped out, even those offences committed by thrice seven generations of ancestors.[63] Kings in particular were assured of attaining overlordship (*adhirājya*) by celebrating *tulāpuruṣa*.[64] Some inscriptions also provide information about the purposes these *tulāpuruṣa* ceremonies should serve. Pāṇḍya Cendaṇ claimed in the 7th century that he had "chastised" the Kali age by performing the *mahādānas* of *hiraṇyagarbha*, *gosahasra*, and *tulābhāra*, and thereby erased the negative results of the current dark age.[65] Pāṇḍya Varaguṇa

---

[58] APPENDIX 3, nos. 11-15.

[59] APPENDIX 3, no. 16.

[60] APPENDIX 3, nos. 17 & 18.

[61] APPENDIX 3, no. 19.

[62] APPENDIX 3, no. 19 = EI 7: 27, n. 2 and Schmiedchen 2001: 82.

[63] AVPariś 11.2.4: *yat pāpaṃ sve kule jātais triḥsaptapuruṣaiḥ kṛtam / tat sarvaṃ naśyate kṣipraṃ agnau tūlaṃ yathā tathā //.*

[64] AVPariś 11.2.2: *indreṇedaṃ purā dattam adhirājyāptaye varam / sarvapāpapraṇāśāya sarvapuṇyavivṛddhaye //.*

[65] APPENDIX 3, no. 1.

I reported that after celebrating the gifts called *hiraṇyagarbha*, *tulābhāra* and *gosahasra* many times, his great-grandfather and his father showered freely their wealth on brāhmaṇas, beggars, and temples (*surāyatana*), and were thus freed of their sins.[66] With regard to the weighing ceremony, an ancestor of Kacchapaghāta Mahīpāla is said to have reflected on the question of whether any king on earth rivalled him in greatness.[67] This reminds one of Matsyapurāṇa 274.77, the next to last verse on *tulāpuruṣa*:

> On the completion of his store of virtue, the believer who performs thousands of sacrifices is reborn here on earth as an emperor, whose footstool is honoured by the jewels on the foreheads of the kings, and who conquers all of the kings through his shining glory.[68]

Some south Indian kings of the period from the 13th to the 16th centuries celebrated *tulāpuruṣa* not for future conquests but also just after victories in battle, using the booty thereof for the weighing ritual.[69]

SOME UNUSUAL INSCRIPTIONAL REFERENCES

In the following, three particularly remarkable epigraphical references to the weighing ceremony will be presented. They record, first, the alleged refusal of *tulāpuruṣa* gifts by a brāhmaṇa, second, the existence of special temples for this ritual, and third, the application of this purāṇic ritual in a Buddhist context.

(1) An 11th-century Sanskrit stone inscription from Bengal (Bangladesh) furnishes a *praśasti* or eulogistic account of a brāhmaṇa called Prahāsa and his family.[70] The record reports that while making a *tulāpuruṣamahādāna*, king Jayapāla of Kāmarūpa offered a large gift

---

[66] APPENDIX 3, no. 2.

[67] APPENDIX 3, no. 40 = CII 7.3: 542, line 4, verse 7.

[68] MtP 274.77: *karmakṣayād iha punar bhuvi rājarājo bhūpālamaulimaṇirañjitapādapīṭhaḥ / śraddhānvito bhavati yajñasahasrayājī dīptapratāpajitasarvamahīpalokaḥ //.*

[69] APPENDIX 3, nos. 69-71 and for Vijayanagara, e.g., no. 73.

[70] APPENDIX 3, no. 47 = EI 13: 292, lines 19-20.

to this learned brāhmaṇa of Varendrī, who, however, refused to accept it, for reasons that are not mentioned.

(2) At the end of the 10th century, in the ninth year of Coḷa Rājarāja I (985-1016), the village assembly (*mahāsabhā*) of Uttiramerucaturvedimaṅgala assembled in "the sacred temple of the weighing ceremony" (*tulāvāraśrīkoyil*) and decided on a resolution (*vyavasthā*) relating to the responsibility for the payment of fines imposed on the members of different social groups. This was recorded in a Tamil inscription engraved on a stone slab at present-day Uttiramerur (Kanchipuram Dist.).[71]

(3) At the beginning of the 11th century, still during the reign of Rājarāja I, the Coḷas invaded Sri Lanka, to remain there until they were driven out by the Sinhala king Vijayabāhu I (1055-1110). Epigraphical reports state that Vijayabāhu I purified the Saṅgha of the three *nikāyas* and gave three *tulābhāras* to the Buddhist order.[72] Parākramabāhu I (1153-1186), the grandson of Vijayabāhu I, explicitly referred to his grandfather and also celebrated the weighing ritual, which is described in his rock inscription in the same way as in Vijayabāhu's epigraph. He obviously was striving for a revival of the religious policy of his grandfather, whose ideas are said to have been neglected after his death.[73] Kaliṅga Niśśaṅkamalla (1187-1196), a Sri Lankan king allegedly of Indian origin, claimed that he had introduced the (Indian) custom of recording grants on copper plates and that he had distributed *tulābhāra* gifts. He resolved to have mounted the scale pans "as no former kings have ever done", wearing the crown and the other royal insignia, together with other members of his family.[74] Niśśaṅkamalla seems to have regularly performed his *tulābhāra* ceremonies in his capital Poḷonnaruva, as his stone inscriptions report on the donations in the "king's road" following the event. It appears

---

[71] APPENDIX 3, no. 6.

[72] APPENDIX 3, nos. 52-53.

[73] APPENDIX 3, no. 54; the passage concerned is very similar to that in no. 52.

[74] APPENDIX 3, no. 59 = EZ 2: 132, line 5; no. 61 = EI 36: 29, line 6; no. 63 = EZ 1: 131, line 11; see also nos. 64 & 66.

that right from the beginning, the charitable character of these distributions was more comprehensive than that of their Indian counterparts. Besides, Niśśaṅkamalla apparently invaded the territory of the Pāṇḍyas twice, and at Rāmeśvara, he ascended the scales, had columns of victory set up, and had a temple bearing his name built.[75] Niśśaṅkamalla's *tulābhāra* rituals are mentioned in more than a dozen of his inscriptions, but the number of protagonists differs. The number of the participants belonging to the royal family varied between three to five; sometimes up to eight persons seem to have taken part. Besides the king, his senior queen, and the heir apparent, the group could include a second queen, the daughter of the king, his brother, the queen mother, and a maid of honour. In some epigraphs, only the number of the *tulābhāra* ceremonies held annually has been recorded, namely, four or, more often, five.[76]

In contrast to this case from Sri Lanka, often only one weighing ritual is recorded for each of the respective Indian kings; but this might be due to a lack of relevant sources. There is some evidence, however,

---

[75] Niśśaṅkamalla claimed that he searched the Pāṇḍya country for three months but could not find any appropiate adversary, and therefore decided to celebrate the *tulābhāra* ceremony (at Rāmeśvara); see, e.g., APPENDIX 3, no. 64 = EZ 2: 287, line 6. In this context it is worth mentioning that one of this king's relevant inscriptions written in Sinhala is situated at Rāmeśvara (Ramanathapuram Dist., Tamil Nadu); see APPENDIX 3, no. 61. The contents of these epigraphs as well as the location of the Rāmeśvara inscription remind one of the connection between the weighing ceremony, military achievements, and imperial claims that was discussed above.

[76] This figure presumably does not denote the annual frequency of the events, but a kind of individual counting of the rituals according to the number of their participants. The language of some of the relevant royal inscriptions suggests this conjecture; see APPENDIX 3, no. 61. In this stone epigraph the five *tulābhāra* ceremonies are directly associated with the five persons participating; for this interpretation and one additional reference, see also Bell 1915: 85-86. Proceeding from th[illegible] supposition and interpreting the increase chronologically, a hypothetical [illegible]equence of Niśśaṅkamalla's inscriptions, all of them undated, has been fixed for th[illegible] APPENDIX 3: at the beginning, there were three participants (no. 55), then four an[illegible]ual *tulābhāra* rituals (no. 56), and later five ceremonies or the weighing of five persons each year (nos. 57-61) plus either additionally (nos. 62-64) or exclusively (nos. 65-67) a reference to the performance of a weighing ritual at Rāmeśvara / in the Pāṇḍya country, and finally the *tulābhāra* ceremony of eight persons belonging to the royal household (no. 68).

that several monarchs celebrated the ceremony more than once during their periods of reign. Particularly in the general accounts, that is, in the genealogies and eulogies, one finds references to alleged frequent performances of *tulāpuruṣa*, though mainly in connection with ancestors. A survey of the epigraphical material on the weighing ritual dating from the 7th to the 16th centuries is given in APPENDIX 2.

THE WEIGHING CEREMONY SINCE THE 16TH CENTURY

It is noteworthy that the ritual of weighing continued to be popular under the Muslim kings of the Mughal dynasty in northwest India from the 16th to the 18th centuries, as texts and paintings prove. The Mughal ceremony was strongly associated with the birthdays of the emperors and princes, which were celebrated according to both the lunar and solar calendars. The king was weighed against several substances (gold, silver, jewels, iron, rice, salt, etc.), which had been collected as tributes and were later distributed among the needy. Sometimes the Mughal emperors also performed the ritual of weighing on the occasion of solar and lunar eclipses, in order to avert the evil influence of such astrological events.[77]

In the period from the 17th to the 19th centuries, the weighing ceremony is supposed to have been celebrated in the north Indian principalities of Ujjain, Udaipur, Jaisalmer, and Amritsar and in the Nepalese kingdom, as well as in the south Indian princely states of Madurai, Mysore, Tanjore, and Travancore.[78]

In Islamic contexts in recent times, it is worth mentioning that Sultan Muhammad Shah Aga Khan III (1877-1957), the forty-eighth Imam of the Shiite Ismailis, was weighed by his adherents against gold and diamonds on the occasion of certain jubilees in the 1930s, 1940s, and 1950s. These anniversary festivities were held at two places at a time, one in Bombay (Mumbai) and the other in various African cities,

---

[77] See, e.g., Schimmel 2000: 242-243.

[78] See, e.g., EI 24: 74, lines 24-25; EI 36: 127, line 13. See also Vajracharya 2003.

and were designed to support the financing of several educational and charitable projects.[79]

One still encounters the phenomenon of the weighing ritual in India up to present times, although under different circumstances than those of the middle ages. A search in the Internet, for instance, produces numerous results for tulabhara (sic), the expression originally used in Tamil Nadu only. Today this term denotes the weighing ceremony in different regional and social contexts. Religious leaders, for example, are weighed against gold collected by their followers in Maharashtra and Karnataka, sometimes in connection with temple consecrations. This method of fund-raising seems to be also practised by some sects that operate globally, for instance the Chinmaya Mission, whose Gurudev decided to perform a *suvarṇatulābhāra* in 1991 and had the offering required for that purpose supplemented with stones as it weighed only forty-five kilograms.[80] Moreover, ritual weighing is apparently popular not only among the religious elite but also among political, particularly provincial leadership. In 1998, for example, the birthday celebrations of a local Shiv Sena leader in Maharashtra were embellished not only by the opening of an exhibition but also by the performance of a *tulābhāra* ceremony with *pañcāmṛta*, the five holy substances.[81] In 2001, members of the Congress Party planned to hold a *rajatatulābhāra* or weighing against silver, of Sonia Gandhi, in favour of the victims of a disastrous drought in Karnataka, but she refused. Indira Gandhi, however, is reported to have been weighed against gold in favour of the National Defense Fund in Bijapur in the 1960s.[82]

Furthermore, the *tulābhāra* seems to play a role in the religious life in some regions today for which it cannot be documented for medieval

---

[79] http://ismaili.net/sultan/sultan.html (15th October 2003).

[80] http://www.chyk.net/onlinemagazine/aug2001/articles/glimpses.htm (15th October 2003).

[81] http://www.expressindia.com/ie/daily/19980129/02950264.html (15th October 2003).

[82] http://www.hinduonnet.com/thehindu/2001/09/11/stories/0411210c.htm (15th October 2003).

times. In a number of temples in Maharashtra, Karnataka, and Kerala, *tulābhāra* is among the *pūjās* offered, with devotees getting themselves weighed against different metals, sandal wood, rice, sugar, coconuts, bananas, and even against firewood, and presenting these items to the god. This form of *pūjā* is also recommended to promote the recovery of sick children. Sometimes the *pūjā* lists give details about particular dates when this kind of *pūjā* should not be performed.[83]

CONCLUSION

In conclusion, it can be emphasized once again that the *tulāpuruṣa* ceremony is part of an Indian tradition whose origins go back at least to the early middle ages. The oldest epigraphic references to the performance of this important donative ritual (*mahādāna*) come from the Deccan and date from the 7th and 8th centuries. These inscriptions are rather close in time and place to the earliest systematic treatises on the so-called sixteen Great Gifts in the Purāṇas. Due to the nature of the medieval inscriptions, information about the *tulāpuruṣa* for this period of history is almost completely restricted to the courtly environment. The limited source material is probably also the reason that the actual circumstances of the weighing ritual are very often not clearly revealed. This applies, for instance, to the paucity of our knowledge about the actual suppliers and beneficiaries of the gifts redistributed during the ceremony. Modern references prove the possible complexity of the phenomenon, but we cannot, of course, automatically conclude that such a diversity already existed in the middle ages. A comparison of the medieval and the more recent evidence for the weighing ceremony merely elucidates the potential religious, political, and social dimensions of this important ritual of the redistribution of wealth.

---

[83] E.g., *ekādaśī*, *saṃkramaṇa* and *amāvāsyā*; see http://manjeshwar.org/Complete%20Seva%20List.htm (15th October 2003). Certain inauspicious dates should obviously be avoided, but this is in contrast to the medieval epigraphical evidence for the royal ceremony (regarding, e.g., solar eclipses) and to the recommendations of MtP 274.20.

Furthermore, certain popular variants and forms of the present-day *tulābhāra-pūjā* point to a different socio-cultural environment of this phenomenon, which is not yet traceable for medieval times.

REFERENCES

AVPariś = Atharvavedapariśiṣṭa. *The Pariśiṣṭas of the Atharvaveda, Vol. I: Text and Critical Apparatus, Pt. 1*. Ed. by G.M. Bolling & J. von Negelein. Leipzig 1909.

BELL, H.C.P. 1915. King Kirtti Nissanka and the "Tulá-bhára" Ceremony. *The Ceylon Antiquary and Literary Register* 1: 83-86.

CVC = Caturvargacintāmaṇi. Hemādri, *Caturvargacintāmaṇi, Vol. I: Dānakhaṇḍa, Pt. 1*. Ed. by Bhāratacandra Śiromaṇi. (Bibliotheca Indica, 72.1.1.) Calcutta 1873.

DS = Dānasāgara. Ballālasena, *Dānasāgara. Critically Edited with Introduction and Index, Vol. I*. Ed. by Bh. Bhattacharya. (Bibliotheca Indica 274.1.) Calcutta 1953.

GAI, G.S. 1946. *Historical Grammar of Old Kannada*. Poona.

HAZRA, R.C. 1975. *Studies in the Purāṇic Records on Hindu Rites and Customs*. Second edition. Delhi.

HOHENBERGER, A. 1967. *Das Bhaviṣyapurāṇa*. Wiesbaden.

HULTZSCH, E. (ed.) 1916. *South Indian Inscriptions* 2, Pts. 3-5. Madras.

INDEN, R. 1979. The Ceremony of the Great Gift (Mahādāna): Structure and Historical Context in Indian Ritual and Society. In: M. Gaborieau & A. Thorner (eds.), *Asie du Sud: Traditions et changements*: 131-136. Paris.

[Institute of Kannada Studies] 1974. *Epigraphia Carnatica* 3. Revised edition. Mysore.

[Institute of Kannada Studies] 1976. *Epigraphia Carnatica* 5. Revised edition. Mysore.

[Institute of Kannada Studies] 1977. *Epigraphia Carnatica* 6. Revised edition. Mysore.

[Institute of Kannada Studies] 1979. *Epigraphia Carnatica* 7. Revised edition. Mysore.

[Institute of Kannada Studies] 1984. *Epigraphia Carnatica* 8. Revised edition. Mysore.

[Institute of Kannada Studies] 1990. *Epigraphia Carnatica* 9. Revised edition. Mysore.

[Institute of Kannada Studies] 1997. *Epigraphia Carnatica* 10. Revised edition. Mysore.

[Institute of Kannada Studies] 1998. *Epigraphia Carnatica* 11. Revised edition. Mysore.

KANE, P.V. 1974. *History of Dharmaśāstra. Ancient and Mediaeval Religious and Civil Law in India, Vol. II, Pt. 2.* Second edition. Poona.

—— 1975. *History of Dharmaśāstra. Ancient and Mediaeval Religious and Civil Law in India. Vol. I, Pt. 2.* Second edition. Poona.

KOSKIKALLIO, P. 2002. The *Gargasaṃhitā* and the *Ānandarāmāyaṇa*: additional sources for studying the pseudo-Vedic ritualism in post-epic texts. In: M. Brockington (ed.), *Stages and Transitions: Temporal and Historical Frameworks in Epic and Purāṇic Literature*: 313-336. Zagreb.

KRISHNAN, K.G. (ed.) 2002. *Inscriptions of the Early Pāṇḍyas (from c. 300 B.C. to 984 A.D.)*. New Delhi.

LAKSHMINARAYAN RAO, N. (ed.) 1940. *South Indian Inscriptions* 11, Pt. 1. Madras.

—— (ed.) 1952. *South Indian Inscriptions* 11, Pt. 2. Madras.

LiP = Liṅgapurāṇa. *Liṅgapurāṇa of Sage Kṛṣṇa Dvaipāyana Vyāsa. With Sanskrit Commentary Śivatoṣiṇī of Gaṇeśa Nātu.* Ed. by J.L. Shastri. Delhi 1980.

MAHALINGAM, T.V. (ed.) 1988. *Inscriptions of the Pallavas*. New Delhi.

MIRASHI, V.V. (ed.) 1955. *Inscriptions of the Kalachuri-Chedi Era, Vol. I.* (Corpus Inscriptionum Indicarum, 4.) New Delhi.

—— (ed.) 1977. *Inscriptions of the Śilāhāras*. (Corpus Inscriptionum Indicarum, 6.) New Delhi.

MtP = Matsyapurāṇa. *Śrīmad-dvaipāyanamuni-praṇītaṃ matsyapurāṇam*. Ed. by the Pandits of the Ānandāśrama ("*etad pustakam Ānandāśramasthapaṇḍitaiḥ saṃśodhitam*"). (Ānandāśrama Sanskrit Series, 54.) Poona 1981. (Reprint of the edition of H.N. Apte of 1907.)

NARASIMHASWAMI, H.K. (ed.) 1972. *South Indian Inscriptions* 16. Madras.

NATH, V. 2000. *Mahādāna*: The Dynamics of Gift-economy and the Feudal Milieu. In: D.N. Jha (ed.), *The Feudal Order*: 411-440. New Delhi.

NILAKANTA SASTRI, K.A. 1975. *A History of South India. From Prehistoric Times to the Fall of Vijayanagara.* Fourth edition. New Delhi.

PARANAVITANA, S. (ed.) 1933. *Epigraphia Zeylanica* 3. London.

RICE, B.L. (ed.) 1903. *Epigraphia Carnatica* 11. Bangalore.

—— (ed.) 1904. *Epigraphia Carnatica* 12. Bangalore.

SALOMON, R. 1998. *Indian Epigraphy. A Guide to the Study of Inscriptions in Sanskrit, Prakrit, and the Other Indo-Aryan Languages.* New York.

SCHIMMEL, A. 2000. *Im Reich der Großmoguln: Geschichte, Kunst, Kultur.* München.

SCHMIEDCHEN, A. 2001. Dorfverleihungen an Brahmanen und brahmanische Aktivitäten im frühmittelalterlichen Reich der Rāṣṭrakūṭas. In: M. Njammasch, A. Schmiedchen & F. Virkus (eds.), *Sozialgeschichte des Brahmanentums im frühen Mittelalter in Gujarat, Maharashtra und Karnataka* (Beiträge des Südasien-Instituts, Sonderheft 3): 63-105. Berlin.

SCHOPEN, G. 1991. Archaeology and Protestant Presuppositions in the Study of Indian Buddhism. *History of Religions* 31: 1-23.

SHAMA SHASTRY, R. & N. LAKSHMINARAYAN RAO (eds.) 1941. *South Indian Inscriptions* 9, Pt. 2. Madras.

SIRCAR, D.C. 1966. *Indian Epigraphical Glossary*. New Delhi.

SRINIVASA RAO, G.V. (ed.) 1979. *South Indian Inscriptions* 23. New Delhi.

SUBRAHMANYA SASTRY, S. (ed.) 1984, *Early Inscriptions, Vol. I*. Second edition. Delhi (originally: Madras, 1930-1938).

TRIVEDI, H.V. (ed.) 1989. *Inscriptions of the Paramāras, Chandellas, Kachchhapaghātas and Two Minor Dynasties, Vol. III*. (Corpus Inscriptionum Indicarum, 7.) New Delhi.

VAJRACHARYA, G.V. 2003. Painted History: The *Tuladana* Ceremony in a Medieval Nepalese Palace. *Orientations* 34.10: 46-51.

VENKATASUBBA AYYAR, V. (ed.) 1943. *South Indian Inscriptions* 12. Madras.

VR = Vivādaratnākara. Caṇḍeśvara, *The Vivāda-Ratnākara. A Treatise on Hindu Law by Caṇḍeśvara Ṭhakkura*. Ed. by Kamalakṛṣṇa Smṛtitīrtha. (Bibliotheca Indica, 103.) Calcutta 1931.

DE ZILVA WICKREMASINGHE, D.M. (ed.) 1912. *Epigraphia Zeylanica* 1. London.

—— (ed.) 1928. *Epigraphia Zeylanica* 2. London.

APPENDIX 1:
Table of the distribution of the references to the weighing ceremony

Kings	Regions	Periods, materials	Languages	Technical terms	Nos. in appendix 3
Pāṇḍya Cendan and Varaguṇa I	Tamil Nadu, Madurai Dist.	7th/8th cent. A.D., copper, stone	Tamil, Sanskrit	*tulābhāra*	nos. 1-3
Pallava Nṛpatuṅgavarman	Tamil Nadu, Thanjavur Dist.	9th cent. A.D., stone	Tamil	*tulābhāra*	no. 4
Coḷa Parāntaka and Rājarāja I	Tamil Nadu, several districts	10th/11th cent. A.D., copper, stone	Tamil, Sanskrit	*tulābhāra/ tulāvāra*	nos. 5-7
Rāṣṭrakūṭa (several kings)	Maharashtra, Karnataka, Gujarat	8th-10th cent. A.D., copper, stone	Sanskrit, Kannaḍa	*tulāpuruṣa/ tuḷāpuruṣa*	nos. 8-20
Cāḷukya Vikramāditya VI	Karnataka, Dharwad Dist.	11th/12th cent. A.D., stone	Kaṇnaḍa, Sanskrit	*tulāpuruṣa/ tuḷāpuruṣa*	nos. 21-22
Hoysaḷa Viṣṇu-vardhana et al.	Karnataka, several districts	12th/13th cent. A.D., stone	Kannaḍa	*tulāpuruṣa/ tuḷāpuruṣa*	nos. 23-31
Coḍa-Cāḷukya Rājendra II	Andhra Pradesh, Guntur Dist.	12th cent. A.D., copper	Sanskrit	[*tulāpūruṣadāna*]	no. 32
Śilāhāra Bhoja II	Maharashtra, several districts	12th cent. A.D., copper, stone	Sanskrit	*tulāpuruṣadāna*	nos. 33-35
Candella Dhaṅga	Madhya Pradesh, Chhatarpur Dist.	11th cent. A.D., stone	Sanskrit	*tulāpuruṣa*	no. 36

Kalacuri Yaśaḥkarṇa	Madhya Pradesh, Jabalpur Dist.	11th cent. A.D., copper	Sanskrit	*tulāpuruṣa*	nos. 37-39
Kacchapaghāta Mahīpāla	Madhya Pradesh, Gwalior Dist.	11th cent. A.D., stone	Sanskrit	*tulāpuruṣa*	no. 40
Gāhaḍavāla (several kings)	Uttar Pradesh, Varanasi Dist.	11th/12th cent. A.D., copper	Sanskrit	*tulāpuruṣa*/(*tulā*)	nos. 41-45
Sena Vijayasena	West Bengal, 24-Parganas Dist.	11th/12th cent. A.D., copper	Sanskrit	*tulāpuruṣa-mahādāna*	no. 46
(Kāmarūpa) Jayapāla	Bangladesh, Rajshahi, Bogra	(11th cent. A.D.), stone	Sanskrit	*tulāpuruṣa*	no. 47
Eastern Gaṅga Anaṅgabhīma III	Orissa, Mayurbhanj Dist.	13th cent. A.D., copper, stone	Sanskrit	*tulāpuruṣadāna*	nos. 48-51
Vijayabāhu I and Niśśaṅkamalla I	Sri Lanka, several districts	12th cent. A.D., stone	Sinhala, Tamil, Sanskrit	*tulābhāra*/ (*tulātala*)	nos. 52-68
Pāṇḍya Sundara I	Tamil Nadu, Tiruchchirappalli	13th cent. A.D., stone	Sanskrit	*tulādhirohavidhi*	no. 69
Kāḍava Kopperuñjiṅga II	Andhra Pradesh, Kurnool Dist.	13th cent. A.D., stone	Tamil	*tulārohaṇa*	no. 70
Yādavarāya Vīranṛsiṃha	Andhra Pradesh, Chittoor Dist.	13th cent. A.D., stone	Tamil	*tulārohaṇa*	no. 71
(Vijayanagara) Saṅgama kings	Karnataka, Andhra Pradesh	14th/15th cent. A.D., copper, stone	Sanskrit, Kannaḍa	*tulāpuruṣa*/ *tulāpūruṣa*	nos. 72-77
(Vijayanagara) Tuḷuva kings	Karnataka, Andhra Pradesh, Tamil Nadu	15th/16th cent. A.D., copper, stone	Sanskrit, Kannaḍa/Telugu	*tulāpūruṣa*/ *tulāpuruṣa*	nos. 78-106
(Vijayanagara) Āravīḍu kings	Tamil Nadu, Karnataka	16th cent. A.D., copper	Sanskrit	*tulāpūruṣa*	nos. 107-109

APPENDIX 2:
Descriptive survey of references to the weighing ceremony

Pāṇḍya Cendaṉ (7th century) claimed that he had "chastised" the Kali age by celebrating the *mahādānas* of *hiraṇyagarbha*, *gosahasra*, and *tulābhāra* in the fiftieth year of his reign (no. 1: Tamil Nadu, Madurai Dist.). Pāṇḍya Varaguṇa I (768-811), his descendant in the fourth generation, reported that, having performed the gifts called *hiraṇya-garbha*, *tulābhāra*, and *gosahasra* many times, his great-grandfather and his father freely showered their wealth on brāhmaṇas, beggars, and temples (*surāyatana*) and were thereby freed of their sins (nos. 2-3: Tamil Nadu, Madurai Dist.). In the twenty-second year of Pallava Nṛpatuṅgavarman's reign (= 891 A.D.), his queen Vīramahādevī celebrated her own *hiraṇyagarbha* and *tulāpuruṣa* ceremonies in a Mahādeva temple (no. 4: Tamil Nadu, Thanjavur Dist.). According to a grant (no. 5: Tamil Nadu, North Arcot Dist.) of his Gaṅga vassal Pṛthivīpati II, the Coḷa sovereign Parāntaka I (907-955) performed *hemagarbha*, *tulābhāra*, etc. Under the rule of Coḷa Rājarāja I (985-1016), the great-grandson of Parāntaka I, there existed a separate temple for the weighing ritual (*tulāvāraśrīkoyil*) in ancient Uttirameru (no. 6: Tamil Nadu, Kanchipuram Dist.). Coḷa Rājarāja I held a *tulā-bhāra* ceremony in his twenty-ninth regnal year (= 1013 A.D.), while his consort Lokamahādevī simultaneously celebrated the *hiraṇya-garbha* rite in the Mahādeva temple of Tiruviśalūr (no. 7: Tamil Nadu, Thanjavur Dist.).

According to the testimony of a copper-plate grant dating from the middle of the 8th century (no. 8: Maharashtra, Kolhapur Dist.), the Rāṣṭrakūṭa king Dantidurga, a contemporary of the father of Pāṇḍya Varaguṇa I, donated a village to a brāhmaṇa on the occasion of a royal *tulāpuruṣa* ritual. With the consent of his queen, Rāṣṭrakūṭa Govinda III, the son of Dantidurga's cousin and an adversary of Pāṇḍya Vara-guṇa I, granted a village to thirteen brāhmaṇas (no. 9: Maharashtra, Amravati Dist.) when he performed the weighing ceremony in his residence at Mayūrakhaṇḍī on the occasion of a solar eclipse in the year 800 A.D. A Kannaḍa stone epigraph records that Rāṣṭrakūṭa Amoghavarṣa I, the son of Govinda III and a contemporary of Pallava Nṛpatuṅgavarman, bestowed a village on an astrologer during such a ritual being held on the occasion of a solar eclipse in 862 A.D. (no. 10: Karnataka, Bijapur Dist.). According to at least five copper-plate records (nos. 11-15: Maharashtra, Aurangabad and Nasik Districts; Gujarat, Surat Dist.), Rāṣṭrakūṭa Indra III, great-grandson of Amoghavarṣa I and contemporary of Coḷa Parāntaka I, celebrated the *tulāpuruṣa* ceremony on the occasion of his coronation in the year 915 A.D. and endowed brāhmaṇas as well as Jaina monasteries with a number of villages. Rāṣṭrakūṭa Govinda IV, a son of Indra III, is supposed to have performed at least three weighing rituals between the end of 929 and the middle of 930 A.D., on the occasic , among others, of his own and his queen's coronations, and to ł ıve given villages to brāhmaṇa priests and generals (nos. 16-19: M aharashtra, Akola Dist.; Karnataka, Dharwad and Gulbarga Districts; Gujarat, Kheda Dist.). Under the rule of Rāṣṭrakūṭa Amoghavarṣa III, one of his vassals also celebrated this famous ceremony in 937 A.D. (no. 20: Karnataka, Chitradurga Dist.).

In Karnataka, the tradition of the ritual weighing of kings and other nobles against gold was continued by several vassals of Cāḷukya Vikramāditya VI (1076-1126) and the Hoysaḷa kings. On the occasion of a lunar eclipse in the year 1077 A.D., the brother of Vikramāditya VI performed the *tuḷāpuruṣa* and *hiraṇyagarbha* ceremonies and granted land (no. 21: Karnataka, Dharwad Dist.). In another inscription (no. 22: Karnataka, Dharwad Dist.), the Kadamba vassal Jayakeśin II mentions the performance of numerous weighing rituals by his great-grandfather and his grandfather. Hoysaḷa Viṣṇuvardhana, who had previously also ackowledged the supremacy of Vikramāditya VI, and his successors celebrated *tuḷāpuruṣa* and *hiraṇyagarbha* ceremonies in the first half of the 12th century. The relevant references are provided by the epigraphs of local chiefs (nos. 23-31: Karnataka, Chikmagalur, Hassan and Mandya Districts), who reported that they had passed on land which they had received on the occasion of *tuḷāpuruṣa* rituals held by the Hoysaḷa kings to religious beneficiaries.

The *tulāpuruṣa* tradition probably spread from Karnataka eastwards to Andhra Pradesh. Thus a Coḍa-Cāḷukya ruler of the 12th century recorded (no. 32: Andhra Pradesh, Guntur Dist.) that king Amma I of the Eastern Cāḷukya dynasty, one of his very ancient predecessors, had performed this ceremony annually, during his short reign of only seven years, at the beginning of the 10th century.

In Maharashtra, the tradition of the ritual weighing was continued by the Śilāhāras. The genealogical passages in the copper-plate and stone inscriptions of Śilāhāra Bhoja II dating from the end of the 12th century (nos. 33-35: Maharashtra, Kolhapur and Ratnagiri Districts) contain a verse reporting that his grandfather Gaṇḍarāditya had celebrated *tulāpuruṣa* and other rituals.

By the late 10th century, the practice of the weighing ceremony had spread to the north. Candella Dhaṅga boasted about the hundreds of *tulāpuruṣa* rituals he supposedly held in the eulogy of his Khajuraho stone epigraph, which had been originally written in the year 1003 A.D and renewed at the beginning of the 12th century (no. 36: Madhya Pradesh, Chhatarpur Dist.). The Kalacuri king Yaśaḥkarṇa is also eulogised for the performance of this ceremony in some of his copper-plate grants from the second half of the 11th century (nos. 37-39: Madhya Pradesh, Jabalpur Dist.). In an inscription dating from the end of the 11th century (no. 40: Madhya Pradesh, Gwalior), Kacchapaghāta Mahīpāla recalled one of his ancestors, who had celebrated several *tulāpuruṣa* rituals in the late 10th century.

General as well as more specific references to the performance of this ceremony are also found in some copper-plate records of the Gāhaḍavāla rulers of Kanauj (nos. 41-45: Uttar Pradesh, Varanasi Dist.). The fifth verse of the stereotyped genealogy of king Candradeva and his successors reports that at the end of the 11th century Candradeva had himself weighed against gold many times and endowed brāhmaṇas with gifts. For the year 1100 A.D., there is also a specific piece of evidence (no. 42) proving that Candradeva celebrated the great donative rituals of *tulāpuruṣa* and *gosahasra* in the presence of an image of Ādikeśava at Benares and granted 32 villages to 500 brāhmaṇas and one village in favour of a temple. A copper-plate grant of Gāhaḍavāla Jayacandra dating from 1174 A.D. (no. 45) cords that after bathing in the Gaṅgā near Benares and performing th Great Gift of *tulāpuruṣa* in the presence of god Kṛttivāsas (Śiva), e king bestowed a village on nine brāhmaṇas.

Presumably at the end of the 11th century, Vijayasena of Bengal granted a piece of land as *dakṣiṇā* for the *homa* performed by a brāhmaṇa during the golden *tulāpuruṣa* ceremony celebrated by his queen Vilāsadevī on the occasion of a lunar eclipse (no. 46: West Bengal, 24-Parganas Dist.). Apparently also on the occasion of a weighing ritual, Jayapāladeva of Kāmarūpa distributed gold coins and presented revenues to brāhmaṇas in the 11th century (no. 47: Bangladesh, Rajshahi Province, Bogra Dist.).

For the 13th and 14th centuries, the *tulāpuruṣa* tradition is also traceable in Orissa. Anaṅgabhīma III (1211-1238) of the Eastern Gaṅga dynasty had a verse inserted into the eulogies of his copper-plate records (nos. 48-49: Orissa, Mayurbhanj and Puri Districts), which established a connection between his coronation and *tulāpuruṣa*. This verse was preserved in the genealogical sections of the epigraphs of his successors (e.g., no. 51: Orissa, Mayurbhanj Dist.). According to a temple inscription (no. 50: Orissa, Cuttack Dist.), a minister of Anaṅgabhīma III celebrated his own weighing ceremony on the sea-shore near Purī.

While the *tulāpuruṣa* practice probably spread from the Rāṣṭrakūṭa territories in Maharashtra northwards, it was obviously the Coḷa kings who were responsible for the dissemination of the *tulābhāra* tradition from Tamil Nadu further south to Sri Lanka. The performance of numerous *tulābhāra* rituals in a Buddhist environment and with a strong charitable orientation has been recorded for several Sri Lankan rulers and their families during the 11th and 12th centuries (nos. 52-68: Sri Lanka, Polonnaruva, Anuradhapura, Kandy, Kegalla, Matale, Monaragalla and Trincomalee Districts; Tamil Nadu, Ramanathapuram Dist.).

In south India, the tradition of "the ascending of the balance" continued to exist under several minor dynasties in the 13th century. According to the inscriptional evidence, weighing ceremonies were held by Pāṇḍya Sundara I (no. 69: Tamil Nadu, Tiruchchirappalli Dist.), Kāḍava Kopperuñjiṅga II (no. 70: Andhra Pradesh, Kurnool Dist.), and Yādavarāya Vīranṛsiṃha (no. 71: Andhra Pradesh, Chittoor Dist.). These kings had the *vimānas* of some temples in Tamil Nadu (Nāṭarāja at Cidambaram, Raṅganātha at Śrīraṅga, and Veṅkaṭagiri at Tirumala) covered with the gold against which they had weighed themselves. The three south Indian rulers performed these rituals immediately after victories in battle and also used part of their booty for it.

The *tulāpuruṣa* tradition also seems to have been very popular in the Vijayanagara empire (nos. 72-109). The epigraphs of the Saṅgama dynasty reveal some evidence for actual weighing ceremonies. The large number of references under Tuḷuva Kṛṣṇarāya and Acyutarāya, however, is mainly due to the fact that two verses mentioning the ritual appear in all the stereotyped royal records. In 1394 A.D., Saṅgama Harihara II celebrated a *tulāpuruṣa* ceremony at the Tuṅgabhadrā and granted two villages to an astrologer on that occasion for, among other services, the composition of the Sanskrit copper-plate grant (no. 72: Karnataka, Shimoga Dist.). Devarāya I, the son of Harihara II, performed this ritual at the Godāvarī after a military campaign in 1397 A.D., when Harihara II was still alive (no. 73: Andhra Pradesh, Karimnagar Dist.). According to a Sanskrit copper-plate record of the year 1448 A.D. (no. 75: Karnataka, Mysore Dist.), Saṅgama Mallikārjuna donated a village on Hoysaḷa territory to a number of brāhmaṇas during a *tulāpuruṣa* ceremony in the city of Vijayanagara (= Hampi), situated close to the Tuṅgabhadrā. In 1497 A.D., Tuḷuva Narasanāyaka celebrated this ritual, endowed a brāhmaṇa with a village in the region of Maisūru, and had the grant registered in a stone inscription in Sanskrit (no. 78: Karnataka, Mysore Dist.). A eulogistic verse in a copper-plate record of 1508 A.D. (no. 79: Tamil Nadu, Kanchipuram Dist.) praises Nārasiṃha, Narasanāyaka's eldest son, for performing the ceremony of weighing and other Great Gifts. Tuḷuva Kṛṣṇarāya, Nārasiṃha's younger brother and successor, adapted this verse for the genealogy of his Sanskrit copper-plate records (nos. 81-83, 85, 87-88, 90-95, 98-101: Karnataka: Mandya, Hassan and Mysore

Districts; Tamil Nadu, Kanchipuram Dist.; see note 5) and of a few stone inscriptions (e.g., no. 80: Karnataka: Bellary Dist.), adding one verse describing his own deeds with regard to the weighing ceremony. In contrast to his copper-plate grants, some of Kṛṣṇarāya's stone epigraphs register particular *tulāpuruṣa* rituals. In June 1515 A.D., for instance, this Tuḷuva king celebrated such a donative ceremony and granted many *agrāhāra* gifts in the presence of god Śūlapāṇi alias Amareśa (no. 84: Andhra Pradesh, Krishna Dist.). Kannaḍa, Telugu, and Tamil inscriptions at a temple in Kāñcī dating from the year 1532 A.D. (no. 96: Tamil Nadu, Kanchipuram Dist.) record that king Acyuta, Kṛṣṇarāya's younger brother, performed a *tulāpuruṣa* ritual together with his senior queen and Prince Veṅkaṭādri, the heir apparent. The three Sanskrit verses of another stone epigraph, which is only a few months younger (no. 97: Andhra Pradesh, Chittoor Dist.), also refer to a weighing ritual celebrated by Acyuta, his consort and the crown prince in Kāñcī. The Tamil introduction of an inscription at the Raṅganātha temple at Śrīraṅga dating from the year 1539 A.D. (no. 102: Tamil Nadu, Tiruchchirappalli Dist.) mentions that a second queen of Acyuta composed two Sanskrit verses on the occassion of a royal *tulābhāra* ritual and had them engraved at several holy places, so that "the descendants of the prince Veṅkaṭādri might rule as emperors." Various versions of these two verses, engraved in different scripts and with diverse introductory and final passages, exist at several places in Karṇataka, Andhra Pradesh and Tamil Nadu.

APPENDIX 3:
List of inscriptions referring to the weighing ceremony

1. Krishnan, K.G. 2002. Vaigai River Bed Inscription of Chendaṇ. In: *Inscriptions of the Early Pāṇḍyas*: 3.

2. Krishnan, K.G. 2002. Veḷvikuḍi Plates of Neḍuñchaḍaiyan (Varaguṇa I). In: *Inscriptions of the Early Pāṇḍyas*: 5-15.

3. Krishnan, K.G. 2002. Chiṉṉamaṉūr Plates of Varaguṇa I. In: *Inscriptions of the Early Pāṇḍyas*: 25-27.

4. Mahalingam, T.V. 1988. Tirukkodikkaval Inscription of Nrpatungavarman. In: *Inscriptions of the Pallavas*: 501-502.

5. Hultzsch, E. 1916. Udayendiram Plates of Prithivipati II. Hastimalla. *SII* 2.3-5: 375-390.

6. Nilakanta Sastri, K.A. 1933-1934. A Chola Inscription from Uttiramerur. *EI* 22: 205-207.

7. Srinivasa Rao, G.V. 1979. No. 42. *SII* 23: 20-22 (Coḷa Rājarāja I, twenty-ninth regnal year, Tamil stone inscription).

8. Fleet, J.F. 1882. Sanskṛit and Old-Canarese Inscriptions: No. CXXI. *IA* 11: 109-115 (Rāṣṭrakūṭa Dantidurga, Śaka 675, Sanskrit copper-plate grant).

9. Mirashi, V.V. & L.R. Kulkarni 1935-1936. Anjanavati Plates of Govinda III; Saka Year 722. *EI* 23: 8-18.

10. Lakshminarayan Rao, N. 1940. No. 9. *SII* 11.1: 5-6 (Rāṣṭrakūṭa Amoghavarṣa I, Śaka 784, Kannaḍa stone inscription).

11. Mirashi, V.V. 1965-1966. Jambgaon Plates of Indra III, Saka 836. *EI* 36: 223-238.

12. Bhandarkar, D.R. 1907-1908. Two Grants of Indraraja III; Saka-Samvat 836: No. I. *EI* 9: 24-33.

13. Bhandarkar, D.R. 1907-1908. Two Grants of Indraraja III; Saka-Samvat 836: No. II. *EI* 9: 33-41.

14. Kolte, V.B. 1969-1970. Two Grants of Rashtrakuta Indra III from Vajirkheda, Saka 836: A. *EI* 38: 5-20.

15. Kolte, V.B. 1969-1970. Two Grants of Rashtrakuta Indra III from Vajirkheda, Saka 836: B. *EI* 38: 20-22.

16. Mirashi, V.V. 1965-1966. Andura Plates of Govinda IV, Saka 851. *EI* 36: 257-272.

17. Barnett, L.D. 1915-1916. Kalas Inscription of Rashtrakuta Govinda IV. Saka 851. *EI* 13: 326-338.

18. Dikshit, K.N. 1935-1936. Three Copper-Plate Inscriptions from Gaonri: A. – Fragmentary grant of the Rāshṭrakūṭa Suvarṇavarsha (Govinda IV): Saka 851. *EI* 23: 101-108.

19. Bhandarkar, D.R. 1902-1903. Cambay Plates of Govinda IV; Saka-Samvat 852. *EI* 7: 26-47.

20. Rice, B.L. 1903. Cd. 76. *EC* 11: 29-30 (Rāṣṭrakūṭa Amoghavarṣa, Śaka 859, Kannaḍa stone inscription).

21. Lakshminarayan Rao, N. 1952. No. 124. *SII* 11.2: 143-144 (Cāḷukya Vikramāditya VI, ca. 1077 A.D., Kannaḍa stone inscription).

22. Barnett, L.D. 1915-1916. Inscriptions at Narendra: A. – Of the Time of Vikramaditya VI and the Kadamba Jayakesin II: A.D. 1125. *EI* 13: 298-316.

23. [Institute of Kannada Studies] 1998. Cm. 210. *EC* 11: 131-136 (Hoysaḷa Viṣṇuvardhana, 1110-1152 A.D., undated Kannaḍa stone inscription).

24. [Institute of Kannada Studies] 1990. Bl. 389. *EC* 9: 352-357 (Hoysaḷa Viṣṇuvardhana, Śaka 1055, Kannaḍa stone inscription).

25. [Institute of Kannada Studies] 1997. Ak. 244. *EC* 10: 313-315 (Hoysaḷa Viṣṇuvardhana, Śaka 1059, Kannaḍa stone inscription).

26. [Institute of Kannada Studies] 1998. Cm. 211. *EC* 11: 136-141 (Hoysaḷa Viṣṇuvardhana, Śaka 1060, Kannaḍa pillar inscription).

27. [Institute of Kannada Studies] 1990. Bl. 340. *EC* 9: 318-320 (Hoysaḷa Viṣṇuvardhana, Śaka 1063, Kannaḍa stone inscription).

28. [Institute of Kannada Studies] 1979. Ng. 64. *EC* 7: 45-49 (Hoysaḷa Narasiṃha I, Śaka 1067, Kannaḍa stone inscription).

29. [Institute of Kannada Studies] 1990. Bl. 410 and Bl. 411. *EC* 9: 377-390 (Hoysaḷa Narasiṃha I, Śaka 1082, Kannaḍa stone inscriptions).

30. [Institute of Kannada Studies] 1990. Bl. 95. *EC* 9: 51. (Hoysaḷa Narasiṃha II, 1220-1238 A.D., undated Kannaḍa pillar inscription).

31. [Institute of Kannada Studies] 1997. Ak. 317. *EC* 10: 387-393. (Hoysaḷa Someśvara, Śaka 1177, Kannaḍa stone inscription).

32. Krishna Rao, B.V. 1951-1952. Nanduru Plates of Velananti Rajendra-Choda: Saka 1091. *EI* 29: 225-247.

33. Mirashi, V.V. 1977. Kolhāpur Stone Inscription of Bhoja II: Saka Year 1104. In: *Inscriptions of the Śilāhāras* (CII, 6): 258-263.

34. Mirashi, V.V. 1977. Kaśeli Grant of Bhoja II: Saka Year 1113. In: *Inscriptions of the Śilāhāras* (CII, 6): 267-273.

35. Mirashi, V.V. 1977. Kutāpur Grant of Bhoja II: Saka Year 1113. In: *Inscriptions of the Śilāhāras* (CII, 6): 282-286.

36. Trivedi, H.V. 1989. Khajurāho Stone Inscription of Dhaṅgadeva of the Year 1059. In: *Inscriptions of the Paramāras, Chandellas, Kachchhapaghātas and Two Minor Dynasties*, III (CII, 7): 381-390.

37. Mirashi, V.V. 1955. Khairha Plates of Yasahkarna: (Kalachuri) Year 823. In: *Inscriptions of the Kalachuri-Chedi Era*, I (CII, 4): 289-299.

38. Srinivasan, P.R. 1971-1972. Barhi Plates of Yasahkarna, [Kalachuri] Year 828. *EI* 39: 57-60.

39. Mirashi, V.V. 1955. Jabalpur Plate of Yasahkarna. In: *Inscriptions of the Kalachuri-Chedi Era*, I (CII, 4): 299-305.

40. Trivedi, H.V. 1989. Gwālior Stone Inscription of Mahīpāla. In: *Inscriptions of the Paramāras, Chandellas, Kachchhapaghātas and Two Minor Dynasties*, III (CII, 7): 535-548.

41. Konow, S. 1907-1908. Chandravati Plate of Chandradeva. Samvat 1148. *EI* 9: 302-305.

42. Sahni, D.R. 1917-1918. Chandravati Plates of Chandra-Deva: V.S. 1150 and 1156: [2] Plate of Vikrama-Samvat 1156. *EI* 14: 197-200.

43. Kielhorn, F. 1896-1897. Twenty-one Copper-Plates of the Kings of Kanauj; [Vikrama-]Samvat 1171 to 1233: A. – Plate of Govindachandra of [Vikrama-] Saṃvat 1182. *EI* 4: 99-101.

44. Barnett, L.D. 1915-1916. Gagaha Plates of Govindachandra of Kanauj: Samvat 1199. *EI* 13: 216-220.

45. Kielhorn, F. 1896-1897. Twenty-one Copper-Plates of the Kings of Kanauj; [Vikrama-]Samvat 1171 to 1233: S. – Plate of Jayachandra of [Vikrama-]Saṃvat 1231. *EI* 4: 124-126.

46. Banerji, [illegible].D. 1919-1920. Barrackpur Grant of Vijayasena: The 32nd Year. *EI* 15: 278-286.

47. Basak, [illegible] G. 1915-1916. Silimpur Stone-Slab Inscription of the Time of Jayapala-Deva. *EI* 1[illegible] 283-295.

48. Sircar, D.C. 1949-1950. Nagari Plates of Anangabhima III; Saka 1151 and 1152. *EI* 28: 235-258.

49. Srinivasan, P.R. 1967-1968. Orissa State Museum Plates of Anangabhima III. *EI* 37: 317-332.

50. Chhabra, B.Ch. 1951-1952. Chatesvara Temple Inscription. *EI* 29: 121-133.

51. Sircar, D.C. 1955-1956. Asankhali Plates of Narasimha II, Saka 1225. *EI* 31: 109-128.

52. de Zilva Wickremasinghe, D.M. 1928. Ambagamuva Rock-Inscription of Vijaya-Bāhu I (1058-1114 A.D.). *EZ* 2: 202-218.

53. Paranavitana, S. 1925-1926. Polonnaruva Inscription of Vijayabahu I. *EI* 18: 330-338.

54. Paranavitana, S. 1933. Devanagala Rock-Inscription of Parākramabāhu I. *EZ* 3: 312-325.

55. de Zilva Wickremasinghe, D.M. 1928. The Slab-Inscription of Kīrti-Niśśanka-Malla (1187-1196 A.D.) at Ruvanavāli-dāgaba, Anurādhapura. *EZ* 2: 70-83.

56. de Zilva Wickremasinghe, D.M. 1928. Poḷonnaruva: Kalā-krīḍa-vinoda Gal-āsana Inscription. *EZ* 2: 128-134.

57. de Zilva Wickremasinghe, D.M. 1928. Poḷonnaruva: Häta-dāgē Portico Slab Inscription. *EZ* 2: 84-90.

58. de Zilva Wickremasinghe, D.M. 1928. Poḷonnaruva: Kāliṅga Forest Gal-āsana Inscription. *EZ* 2: 125-127.

59. de Zilva Wickremasinghe, D.M. 1928. Poḷonnaruva: Kāliṅga Park Gal-āsana Inscription. *EZ* 2: 130-134.

60. de Zilva Wickremasinghe, D.M. 1928. Poḷonnaruva: Rankot-dāgaba Gal-āsana Inscription. *EZ* 2: 134-137.

61. Paranavitana, S. 1965-1966. Ramesvaram Inscription of Nissankamalla. *EI* 36: 23-32.

62. de Zilva Wickremasinghe, D.M. 1928. Poḷonnaruva: Galpota Slab-Inscription. *EZ* 2: 98-123.

63. de Zilva Wickremasinghe, D.M. 1912. Dambulla Rock-Inscription of Kīrti Niśśanka Malla (1189-1198 A.D.). *EZ* 1: 121-135.

64. de Zilva Wickremasinghe, D.M. 1928. Kantalāi Gal-asana Inscription of Kitti Nissaṅka Malla (1187-1196 A.D.). *EZ* 2: 283-290.

65. de Zilva Wickremasinghe, D.M. 1928. Poḷonnaruva: Kir vehera Slab Inscription. *EZ* 2: 148-152.

66. de Zilva Wickremasinghe, D.M. 1928. Poḷonnaruva: A Slab-Inscription of Niśśaṅka-Malla. *EZ* 2: 153-156.

67. Paranavitana, S. 1933. Kaṭugaha-galgē Pillar-Inscription. *EZ* 3: 325-331.

68. de Zilva Wickremasinghe, D.M. 1928. Poḷonnaruva: Häṭa-dāgē Vestibule Wall-Inscription. *EZ* 2: 91-96.

69. Hultzsch, E. 1894-1895. Ranganatha Inscription of Sundara-Pandya. *EI* 3: 7-17.

70. Venkatasubba Ayyar, V. 1943. No. 247. *SII* 12: 154-156 (Kāḍava Kopperuñjiṅga II, 13th century A.D., Tamil stone inscription).

71. Subrahmanya Sastry, S. 1984. No. 91. In: *Early Inscriptions*, I: 122-123 (Yādavarāya Vīranṛsiṃha, 13th century A.D., Tamil stone inscription).

72. Rice, B.L. 1903. Ci. 13. *EC* 11: 315-317 (Saṅgama Harihara II, Śaka 1316, Sanskrit copper-plate grant).

73. Venkataramanayya, N. 1965-1966. Kalesvaram Inscription of Devaraya I, Saka 1319. *EI* 36: 199-202.

74. Rice, B.L. 1904. Tm. 11. *EC* 12: 12-13 (Saṅgama Devarāya II, Śaka 1348, Sanskrit copper-plate grant).

75. [Institute of Kannada Studies] 1974. Gu. 147. *EC* 3: 104-111 (Saṅgama Mallikārjuna I, Śaka 1369, Sanskrit copper-plate grant).

76. [Institute of Kannada Studies] 1977. Pp. 179. *EC* 6: 254-256 (Saṅgama Mallikārjuna, Śaka 1380, Kannaḍa stone inscription).

77. [Institute of Kannada Studies] 1977. Pp. 163. *EC* 6: 247-249 (Saṅgama Virūpākṣa II, Śaka 1393, Kannaḍa stone inscription).

78. [Institute of Kannada Studies] 1976. My. 225. *EC* 5: 322-323 (Tuḷuva Narasanāyaka, Śaka 1419, Sanskrit stone inscription).

79. Venkateswara, S.V. & S.V. Viswanathan 1917-1918. The Kudiyantandal Grant of Vira-Nrsimha: Saka 1429. *EI* 14: 231-240.

80. Hultzsch, E. 1892. Hampe Inscription of Krishnaraya, Dated Saka 1430. *EI* 1: 361-371.

81. [Institute of Kannada Studies] 1979. Ng. 134. *EC* 7: 131-139 (Tuḷuva Kṛṣṇarāya, Śaka 1434, Sanskrit copper-plate grant).

82. [Institute of Kannada Studies] 1990. Bl. 172. *EC* 9: 143-151 (Tuḷuva Kṛṣṇarāya, Śaka 1434, Sanskrit copper-plate grant).

83. [Institute of Kannada Studies] 1974. Nj. 398. *EC* 3: 541-544 (Tuḷuva Kṛṣṇarāya, Śaka 1435, Sanskrit copper-plate grant).

84. Lüders, H. 1902-1903. Amaravati Inscription of Krishnaraya of Vijayanagara; Saka-Samvat 1437. *EI* 7: 17-22.

85. [Institute of Kannada Studies] 1984. Hn. 8. *EC* 8: 218-225 (Tuḷuva Kṛṣṇarāya, Śaka 1437, Sanskrit copper-plate grant).

86. Narasimhaswami, H.K. 1972. No. 52. *SII* 16: 62-63 (Kannaḍa version: Shama Shastry, R. & N. Lakshminarayan Rao 1941. No. 549. *SII* 9.2: 514-515) (Tuḷuva Kṛṣṇarāya, Śaka 1438, Telugu and Kannaḍa stone inscriptions).

87. [Institute of Kannada Studies] 1979. Md. 7. *EC* 7: 189-196 (Tuḷuva Kṛṣṇarāya, Śaka 1438, Sanskrit copper-plate grant).

88. [Institute of Kannada Studies] 1977. Sr. 26. *EC* 6: 367-373 (Tuḷuva Kṛṣṇarāya, Śaka 1438, Sanskrit copper-plate grant).

89. Narasimhaswami, H.K. 1972. Nos. 57 and 58. *SII* 16: 67-69 (Tuḷuva Kṛṣṇarāya, Śaka 1438, Telugu stone inscriptions).

90. [Institute of Kannada Studies] 1997. Cp. 21. *EC* 10: 426-435 (Tuḷuva Kṛṣṇarāya, Śaka 1441, Sanskrit copper-plate grant).

91. [Institute of Kannada Studies] 1976. TN 105. *EC* 5: 504-510 (Tuḷuva Kṛṣṇarāya, Śaka 1442, Sanskrit copper-plate grant).

92. Venkateswara Ayyar, S.V. & S.V. Viswanatha 1915-1916. Conjeeveram Plates of Krishnadeva-Raya: Saka 1444. *EI* 13: 122-132.

93. [Institute of Kannada Studies] 1984. Hn. 83. *EC* 8: 292-299 (Tuḷuva Kṛṣṇarāya, Śaka 1446, Sanskrit copper-plate grant).

94. Venkateswara Ayyar, S.V. & S.V. Viswanatha 1917-1918. Udayambakam Grant of Krishna-Deva Raya: Saka 1450. *EI* 14: 168-175.

95. [Institute of Kannada Studies] 1977. Kr. 99. *EC* 6: 81-90 (Tuḷuva Acyutarāya, Śaka 1453, Sanskrit copper-plate grant).

96. Narasimhaswami, H.K. 1972. No. 97. *SII* 16: 111-112 (Kannaḍa versions: Shama Shastry, R. & N. Lakshminarayan Rao 1941. Nos. 547 and 548. *SII* 9.2: 565-568) (Tuḷuva Acyutarāya, Śaka 1454, Telugu and Kannaḍa stone inscriptions).

97. Shama Shastry, R. & N. Lakshminarayan Rao 1941. No. 549. *SII* 9.2: 568 (Tuḷuva Acyutarāya, Śaka 1455, Sanskrit stone inscription).

98. [Institute of Kannada Studies] 1979. Md. 144. *EC* 7: 339-346 (Tuḷuva Acyutarāya, Śaka 1456, Sanskrit copper-plate grant)

99. [Institute of Kannada Studies] 1997. Ak. 240. *EC* 10: 293-307 (Tuḷuva Acyutarāya, Śaka 1456, Sanskrit copper-plate grant).

100. [Institute of Kannada Studies] 1976. My. 105. *EC* 5: 250-260 (Tuḷuva Acyutarāya, Śaka 1457, Sanskrit copper-plate grant).

101. [Institute of Kannada Studies] 1990. Bl. 195. *EC* 9: 185-193 (Tuḷuva Acyutarāya, Śaka 1461, Sanskrit copper-plate grant).

102. Ramanatha Ayyar, A.R. 1937-1938. Srirangam Inscription of Achyutaraya: Saka 1461. *EI* 24: 285-290.

103. Kielhorn, F. 1894-1895. Unamanjeri Plates of Achyutaraya; Saka-Samvat 1462. *EI* 3: 147-158.

104. [Institute of Kannada Studies] 1979. Ng. 107. *EC* 7: 100-113 (Tuḷuva Sadāśivarāya, Śaka 1467, Sanskrit copper-plate grant).

105. Venkateswara, S.V. & S.V. Viswanathan. 1917-1918. Bevinahalli Grant of Sadasiva-Raya: Saka 1473. *EI* 14: 210-231.

106. [Institute of Kannada Studies] 1984. Hn. 9. *EC* 8: 226-237 (Tuḷuva Sadāśivarāya, Śaka 1483, Sanskrit copper-plate grant).

107. Natesa Aiyar, V. 1911-1912. Maredapalli Grant of Sri-Rangaraya II; Saka 1497. *EI* 11: 326-336.

108. Gopinatha Rao, T.A. 1913-1914. Dalavay-Agraharam Plates of Venkatapati-deva-Maharaya I; – Saka-Samvat 1508. *EI* 12: 159-187.

109. Gopinatha Rao, T.A. 1921-1922. Vellangudi Plates of Venkatapati-Deva-Maharaya I: Saka-Samvat 1520. *EI* 16: 298-321.

The Memorial Stone (*Pāḷiyā*) Inscriptions: The Cultural Heritage of Gujarat, Saurashtra and Kutch

BHARATI SHELAT

In India, rocks, stone slabs, stone or wooden pillars, copper plates or other metal surfaces, tablets and other objects have been used for incising epigraphs. Gujarat, Saurashtra and Kutch are particularly rich in archaeological, epigraphic and literary material. The majority of epigraphs record donations made in favour of religious establishments or the installation of images for worship. Innumerable dedicatory inscriptions, large and small, are engraved on the walls and other parts of important religious establishments and centres of pilgrimage. Eulogistic compositions called *praśasti* were composed and engraved on stone slabs or pillars to commemorate public works such as the excavation of a tank or a step-well or the construction of a temple by a royal or ordinary personage or group of individuals. These *praśastis* were composed by poets of great ability and their compositions are of high order. They provide valuable information for the reconstruction of political and cultural history. The epigraphs recording royal grants of land were generally engraved on copper plates. Memorial stone (*pāḷiyā*) inscriptions and *satī* stone inscriptions commemorate such events as the fall of a hero in battle or social customs such as the self-immolation of a widow and the head-offering of a devotee (*kamala-pūjā*). In some cases, an inscription may embody a *kāvya* in many cantos or a drama in several acts; for example, the Udaipur Rāja-samudra inscription called *Rājapraśasti-kāvya* (EI 29-30, Appendix) and the Ajmer *Lalitavigraharāja* and *Harakelināṭaka* inscriptions (IA 20, pp. 201ff.).

Epigraphic records are especially valuable as they are sometimes the only extant contemporary sources. Moreover, they preserve accounts of the past in the original language and the script of the corresponding periods.

MEMORIAL STONES (*PĀḶIYĀ*)

Memorial stones, known as *pāḷiyā* in Gujarati, have been found in large numbers in mainland Gujarat, Saurashtra and Kutch in western India. They are most often referred to as "hero stones" or "*satī* stones". *Pāḷiyās* recording the death of heroes while fighting in battle generally contain three panels. The upper panel on the semi-circular or triangular portion of the stone depicts the symbols of the sun and the moon. The middle panel shows a warrior riding a horse, or a *padāti* (footsoldier), or a woman offering herself for immolation with her arm, decorated with *kaṅkaṇa* (bangles), raised upward; sometimes the widows of the warriors are depicted entering into the fire. The lower panel contains the inscription regarding the event.

Pāḷiyās are raised in memory of persons who died a violent death, or died as martyrs, or who, when living, had been remarkable for holiness or some other notable trait of character. These stones may be set in an enclosure, under a pipal tree, on the border of a village, near the village reservoir, or at the spot where the person was slain. The stones, which have sometimes one of their corners flattened, are generally oblong, about 122 cm high, 61 cm broad and 15-30 cm thick. They are sometimes set on a masonry platform, or are sunk about 29 cm deep in the ground.

Dates and ceremony for setting up *pāḷiyās*

Memorial stones are set up either on the fourteenth day of the dark fortnight of *Āśvina* (September-October) or on the fourteenth day of the bright fortnight of *Kārttika* (October-November). When they are set up, the people of the village assemble and the stone is washed with milk and smeared with red lead and clarified butter. Palm juice liquor and sesame oil are poured over it and the flesh of the sacrificial animal is cooked and served to the guests. On Sundays, Tuesday and Thursdays, on their yearly death days, on the second, fifth, thirteenth, fourteenth and fifteenth days of the bright fortnight of *Kārttika*, on the *Holi* festival in March, on the thirteenth, fourteenth, and fifteenth days of the dark fortnight of *Śrāvaṇa* (July-August), on the fourteenth day of the dark fortnight of *Bhādrapada* (August-September), and on the tenth day of the bright fortnight and the fourteenth day of the dark fortnight of *Āśvina*, the members of the deceased family wash the stone with milk, paint it with red lead, scatter flowers over it, lay a sesame oil lamp near it, and set a flag over it (BG 9.1, pp. 363f.).

Types of memorial stones

Traditionally, memorial stones are divided into five types: *pāḷiyā*, *khāṃbhī*, *śūrapūrā*, *ṭhesa*, and *sūradhana*.

1. Pāḷiyā

The word *pāḷiyā* may be derived from the Sanskrit root *pāl* "to protect", and *pāḷiyā* is explained as "the death of the hero while protecting the cows from the ememies' freebooters". Some scholars derive *pāḷiyā* from *pālayitṛ* > *pālayiu* > *pāliu* > *pālio*. In the Kutch region, the terms for *pāḷiyā* are *pālīu*, *pālīa*, *palaa*, *pāvaḷiyo*, and *pārio*, as well as the sanskritised *puṣkalaka*. In Gujarati, *pāḷa* means "a group of soldiers in a skirmish" or "army". When a brave man in a *pāḷa* is killed in battle, his memorial stone is raised at the very place where he died. Thus the hero stone of a brave man who died in *pāḷa* is called *pāḷiyā* (Bhatti 1987: 8).

In Saurashtra, among the Kathis, Khuman, Bala and other groups of Scythic descent, *pāḷiyā* or *jujhar* (sacrificial pillars) are conspicuous under the walls of every town, arranged in lines, irregular groups and circles. On each is displayed in rude relief the warrior, with lance in hand, generally on horseback though sometimes in his chariot, and the manner of his death. On the coast, the pirates of Budha, at Dwarka, are depicted boarding from the shrouds (Tod 1920, I: 90).

Jujhars are a type of cenotaphs, also known as *pāḷiyās*, which are common in Gujarat and Rajasthan. The word *jujhar* may have been derived from *jodhā* (Sanskrit *yoddhā* "warrior"). Another term for *pāḷiyā* is *sara*, which is used in the phrases "erect a *sara*" (Gujarati *sara khoḍavī*) "set up a *sara*" (*sara maṇḍavī*), or " place a sara" (*sara mūkavī*). According to one belief, when the head of the warrior falls down a *sara* is set up, and when his trunk falls, a *pāḷiyā* is raised. In Kutch too, the word *sara* is used in the sense of *pāḷiyā*. *Sara* seems to be derived from *śura* "brave".

The terms *cago, cagaliyo, cagā, chagā, sagā or śaga* ("heap") are used to refer to small stones or small pieces of mud raised in commemoration of an individual. *Śaga* seems to be derived from Sanskrit *śṛṅga* "top". *Pārso* is also used in the sense of *pāḷiyā*. It seems to be derived from Sanskrit *pauruṣa*/Prakrit *porasa* "heroism, bravery". In Kutch it is used to mean "golden man".

2. Khāṃbhī-khāṃbhā

The word *khāṃbhī* or *khāṃbhā* is derived from Sanskrit *[illegible]ambha* > *khaṃbha* > *khāṃbhā* > *khāṃbhī*, although some schola[illegible] derive it from Sanskrit *stambha* (> *thaṃbha* > *khaṃbha*). The wor[illegible] *stambha* is used in the sense of *khāṃbhī* in the following lines:

> *Gāma gāma ubhā stambha, pokāratā śuranā guṇani gāthā varaṇī*
> (UNR 46, pp. 6, 420)
>
> The *stambhas* (i.e., *khāṃbhīs*) raised at the outskirts of the villages sing the stories of the virtues of the brave men.

The word *khāṃbhī* is used in these lines:

> *Loṛaṇa caḍhāve lohī tārī khāṃbhī māthe khīmrā* (UNR 46, p. 568)
>
> Khimarā, Loṛaṇa is pouring blood on your *khāṃbhī*.

Heavy stone slabs raised vertically at the edge of the village are called *khāṃbhā*. In Saurashtra, *khāṃbhīs* from five to eight feet tall are seen at Pālakhaḍa and Mahaḍeśvara near Porbandar and at Mandor Ṭimbā near Prabhās. *Khāṃbhīs* are crude tall stone slabs without any engraving. They are raised in the memory of a warrior on the spot, immediately after his death.

3. Śūrāpurā

The Kāṭhī people made Saurashtra their home and fought for their country, women and vows. When they died while fighting, their hero stones were raised at the edge of the village. These Kāṭhīs were brave warriors and their *pāḷiyās* are called *śūrāpurā*. On these *śūrāpurās* are shown the figure of a horse rider and a barber holding a hookah. Such *śūrāpurās* are seen in Gadhada and Jasdan and in villages populated by Kāṭhīs. At Bodidar (Kodinar), there is a *śūrāpurā* of Ugābodara from the Bodara family of Āhiras, dating from about the 11th century A.D. (UNR 46, p 541).

4. Ṭhesa

Small crude stones or roughly hewn blocks of stone with rubbed red lead, raised along with *pāḷiyās*, are called *ṭhesa*. People who could not afford to raise *pāḷiyās* would set up *ṭhesa*.

5. Sūradhana

If a man dies of accident, suicide or murder, his family members raise a *khāṃbhī* for him, which is called *sūradhana*.

Trāga pāḷiyās

Trāga pāḷiyās are peculiar to the regions of Kutch and Saurashtra. In these reliefs a man is shown standing, squatting or riding a horse while piercing his own neck with a dagger. In popular belief, *cāraṇa* women are believed to be living deities and their men call themselves *devīputras*. Their curse was very much dreaded because of their capacity to perform *trāgu*, that is, killing themselves in the presence of their opponent with a dagger or sword and sprinkling blood over the enemy, cursing him with total destruction. *Trāgu* was considered one of the proofs of the divine powers of the *cāraṇas*. Those who died such a death are worshipped as gods, and hero or *satī* stones are installed for them. This practice seems to have been also adopted by brāhmaṇa and other communities.

Avagatiyā stones

Memorials for those who died of snakebite or attack by wild animals, known as *avagatiyā,* are generally indistinguishable from hero and *satī* stones. In Porbandar and vicinity, the snake or wild animal that caused the death is shown along with the deceased. A memorial stone for a woman bitten by a snake has been found at Ratdi, near Porbandar (Fischer & Shah 1970: 132, pl. 43).

Govardhana pāḷiyās

Govardhana stones are found in Rajasthan and with slight differences in Saurashtra.[1] A *govardhana* is shaped like a cube with a rounded or pyramidal roof, with three of its sides sculpted (Fischer & Shah 1970: 157ff.).

Tribal memorials in Gujarat

Tribals erect memorials for heroes, priests or commoners, whether they died a natural or an accidental death. Among the Chaudhari tribe, each individual is installed as an orange-coloured figure on a stone under a clay dome about 1 to 2 meters high. These memorials have different names among different regions and tribes of Gujarat, such as *gaṭlā* (Panchmahals: Bhils), *khāṃbhā* (Nizar area, south Gujarat: Vasāvās), *rihama* (Banaskantha and Sabarkantha: Garāsias), *sokli* (for women) and *agath* (for men; Sabarkantha: Garāsias), *vetra* (Surat area: Chaudhari, Gāmitas), *cīra* (Panchamahals: Bhils), *khatrī* (Baroda area: Rathvas, Naiks), and *khatru* (Surat area: Chaudhari, Gāmitas).

Khatrīs are erected in honour of those who died accidental deaths, who were murdered, or who were distinguished persons such as priests, heads of villages etc. They are worshipped on all festivals. *Khatrus*, generally around 10 to 30 cm in size, are installed in memory of individuals in the Chaudhari tribe. The Gāmitas also install *khatrus* for the dead. *Gaṭlās* are mostly seen in Panchamahal District. They are in stone and erected for those who die of old age as well as for those

---

[1] *Kumar*, no. 574, p. 393.

who met an accidental death. *Vetras* are installed after the death of a pregnant woman or when the spirit of a dead woman is believed to be haunting the area (Fischer & Shah 1970: 101ff.).

ANTIQUITY OF THE *PĀḶIYĀ* TRADITION

No primitive or prehistoric memorials of pre-Harappan times have yet been discovered. Excavations at Rupar, Lothal (Dist. Ahmedabad), and Rangpur (Surendranagar) in Gujarat and other contemporary sites in India have not yielded stone memorials of any sort, although burial sites have been brought to light. Numerous megaliths, which to a certain extent approximate stone memorials, have been found in South India, but they have not been dated earlier than the 3rd and 2nd centuries B.C. But a megalith is purely sepulchral in character, while a memorial stone is commemorative, raised in memory or in honour of the dead, and does not form part of the actual ceremony of the disposal of the dead. The main purpose of the memorial is to keep alive or revive the memory of the deceased and to pay homage or respect to him on certain occasions, according to the social and religious practices of the community. No such memorial either in stone or any other form is known to have been erected before Vedic times in India. The Vedic Āryans usually cremated or burnt the dead, although in the cases of infants, unmarried youths, and *sannyāsins*, they practised burial. They did not favour the erection of monuments over the remains, relics, or ashes of the dead, though there are certain Vedic texts which provide for such erections. These texts prescribe four stages of the disposal of the dead: cremation; collection of the charred bones and depositing them in an urn or throwing them into sacred waters or rivers; expiatory rites called *śānti-karma*; and erection of a monument over the bones or relics. The Śatapatha-brāhmaṇa also gives details about the erection of a mound.[2]

In certain specified cases, sepulchral monuments like *loṣṭa-cittis* (tumuli or mounds), partly of earth and partly of bricks, were erected

---

[2] For memorial monuments, see Śatapatha-brāhmaṇa 13.8 (and Kāṇva recension 11.8); Baudhāyana-pitṛmedhasūtra 1.13-16.

by the Vedic Āryans over the relics of their dead. A similar practice prevailed amongst the non-Āryan societies of eastern India in those days. A few scattered references to pillars are found in the Ṛgveda in connection with the funeral practices of the Āryans. The Ṛgveda (10.13.12; 10.18.13) refers to a *sthāṇu* or pillar, probably meaning a wooden post. But the significance of the references to pillar or pillars as part of the sepulchral mound (*loṣṭa-citti*) is not very clear from the Vedic texts. Whether the pillars were mentioned in poetic vocabulary referring to a house to shelter the mound, or whether a pillar or pillars were erected as part of the mound, and if so how they were erected, are also not clear. The later Vedic sūtras are also silent, presumably because this was not a normal practice in later times (Kane 1973: 200). Interesting evidence is found from the excavations of the post-Vedic burial mounds of Lauria-Nandangadh in north Bihar. Here a wooden post was found in the centre of each of the two mounds at the spot where the bones were deposited, though whether the pillar was connected or not cannot be ascertained (Settar & Sontheimer 1982: 74ff.).

The primitive menhirs of the prehistoric period represent the same tradition of raising memorial steles or stones. Some menhirs in the Kerala country are rooted to the laterite and scattered far and wide. Usually they are monolithic rude granitic slabs oriented north-south and standing high above the laterite ground. The menhir at Ānapāra near Trichur (Cochin) is locally known as *paṭakallu*, a memorial stone on a battlefield, or *pulachikallu*, commemoration of a *pulachi* who died on the spot. Similar monoliths are seen at Kuttur, Choorakattukara and Muttam (AI 5, pp. 39f.).

In the historical period, traces of the *pāliyā* tradition are found from the 2nd century A.D. The erection of memorial pillars similar to hero and *satī* stones in honour of dead relatives is referred to in several records of the early centuries of the Christian era, which characterize the object on which they are engraved as *yaṣṭi*. The erection of memorial pillars in honour of one's dead relatives is referred to in early records like the Suivihār (Bahāwalpur, Pakistan) copper plate inscription of the regnal year 11 of Kaniṣka I (= A.D. 89 or 139), in which it is recorded that Balanandi made the *yaṣṭi* for Nāgadatta, Damatrāta's disciple (SI no. 41). The five inscriptions of the Kārdamaka Kṣatrapa Cāṣṭana found at Andhau (Kutch), dated Śaka era 11 (JAIH 2, pp. 104f.) and 52 (SI nos. 63-66), are memorial *yaṣṭi* inscriptions. The inscriptions of Śaka 52 (A.D. 130) refer to the *yaṣṭis* raised by Madana in the memory of his sister, brother and wife, and by Śreṣṭhadatta, a Buddhist monk, in the memory of his son. The Daulatpur *yaṣṭi* inscription records that the *yaṣṭi* was erected by the Ābhira Regareśvaradeva, son of Varāhadāsa and grandson of Jaitraka, for Prītisvāmī, son of Vasudotaka, who was of the Vasu gotra, for the well-being of their family (JOIB 27, pp. 34ff.).

Sometimes the memorial pillar bore the representation of the person in whose memory it was raised. Such a pillar was called *chāyā-stambha* or "image pillar" (ARIE 1957-58, no. B26).[3] Examples are the Nagarjunakonda pillar inscriptions (*chāya-thabho*) of the time of Ikṣvāku Vīrapuruṣadatta, dated in the year Vijaya (= A.D. 273-274; SI no. 102A) and of the time of Rudrapuruṣadatta (*chāyā-khambho*), regnal year 11 (mid-4th century A.D.; SI no. 104A)

The Khāvḍā (Kutch) *yaṣṭi* inscription of the time of King Rudradāman I, dated Śaka [6]2, Śrāvaṇa [śu./ba.?] 15 (= A.D. 140), records the erection of a *yaṣṭi* in memory of A....ka, son of Śatruṃsaha, a *śrāmaṇera* (novice Buddhist monk), by his son Dhanadeva. (The names of the *śrāmaṇera* and his *gotra* are not preserved completely.) The record belongs to the reign of king Rudradāman I, the son of Jayadāman, grandson of Cāṣṭana, and great-grandson of Ysāmotika of the Kārdamaka Kṣatrapa family. The record is incised in Brāhmī characters of the 2nd century A.D. and the language is Sanskrit influenced by Prakrit (JOIB 11, pp. 237f.).

The Mūlavāsara (near Dwarka) inscription of the time of Mahākṣatrapa Rudrasena I (Gadre 1943: 1ff.) is also a sepulchral stele inscription for the son of Vaṇijaka, who sacrificed his own life for the

---

[3] Sometimes a lamp would be placed in the hands of the image of a dead person which had been made expressly for the purpose of burning a perpetual lamp before a deity. Such lamps were called *chāyā-dīpa* (SII 5, no. 1205).

sake of his friend on Śaka 122, Vaiśakha ba. di. 5 (= 21 April, A.D. 200).

The Gaḍhā (Jasdan) *yaṣṭi* inscription of the time of Rudrasena I, Śaka year 127 (= A.D. 205), Bhādrapada ba. di. 5, refers to a *śilāmayī yaṣṭi* (*lāṭha*) raised in memory of Kharapārtha by his brothers (SI no. 72; EI 16, p. 238). Such *lastis* or *yaṣṭis* were frequently raised during the Kṣatrapa period.

During the Gupta period, the Eran posthumous ṣtone pillar inscription of the time of King Bhānugupta, dated Gupta era 191, Śrāvaṇa ba. di. 7 (= 12 Aug., A.D. 510; CII 3, pp. 91ff.), records that a chieftain or noble named Goparāja came in King Bhānugupta's company to the place where the pillar was set up and fought a battle in which he was killed, his wife accompanying him by cremating herself on his funeral pyre (i.e., she became *satī*). This is one of the earliest recorded instances of the pratice of *satī.* In the Nepal inscription of Mānadeva (IA 9, pp. 164-165, ll. 7f.), Rājyavatī, the widow of Dharmadeva, bids her son Mānadeva take up the government in order that she may follow her deceased husband to the other world.[4] This took place in A.D. 705 (IA 14, pp. 344, 350). As noted by Alexander Cunningham, therc are several other *satī* pillars at Eran, but of much later date.

Numerous hero stones are scattered around different parts of the country, especially in western India, the Deccan and South India. They generally began to appear from the 6th century A.D. and continued till late medieval times. The custom is in vogue even today among many tribes in the country. The evidence of the hero stones indicates that cattle raids were common in post-Gupta times, and prote ting cattle from raiders had become a major concern. Village youth often encountered cattle-lifters and sometimes were killed in t e ensuing skirmish. It is in memory of such heroes that memorials in he form of hero stones were erected. This suggests that cattle keeping had become more widespread than agriculture; pastoralism had become a mode of subsistence, resulting in frequent cattle-raids. A similar situation pre-

---

[4] *kṛtvā ca yuddhaṃ sumahatprakāśaṃ svargaṃ gato divyanarendrakalpaḥ / bhaktānuraktā ca priyā ca kāntā bhāryānugatāgnirāśim //*

vailed in medieval times, too, when the menace of freebooters (*thugs* and *peṇḍharis*) became rampant. It should be noted in this context that many village deities were originally *vīras* (heroes), for instance, Śrī-Viṭṭhala of Pandharpur, the most important god of the Deccan. He has been referred to by Candradhara Svāmī, the founder of the Mahānubhāva sect in the 13th century A.D., as a hero who died while protecting cattle. Khaṇḍobā, another important deity, also was a *vīra* (Dhavalikar 2003: 173f.).

Opinions differ on the origin of the practice of raising *pāḷiyās*. Some scholars see its origin in hero worship. Others believe that the heroic tribes of Kutch and Saurashtra did not hesitate to sacrifice their lives for the country, vows, justice, morality, etc. The practice seems to reflect a sense of the uncertainty and fragility of life. When a primitive sailor drowned in the ocean, his last wish was that a *pāḷiyā* be raised for him; a *bhuvā* would speak and the sailor's *pāḷiyā* would be raised. This primitive tradition of setting *pāḷiyās* is mixed with superstitions.

MEMORIAL STONE INSCRIPTIONS FROM GUJARAT

Memorial stones abound in the Gujarat region and are found in great numbers in villages. The practice of carving sculptures and inscriptions on memorial stones was widely in vogue in Gujarat, Saurashtra and Kutch during the medieval period. The earliest known *pāḷiyā* inscription is from Abhapur in the Poḷo forest area of Vijaynagar District (Sabarkantha, north Gujarat). It is a *govardhan*-type *pāliyā* of a *padāti* (footsoldier) dated V.S. 812 (= A.D. 756; UNR 46, p. 435). From this area thirty-four *pāliyās* bearing inscriptions dated before the 14th century A.D. have been found. On a *pāliyā* from Poḷo dated V.S. 1350 (= A.D. 1293-94), the thin garments of the male and the female figures are carved in Greek style (UNR 46, p. 436). A *pāliyā* from Ujedia (near Prantij, Sabarkantha), dated V.S. 1362 (= A.D. 1305-06), shows the figure of King Samarasiṃha on horseback, with the horse decorated with long armour in the Greek style. A *pāḷiyā* of a decorated camel-rider dated V.S. 1722 (= A.D. 1665-66) was found in Kokta

(Viramgam, Dist. Ahmedabad; UNR 46, p. 434). An elephant rider is carved on a *pāḷiyā* at the village Rupal (Himmatnagar-Sabarkantha). A decorated *padāti pāḷiyā* dated V.S. 1758 (= A.D. 1701-02) was found in Kasor (Nadiad Dist., Kheda; UNR 46, p. 435). A noteworthy *khāṃbhī* of the Yelu wrestler and his wife Kuñjā along with four other *khāṃbhīs* depicting wrestler couples has been raised at the village of Delmal (Dist. Mehsana, north Gujarat; UNR 46, p. 437).

In Dolariya Lunavada (Pancamahal) a *pāḷiyā* of a warrior is carved in Greek style. Also in Thānāsāvaḷī (Lunavada) there is a round *ranacagā* of a warrior with an oval top on which are carved the figures of the sun and the moon (UNR 46, p. 433).

A *pāḷiyā* from Vadali (Idar, north Gujarat) from about the 16th century A.D. depicts the hero with a sword and shield fighting a tiger to protect the cows of the village. At the top are figures of the [illegible]n and the moon and below, a badly worn inscription (Inamdar 1936: [illegible]3, pl. XX, 43a).

A *ranacagā* found at Delmal (Mehsana) shows King Ajayapāla of Ajmer hunting a boar, depicted with Greek style helmet and armour. A horizontal *khāṃbhī* from Harsoli (Ahmedabad) depicts the Devasenā of king Ajayapāla (UNR 46, p. 432).

Four *pāḷiyā* inscriptions with sculptures of warriors have been found from Desar (Halol, Panchamahal Dist.):

1. Inscription dated V.S. 1347, Kārttika ba. di. 12, Budha (= 29 Nov., A.D. 1290), recording that in Dahisara village a warrior who was the son of Mehr Sāmanta was slain in a fight.
2. Inscription dated V.S. 1358, Phālguna ba. di. ... (= Feb. ..., A.D. 1302), with a horseman with sword in his hand in the lower portion.
3. Inscription dated year V.S. 1369 (= A.D. 1312-13), with depiction of a warrior with sword and shield in his hands.
4. Inscription dated V.S. 1372, Māgha ba. di. 11, Budha (= 21 Jan., 1316), recording that during the reign of Rāṇaka Jayantasiṃha, Punāka was slain in battle.[5]

[5] *Bulletin of the Chunilal Gandhi Vidyabhavan* 6-7 (1959-60), pp. 109f.

Three *pāḷiyā* incriptions have been recently found at the village Tajpur (Dist. Ahmedabad). All three are of the *padāti* type, with figures of foot-soldiers holding sword and shield carved on the upper panel. Of the three *pāḷiyās,* one is dated V.S. 1761 (= A.D. 1704-05) and the other two seem (on the basis of my own observation) to belong to the 19th century A.D.

Plenty of *satī* stones have been found from Gujarat, for example, one from Rupal (Himmatnagar, north Gujarat) depicting a *satī* woman lying on the fire (UNR 46, p. 436). A *pāḷiyā* with an inscription of the 17th century depicting the horse-rider king Arjunjī and his two *satī* queens Padmābāī and Amarībāī was found at Chadotara (Palanpur – Banaskantha; UNR 46, p. 437).

At the Dudheśvara cistern in Ahmedabad, there was found in the basin of a well a mutilated marble *satī pāḷiyā* (FIGURE 1) of one Rūpachanda with an inscription dated V.S. 1672, Vaiśākha śu. di. 3, Guru (= 20 April, A.D. 1615).[6] In the two corners of the upper panel are carved the figures of the sun and the moon. The middle of the upper panel shows a horse-rider and three female figures, with the heads mutilated. In the margin is an inscription in Devanāgarī script and Gujarati language, recording that three wives of Rūpacanda, named Rūpaśrī, Komā and Kesarajanī, became *satī* (*traṇe sāgamana kīdho*) after the de th of Rūpacanda, who was the son of Sonapāla and grandson of Ṛṣ hadāsa. They belonged to the Osval caste, Vṛddha Śākhā, and Loḍhā Gotra.

A beautifully carved unique *satī* stone of Tejabā was found in a Śiva temple at Kanisa (Tal. Khambhat, Dist. Kheda). The upper panel shows the figures of the sun and the moon. In the middle panel are two beautiful *thāpās* (impression of open hands with red power) and a figure of Gaṇeśa in the middle, with *buddhi siddhi* on either side. In the lower panel the goddess Siṃhavahinī Durgā is represented (UNR 46, p. 433).

---

[6] Jote 1953: 667; *Jain Sāhitya Saṃshodhak* 3, (Ahmedabad, V.S. 1984), pp. 393ff.

Some *pāḷiyā* inscriptions record the *jauhara* practiced by Rajput women when their husbands' death on the battlefield is inevitable. One such *pāḷiyā* depicting *jauhara* is found from the village Gaṇeragadh (Tal. Khedabrahma, Sabarkantha; UNR 45, pp. 223f.).

Other *pāḷiyā* inscriptions record the *kamalapūjā* or offering of one's head to Lord Śiva. For example, a *pāḷiyā* inscription dated V.S. 1968 (= A.D. 1911-12) refers to the *kamalapūjā* by Cāraṇa Śaṅkara Jīvā, who cut his head and offered it to Śiva. There is another *kamalapūjā pāḷiyā* in the Śaraneśvara temple near Abhapura in the Poḷo forest area (Vijaynagar, Sabarkantha; UNR 46, p. 439). At Sondarada (Tal. Keshod, Dist. Junagadh), there is a *khāṃbhī* of Rāyajādā (Rajput) Amarasaṅghjī, who could not protect the cow of a tailor which was being stolen by the Mahiyā people. As headman of the village, Amarasaṅghajī felt remorse for failing to protect the cow, and immediately went to a Śiva temple and offered his head as a *kamalapūjā*. On every fourteenth dark night of Āśvina, the village people worship Amarasaṅghjī at his *khāṃbhī* (UNR 46, p. 460).

The Khambhalia (Navanagar) *pāḷiyā* inscription dated V.S. 1749/ Śaka 1615, Vaiśākha śu. di. 10 (= 5 May, A.D. 1693) records that a Gujaratī brāhmaṇa woman named Lāḍabāī became *satī* at the death of her husband Śaṅkara Raghunātha, who offered his head as *kamalapūjā* (IK no. 151).

Two hero stone inscriptions were found on the bank of the stream Raya, a tributary of the Narmada from the south, at the village Vaghodia, near Rajapipala. They appear to record the death of two persons, one of them belonging to the Chāpotkaṭa clan, in a battle at the village Padriaka during the reign of the ruler Viśāla in V.S. 1311, Phālguna śu. di. 6, Śani (= 13 Feb., A.D. 1255; VVRB 1, pp. 6f.). According to the copper-plate of Jaitrasiṃha (V.S. 1473), this King Viśāla was a contemporary of Arjuna Deva Vaghela of north Gujarat.

Two inscriptions of the Bhīl Vasavās (i.e., the headmen of Bhīl villages), dated V.S. 1419 (= A.D. 1362-63; IK no. 16) and V.S. 1514, Jyestha śu. di. 13, Ravi (IK no. 17), were found on memorial columns at Maṇḍālā on the river Karjan (Dist. Bharuch). At Vadava (north-west of Umarpada-Bharuch), there stands a Bhīl memorial stone bearing an inscription dated V.S. 1476, Phālguna śu. di. 2[6*], Maṅgala (= 20 Feb., A.D. 1420; IK no. 18). The *khāṃbhī* on which the inscription is carved has panels depicting the portrait and mode of living of a Vasāvā brāhmaṇa who seems to have ruled over the hilly tract of the Rajpipala area in the beginning of the 15th century. A similar inscription occurs at Paṭāvalī near the Dhāmaṇmāḷ peak of the Gujarat Satpuras. It is dated V.S. 1481, Māgha ba. di. 5 (= 7 Feb., A.D. 1425; IK no. 19).

An inscribed *khāṃbhī* in Gujarati, found at Chiklota near Netrang (Vasāvā Dungar, Narmada Valley), dated V.S. 1571, Phālguṇa ba. di. 5, [So]ma (= 5 March, A.D. 1515) discloses the existence of such Bhīl principalities in the area (IK no. 25).

MEMORIAL STONE INSCRIPTIONS FROM SAURASHTRA

One of the oldest *pāḷiyās*, found at Amaratvel (Bhavnagar), is dated V.S. 1042 (= A.D. 986) and records the death of a brāhmaṇa man in a fight and his wife's *satī*.[7] James Tod visited Ghumli (Dist. Jamnagar) in 1822 and read five *pāḷiyās* there dated V.S. 1112, Kārttika [śu./ba.?] 13, V.S. 1118, Phālguna śu. di. 15, Soma, and V.S. 1119, Kārttika [śu./ ba.?], but they are no longer at the site. In 1837 Captain LeGrand Jacob noted about a hundred *pāḷiyās* in Ghumli, depicting *padātis* with sword and shield and horsemen with bow and umbrella. Their language is Sanskrit with Prakrit influences, and the script is early Nāgarī. Two *pāḷiyā* inscriptions from Ghumli are dated V.S. 1318, Phālguna śu. di. 15, Bhauma (= 7 March, A.D. 1262, a lunar eclipse day).[8]

A *khāṃbhī* inscription of the time of Jethvā Rāṇā Rāmadevajī dated V.S. 1460, Māgha ba. di. 5, Śukra (= 1 Feb., A.D. 1404) found at Ghumli (Dist. Jamnagar) records that during the reign of Rāmadevajī [III] the tax on cows and pasture land was cancelled, and that anyone who would break this order would suffer the sin of killing a cow (UNR 46, pp. 445f.).

---

[7] *Kathiawad Sarvasangraha* 1987: 282; Shah 1992: 24.

[8] IK no. 1[illegible]. *Vāk* (Saurashtra University, Rajkot), March 1972, p. 110, no. 3.

A memorial stone lying in the public library at Somanath Patan, dated V.S. 1355, Āṣāḍha śu. di. 7, Śani (= 6 June, A.D. 1299), records that two Vājā warriors named Padmala and their brother Depālasiṃha fell at the door of Somanātha temple while fighting with the Turuṣkas, that is, the forces of Ulugh Khān, the General of Alauddin Khilji of Delhi, who invaded and destroyed the town (IK no. 17).

A *pāḷiyā* dated V.S. 1966 (= A.D. 1909-10) belonging to two brave men of the famous businessman Lohāṇā Thakkar Premjī Devarāja Māvāṇi's family was raised near the Sākshī Gopāla temple at Dwarka (Saurashtra; UNR 46, p. 488). These two men lost their lives while protecting Dwarka from attacks by outsiders. Two other *pāḷiyās* of Rajgor brāhmaṇas have been found underneath the umbrella-like stone structure near the temple. One of them, dated Saṃ. 1889 (= A.D. 1832-33), contains the name Rājagara Jeṭhā. The upper panel shows the figures of the sun and the moon and the middle portion, the figures of two warriors in royal garments. These Rājagara brāhmaṇas were the priests of the Vaghera rulers.

In two small shrines near the adjoining *chatrī* there are two *pāva-riyās*, dated V.S. 1780 (= A.D. 1723-24), for two Gugaḷī brāhmaṇas named Pādha Kāśīrāma and Pādha Makanjī (UNR 46, p. 489). These two brothers sacrified their lives in fighting against the invasion of the Muslims. About twenty *pāḷiyās* of Gugaḷī and Aboṭī brāhmaṇas are found on the way to Dvarkādhīś temple. These brāhmaṇas sacrificed their lives for the protection of the temple.

Four *pāḷiyā* inscriptions have been found at Mesvāṇa (Junagadh) with the dates V.S. 1444, Māgaśara, *kṛṣṇa-amāvāsyā* (= 11 Dec., A.D. 1387, a solar eclipse day), V.S. 1470, Āsāḍha ba. di. 7, Soma (= 9 July, A.D. 1414), V.S. 1488, Māgaśara śu. di. 5(2*), Budha (= 7 Nov., A.D. 1431), and V.S. 1495, Māgha śu. di. 3, Ravi (= 18 Jan., A.D. 1439). The *pāḷiyā* of V.S. 1444 depicts the sun, moon, and Śiva liṅgas. Three of the *pāḷiyās* record the death of the warriors in battle, while the fourth commemorates the death of Ghaṇāṇiyā Puñjā in a fight while protecting cows during the reign of the Cūḍāsamā King Mahi-pāla. In all four epigraphs the name of the village is given as Mesuāṇa or Mesuāṇaka (IK nos. 46, 65, 70, 71).

Five *pāḷiyā* inscriptions from Vanthali (Junagadh) dated V.S. 1469, Jyeṣṭha śu. di. 7, Ravi (= 7 May, A.D. 1413) refer to the reign of the Cūḍāsamā King Meligadeva, son of Mokalasiṃha, who ruled at Junagadh and Vanthali. Several soldiers of King Meliga fell in a battle while fighting with the Muslims. Their names are given as Pātāka, son of Veṇu Būbā of the Yādava family, Nūbhā, son of Noghaṇa of the Bārada community, Velāyulu, son of Dāsā Cācā, Meghā, son of Jādhava Merā, and Rāuta Cāṃpā, son of Paḍhiyāriā Jhāṭā. The fifth inscription is in both verse and prose. The old names of Vanthalī and Junagadh are given as Vāmanapura and Jīrṇa Prākāra in these epigraphs (IK no. 64). The *Mirat-i-Sikandarī* states that a battle between the Gujarat Sultan Ahmad Shah and the Cūḍāsamā King Meliga took place at Vanthali, in which latter was defeated and driven towards Junagadh. This statement is supported by the present inscription.

There is a noteworthy *pāḷiyā* inscription at the north side of the Bhūtanātha Mahādeva temple in the place known as Bhuchara Morī near Dhrol (Jamnagar). Dated V.S. 1647, Śrāvaṇa ba. di. 8, Ravi (= 1 Aug., A.D. 1591), it records the death of a warrior named Gopāladās Bārada while fighting together with prince Ajājī against Azam Khan, the Gujarat Viceroy of Emperor Akbar of Delhi. The battle was fought between the armies of Azam Khan and those of Jam Satājī of Navānagar, Lomākhumāṇa of Kherādī, and Dolatkhan Gorī of Junagadh. The *pāḷiyās* of the warriors Ajājī and Gopāladas were raised on the Bhuchara Mori battle field along with a *satī* stone and a small shrine of Ajāji's *satī* queen (IK no. 105).

A *pāḷiyā* inscription from Vartej (Bhavnagar), dated V.S. 1674/ Śaka 1539, Kārttika śu. di. 6, Śani (= 25 Oct., A.D. 1617) records the death of a *satī* belonging to the Kaṇḍoḷiā brāhmaṇa community. It states that Rāwal Dhunājī granted a sum of rupees for raising a memorial stone and a small shrine over it in honour of the brāhmaṇa *satī* (IK no. 116).

Ten *pāḷiyā* inscriptions of the 15th and 16th centuries have been discovered from Nagichana (Mangrol-Junagadh). Six of these memorial inscriptions record the death of warriors on the battlefield. They are dated V.S. 1434, Māgaśara va di. 9, Soma (= 26 Oct., A.D. 1377),

V.S. 1526, Phāgaṇa śu. di. 13, Śani (= 6 March, A.D. 1479), V.S. 1547/Śaka 1412, Caitra ba. di. 8, Soma (= 12 April, A.D. 1490), V.S. 1559/Śaka 1425, Vaiśākha ba. di. 13(11), Ravi (= 21 May, A.D. 1503), V.S. 1569, Āsāḍha ba. di. 11, Soma (= 30 May, A.D. 1513), V.S. 1590, Bhādaravā ba. di. 11, Ravi (= 14 Sept., A.D. 1533; Shastri 1948: 55ff.), and V.S. 1758, Jeṭha śu. di. 9 (= 24 May, A.D. 1702; IK no. 160). Two are *satī* stones dated V.S. 1489, Śrāvaṇa śu. di. 11, Soma (= 27 July, A.D. 1433) and V.S. 1512, Pauṣa śu. di. 11 (14), Bhoma (= 23 Dec., A.D. 1455). One *pāḷiyā* inscription is dated V.S. 1540, Caitra śu. di. 6, Budha (= 31 March, A.D. 1484).

Four *pāḷiyā* inscriptions in Gujarati from the village of Nagvada (Dist. Surendranagar) have been recently read and published. They are dated V.S. 1739, Mahā śu. di. 1 (= 18 Jan., A.D. 1683), V.S. 1768, Kārttika śu. di. 2 (= 1 Nov., A.D. 1711), V.S. 1775, Āsoja śu. di. 14, Śukra (= 16 Oct., A.D. 1719) and V.S. 1775, Phāgaṇa va. di. 13 (= 7 March, A.D. 1719). In the upper panel they depict the warriors on horseback, while the lower panel contains the inscription.[9]

The Wadhwan *pāḷiyā* inscription dated V.S. 1797/Śaka 1663 (= 20 Aug., A.D. 1741) records that Devakuṅvarabāī, daughter of Hāḍā Amarasiṃhajī, burnt herself with her husband Mahārāṇā Arjun Simhajī (IK no. 171). A *derī* was built in her honour by Mahārāṇā Sabalasiṃhajī, son of Achābā of the Parmār family.

Six *pāḷiyā* inscriptions from Beyt (Okha) dated V.S. 18[illegible]5, Phālguṇa ba. di. 11, Ravi (= 31 March, A.D. 1799) now stand in front of the new Śaṅkha-Nārāyaṇa temple (IK no. 183). One of them records the death of Bhāṇajī Pūjājī in the fight with the English, who had attacked the island in 1799.

Many memorial stone inscriptions are found near the Gopanātha temple on the way to Bhavnagar. These *pāḷiyās* depict the figures of mounted warriors with sword and shield in hand. Some of the warriors have a staff, while others hold a spear.

At Pithalpura near Mahuva many *pāḷiyās* are raised in an open space outside the back wall of the old houses. They show mounted

---

[9] *Sāmīpya*, April-September 1992, pp. 39ff.

warriors with spear in hand, held behind the head. A *pāḷiyā* with a composite *vyāla* figure with goad in hand (FIGURE 2) is also found at Pithalpura (author's personal observation).

Three notable *pāḷiyās* with the figure of the *nāgabandha* have been found from the Bhutakaḍā Ṭimbā at Odedar near Porbandar. They contain a *kīrti-lekha* in the lower portion (UNR 46, p. 428).

MEMORIAL STONE INSCRIPTIONS FROM KUTCH

Many hero stones and *satī* stones have been found in the Kutch region. In Bhuj, near the Bihārilal temple there is a *satī* stone inscription which records that in V.S. 1887, Mārgaśīrṣa śu. di. 13 (= 28 Nov., A.D. 1830) Rūpabāī perfomed a *trāga* in Navanagar, putting her daughter in her lap, entering into the funeral pyre, and burning herself and her daughter. Her *pāvaḷiyo* was raised in Bhuj fifteen years later, in V.S. 1902, Māgha ba. di. 2, Śani (= 14 Feb., A.D. 1846; Bhatti 1987: 31).

Near the Santoshi Mātā temple at Bhuj, a *satī* stone dated V.S. 1872, Jyestha śu. di. 10, Budha (5 June, A.D. 1816) records that Bāī Lādhī became *satī* when husband sacrificed his life in battle (Bhatti 1987: 31). Another *satī* stone inscription at Bhuj records that Duda's son Mādhava sacrificed his life in battle and his wife became a *satī*. Their son Rāmadās had a small shrine built in V.S. 1828, Śrāvaṇa va. di. 12(10*), Ravi (= 23 Aug., A.D. 1772), during the reign of Prāgmaljī (Bhatti 1987: 72). The stone depicts the *satī*'s raised hand with bangles.

From Gedi, two early *pāḷiyās*, dated V.S. 1268 and V.S. 1277, are found. The later one belongs to a Ṣachorā brāhmaṇa named Dalasukh Joshi, who had some dispute with the Darbāras. When he could not settle the dispute, he sacrificed his life by putting on an oily coat and setting it afire. This is a *trāgā* type of *pāḷiyā*, ten feet high (Bhatti 1987: 55). Another beautiful inscribed *satī* stone from the same place, dated V.S. 1686, Mahā ba. di. 4 (= 22 Jan., A.D. 1630), is worthy of special note. On the two sides of the upper panel the sun and the moon are engraved. In the middle portion is a beautifully carved parrot and the *satī*'s hand with a lotus flower. In the corner of the lower panel is represented a peacock (Bhatti 1987: 92). A Bhuj *pāḷiyā* of V.S. 1769, Māgaśara va. di. 14, Bhauma (= 16 Dec., A.D. 1712) depicts a Vaiṣṇava male figure with *tilaka* on the forehead, who has slain himself by cutting his neck with a sword. Another *satī pāḷiyā* inscription from Bhuj, dated V.S. 1813, Kārttika śu. di. 2 (= 25 Oct., A.D. 1756), shows a trident in the raised hand of a *satī*.

At Tera village, the inscription on a *pāḷiyā* of a horseman with sword and shield records that in V.S. 1800, Śrāvaṇa śu. di. 12 (= 8 Aug., A.D. 1744) Jam of Puarā sacrificed his life in Koṭhārā (Bhatti 1987: 58).

A *pāḷiyā* insciption dated V.S. 1819, Śaka 1684, Mārga īrṣa śu. di. 10, Bhṛgu (= 26 Nov., A.D. 1762), kept in the Bhuj Mu eum, commemorates the death of Khavāsa Govardhana in the ba tle of Zārā (FIGURE 3). The small shrine with *pāḷiyā* was built in V.S. 1926, Mahā śu. di. 6, Ravi (= 6 Feb., A.D. 1870; Bhatti 1987: 56).

A *pāḷiyā* inscription dated V.S. 1842, Āṣāḍha śu. di. 2 (= 28 June, A.D. 1786) from Lakhāṇiyā (Tal. Abdasa, Kutch) records that Jetabāī, wife of Bhānuśālī Savajī, became *satī* after her husband's death at Lakhāṇiyā (Bhatti 1987: 93). A *pāḷiyā* at the small shrine of Manubhā at Mandvi bears an epigraph dated V.S. 1845/Śaka 1790, Pauṣa ba. di. 2, Bhauma (= 13 Jan., A.D. 1710) recording that Khavāsa Kāniyo sacrificed his life during the reign of Rao Rāyadhaṇajī, and that a small shrine for him was built in V.S. 1846, Phālguna śu. di. 9 (= 23 Feb., A.D. 1790; Bhatti 1987: 79). The inscription includes the phase in Gujarati *Raṇachoḍajī satya che*, "Raṇachoḍaji [the Trivikrama form of Viṣṇu] is truth." A *pāḷiyā* from Nānī Aral village near Dhinodhara mountain (Tal. Nakhatrana), dated V.S. 1941, Pauṣa śu. di. 5,"[10] Guru, states that it is the *pārīo* of Barot Rājavīra Dosānī, and that the small shrine was built at an expense of 300 *koris*.

At Anjar, there are many memorial stones belonging to the brāhmaṇa community in small shrines in the Bhareśvara Mahādeva

[10] The given *tithi*, ba. di. 2, does not tally with the week-day, Bhauma, in V.S. 1941; it should have been either śu. di. 1 or śu. di. 8. In that case the date would correspond to either 18 Dec. or 25 Dec., 1884 A.D.

temple. On the back wall of the shrines are inscribed a Sārasvata brāhmaṇa *satī* stone, an Audicya brāhmaṇa *satī* stone, the raised hand of a *satī* on the *pāḷiyā* of a Trivedī brāhmaṇa, the raised hand of a Puṣkaraṇā brāhmaṇa *satī*, a *satī* stone of an Oza brāhmaṇa, and a *satī* stone of a Vyāsa brāhmaṇa (Bhatti 1987: 72). For a sailor's *pāḷiyā* and a *savatsa* cow *pāḷiyā*, see FIGURES 4 and 5.

LANGUAGES AND SCRIPTS OF MEMORIAL STONE INSCRIPTIONS

The memorial pillars called *yaṣṭi* from the Kṣatrapa period were written in Prakrit influenced by Sanskrit, as in *opaśati sagotrāye laṣṭi utthāpitā* (Andhau inscription of Cāṣṭana, ins. 1, l. 4) and *bahulasa dvitīya vāre* (ins. 3, l. 2). *Pāḷiyā* inscriptions from 11th to 13th century A.D. were written in Sanskrit, whereas from the 14th century onwards they seem to have been written in medieval Gujarati with influences from Sanskrit. The earliest memorial stone inscription which has a sprinkling of Gujarati words and which, therefore, helps us to determine the origin and the history of the Gujarati language, is the Osa *pāḷiyā* inscription of V.S. 1435, with the Gujarati expression *haragāganī mā* "mother of Haragāga" and *kāṭhīsanna*, i.e. *kāṭhīsaṃga*, "with the Kāṭhīs" (IK no. 38). Other examples are *saṃgrāme gāma bhāṅgatā mṛtyaḥ* (IK no. 65), *bāiśrī vāhālabāī sāhāgamana kīdhū* (IK no. 119), *svaraga padhāra* (IK no. 120), *gāyinī vāhāre svaragī thiā* (IK no. 122), *devāṭaṇa pāmā che* (IK no. 126), *gograhe mṛtyaḥ viṣṇucaraṇe vāsaḥ* (IK nos. 70, 71), *devaloka prāptā* (IK no. 119), *taraka sīdī dādaṣānanī p[illegible]oj śāmā laḍhī muā* (IK no. 148), *sāhānī pūtrīo sāgavana kīdho che, bāīne putre darī maṃḍavī cha* (IK no. 129), *jāgaro thao tyāhi kām[illegible] āvyā svarganā lokanā dhaṇī che, satyaśrī raṇachoḍa* (IK no. 158), [illegible]nd *pāliyo coḍo che, ubho kīdha che* (IK nos. 169, 170).

Some of the *khāṃbhīs* and memorial stones of the Vasāvā Bhils from South Gujarat with 15th-century inscriptions carry the antiquity of the Gujarati language even earlier than the 16th century. For example, the Gujarati text of the two Maṇḍālā and one Vadvā inscriptions, dated V.S. 1410, V.S. 1514 and V.S. 1476, of the Vasāvā Bhils reads:

vivā māṃkaḍanuṃ ṣāṃbhu vasāvi pāṃḍisi ghaḍāvyuṃ /
vasa(sā)vā mālabhimoḍhā ṣāṃbhu kotarāvyu //
vasāvā brāmaṇanuṃ ṣāṃbhu vasāvi ne ri ghaḍāvyu ///

The language of the Gujarati *pāḷiyā* inscriptions from south Gujarat, as spoken by the local forest tribes during the 14th and 15th centuries, was nearer the current form of Gujarati language than is the so-called old Gujarati or Western Rajasthani employed by the people inhabiting the plains during this period. Some of the peculiar grammatical usages in these inscriptions are *satī theāṃ che* (Bhuj *pāḷiyā* inscription of V.S. 1789), *svarga pāmatāṃ havāṃ, panara strīuṃ satīuṃ thīuṃ* (Bhuj *pāḷiyā* inscription of V.S. 1928), and *saṃgrāma karate* (Bhuj *pāḷiyā* inscription of V.S. 1746).

Examples of Sanskrit language

Most of the *pāḷiyā* inscriptions are very simple and short, but in rare cases they contain *praśastis* composed in verse. A *pāḷiyā* inscription in the Nāganātha temple in Chorwad (Junagadh) dated V.S. 1450, Bhādrapada śu. di. 9, Śukra (= 4 Sept., A.D. 1394) reads like a Sanskrit *praśasti*; for example, in *anuṣṭubh* meter:

evaṃ rathāśvapādātair asaṃkhyātair anekadhā /
yadā mamāra saṃgrāme surastrībhis tadā vṛtaḥ //

In the Phulka *pāḷiyā* inscription the Gujarati expression *sarovaru prāsāda baṃdhāvyā* occurs within the incorrect Sanskrit text. *Pāḷiyā* inscriptions from the middle of the 16th century A.D. have the appearance of Sanskrit, but are mostly written in Gujarati. Thus, the Bhuj Sārasvata *satī* stone inscription, dated V.S. 1728, Āṣāḍha ba. di. 7, Soma (= 19 June, A.D. 1761) is written in Sanskrit mixed with Gujarati; for example, *sarabāī sāgavana kīdhuṃ*. The Bhuj *pāḷiyā* inscription dated V.S. 1818/Śaka 1684, Vaiśākha ba. di. 5, Guru (= 13 May, A.D. 1762) uses the Sanskrit word *puṣkalaka* for *pāḷiyā* (*puṣkalakaḥ sthāpitaḥ*; Bhatti 1987: 103).

Examples of Gujarati language

The words and phrases used for death are *devaloka thīā* (Bhuj *pāḷiyā* inscription), *saṃgrāma karate rāmasaraṇa thayā che* (Bhuj *pāḷiyā* inscription dated V.S. 1746), *dhāḍāmāṃ marāṇāṃ* (Kanmer *pāḷiyā* inscription), *haricaraṇa pāmā* (Kanthkot *pāḷiyā* inscription), *aṃjāranā lasakaramāṃ kāma āvīu* (Bhuj *pāḷiyā* inscription dated V.S. 1845), *svarga prāpta thīā* (Bhuj *pāḷiyā* inscription), *raṭhoḍ lālā vanājī sāthi paḍā* (Palāsvā *pāḷiyā* inscription of V.S. 1633), *koṭhārāmāṃ marāṇā* (Tera *pāḷiyā* inscription of V.S. 1800), etc.

The Gujarati words used for *satī* are *sāgavana kīdhu* (Bhuj *pāḷiyā* inscription of V.S. 1728), *sahagamana kīdhuṃ* (Bhuj *pāḷiyā* inscription of V.S. 1717), *satī thayā* (Bhuj *pāḷiyā* inscription of V.S. 1788), etc.

From the 16th century on Gujarati, the language of the ordinary people, began to be used frequently in the inscriptions, but it was not in the pure form, especially since the majority of inscriptions on *pāḷiyās* in later times were composed by uneducated men.

SCRIPTS

The memorial pillars of the Kṣatrapa period are inscribed in Brāhmī script of the 2nd century A.D. The hero stones and *satī* stones from the 12th to 15th centuries are written in the Nāgarī script of the medieval period. From about V.S. 1500, Devanāgarī characters sometimes took the forms of Gujarati script, or Boḍiā characters as they are popularly called, though all along we find a decided preference for the Devanāgarī script, even in the modern inscriptions composed in Gujarati. But in comparatively modern memorial stone inscriptions, Devanāgarī script, or rather *Śāstrī-lipi*, began to give place to Boḍiā characters. In the Nāgarī script *paḍī-mātrā* or *pṛṣṭha-mātrā*, with vertical strokes at the left side of the letter, is used. In the *pāḷiyā* inscription from Kanmer (Kutch), dated V.S. 1818 (A.D. 1761-62), the Gujarati letters are written without vertical and oblique strokes.

CHRONOLOGICAL SYSTEMS

The dates of the *pāḷiyā* inscriptions are expressed in the Vikrama era, accompanied by the corresponding Śaka era in some cases. The dates contain the year, month, fortnight, *tithi* and week-day. Sometimes they also refer to the seasons, for example, *vasanta* (IK nos. 120, 135), *varṣā* (IK no. 171), *hemanta* (IK no. 153), *śarad* (IK nos. 53, 116, 129) and *śiśira* (IK nos. 52, 119, 139). There are also some references to the *ayanas*, namely *uttarāyana* (IK nos. 119, 120, 135, 139, 162) and *dakṣiṇāyana* (IK nos. 52, 53, 92, 129, 153, 170 and 171). Other astronomical terms that occur include *nakṣatras* such as *pūrva* (IK nos. 46, 52) and *aśvinī* (IK no. 53), *rāśis* like *dhana* (IK no. 46) and *meṣa* (IK no. 53), *yogas* like *saubhāgya* (IK no. 52) and *vyāghāta* (IK no. 53), *saṃvatsaras* like *vikrama* (IK no. 52), and *ghatīs* like "10 *ghatis*" (IK no. 116).

In a few dates the names of the eras are expressed by phrases like *nṛpavikrama-samvat* (IK no. 53) *nṛpavikramārkasamayātīta* (IK nos. 72, 167), *śālivāhananṛpakāla-śāke* (IK no. 120), and *śrīmannṛpaśālivāhanakṛta-śāke* (IK no. 167).

For the verification of dates expressed in the inscriptions, 124 dates have been referred to the tables given in Swamikannu Pillai's *Indian Ephemeris*. Out of the 124 dates, only 47 are key dates for deciding the systems of years and months. Thirty dates are not helpful in deciding the chronological systems as they fall between the months of Kārttika and Phālguna and belong to the bright fortnight. In 28 dates the week-day, which is the deciding factor, is absent, whereas 16 dates represent only the year of the Vikrama era. Of the three remaining dates, one does not mention a *tithi* and week-day, the second does not mention the fortnight and week-day, and in the third date the fortnight, *tithi* and week-day are not given. Out of the 47 key dates, 31 are useful for deciding the system of years. Among these 31, 23 (74.2%) tally with the *Kārttikādi* system of years, whereas only eight (25.8%) accord with the *Caitrādi* system.

As for the system of months, 28 dates are useful. Of these 28 key dates, 26 (92.86%) tally with the *amānta* system, whereas only two (7.14%) belong to the *pūrṇimānta* system.

From this examination of the key dates, it appears that the *Kārttikādi* system of years and *amānta* system of months predominated in the Gujarat and Saurashtra regions. But in the Kutch and Halar (Jamnagar) regions, *Āṣāḍhādi* years were prevalent.

The following tables represent the key dates with their system of years and months.

TABLE 1: Dates showing the system of years

	Caitrādi	*Kārttikādi*	Total
Number of dates	8	23	31
Percentages	25.8%	74.2%	100%

TABLE 2: Dates showing the system of months

	Amānta	*Pūrṇimānta*	Total
Number of dates	26	2	28
Percentages	92.86%	7.14%	100%

TABLE 3: Dates showing both the system of years and months

	Caitrādi Amānta	*Caitrādi Pūrṇimānta*	*Kārttikādi Amānta*	*Kārttikādi Pūrṇimānta*	*Caitrādi*	*Kārttikādi*	*Amānta*	*Pūrṇimānta*	Total
No. of dates	4	–	6	2	4	16	16	–	48
Percentages	8.5%	–	12.77%	4.26%	8.51%	31.91%	34.04%	–	100%

CONCLUSION

The Sanskrit, Apabhraṃśa and vernacular memorial stone and *satī* stone inscriptions of Gujarat, Saurashtra and Kutch are a valuable source for writing and reconstructing the political and the cultural history of the Gujarat region. They provide ample information about religious beliefs and activities, society, customs, script, language and chronological systems during various periods of the history of Gujarat. The intensive and the extensive survey of the *pāḷiyā* inscriptions can help in restoring and preserving the cultural heritage of the region as well as of India as a whole.

REFERENCES AND ABBREVIATIONS

ARIE = *Annual Report on Indian Epigraphy.*

ba. di. = *bahula-divase*, etc. (also va. di. = *vahula-divase*).

BG = *Bombay Gazetteer.*

BHATTI, N.K. 1987. *Kacchano Sanskritik Vāraso: Pāḷiyā.* Surendranagar.

CII = *Corpus Inscriptionum Indicarum.*

DHAVALIKAR, M.K. 2003. *Archaeology of Western India.* Ahmedabad.

Dist. = District.

EI = *Epigraphia Indica.*

FISCHER, Eberhard & Haku SHAH 1970. *Rural Craftsmen and Their Work.* Ahmedabad.

GADRE, A.S. 1943. *Important Inscriptions from the Baroda State.* Baroda.

IA = *Indian Antiquary.*

IK = D.B. Diskalkar, *Inscriptions of Kathiwad.* Bombay, 1941.

INAMDAR, D.A. 1936. *Some Archaeological Finds in the Idar State.* Himmatnagar.

JAIH = *Journal of Ancient Indian History.*

JOIB = *Journal of the Oriental Institute of Baroda.*

JOTE, R.B. 1953. *Gujarātnun Pāṭnagar: Amadāvād.* Ahmedabad.

KANE, P.V. 1973. *History of Dharmaśāstra, Vol. IV.* Poona.

l(l). = line(s).

MG = *Mysore Gazetteer* (ed. C. Hayavadan Rao, Bangalore, 1930).

Saṃ. = [Vikrama-]saṃvat.

SETTAR, S. & G.D. SONTHEIMER 1982. *Memorial Stones.* Dharwad/New Delhi.

SHAH, Varsha 1992. *Saurashtranā pāḷiyā.* Ahmedabad.

SHASTRI, K.K. 1948. *Anushilana.* Vadodara.

SI = D.C. Sircar, *Select Inscriptions, Vol. I.* Calcutta, 1965.
SII = *South Indian Inscriptions.*
śu. di. = *śukla-divase*, etc.
Tal. = Taluk.
TOD, James 1920. *Annals and Antiquities of Rajasthan.* 3 vols. Bombay.
UNR = *Ūrmi-Navaracanā.*
V.S. = Vikrama-saṃvat.
VVRB = *Vallabh Vidyanagar Research Bulletin.*

APPENDIX:
***Pāḷiyās* in South India and other regions**

In Karṇātaka, *pāḷiyās* are called *vīrakala* (*vīrakkala* or *vīragala*). In Maharashtra they are called *vīraḍagada*. Many *vīrakala* ins riptions of the Rāṣṭrakūtas and Yādavas of the Deccan, Śilāhāras of K lhapur and Cālukyas of Kalyāṇī are found in various places in sou ern India. These inscriptions are very simple and short. Some *vīrak las* of Kolhapur and Karṇātaka are *praśastis* composed in verse. They closely resemble Babylonian stelae and boundary stones in their shape, in the order of figures, and in the inscriptions depicted on them. Both types have on the top the figures of the sun and the moon and record curses on those who would try to destroy them (EI 33, p. 72).

The *vīrakala* inscription at Mavali (Mysore), dated about 800 A.D., contains a spirited description of how Kalemudda fell fighting in an exciting battle at the bidding of Kakkarasa, the Nolamba Pallava general. Similarly the Baraḍavallī (Mysore) *vīrakala*, dated 1300 A.D., tells how Madigauda, at the bidding of Jagadala Gāṅgeya Sāhanī, the great minister of Kāva Devarasa, fell fighting against Ballala Deva, who had marched on Kadabalau. The Hunavalli *vīrakala* in front of the Kalleśvara temple at the same place, dated 945 A.D., records how, while Tailapa Deva was the king of Banavasi, one Piyana saw two murderers and fought and killed them both by stabbing them with his dagger. A number of Kālachūrya inscriptions in Shimoga District are of *vīrakala* type. Many of them record attacks on Gutti, while others refer to fights with Hoysala officers (MG 2, pp. 66f). A *vīrakala* at Hale Sorab belonging to the time of Cālukya Vikramāditya (A.D. 1076-1126), dated in the Cālukya-Vikrama era (= A.D. 1093) contains a sculptural representation of a village exploit (MG 2, p. 175): when Mahāmaṇḍaleśvara Śrīvalla Deva's chiefs entered Naduhalli in Edanad and carried off the cows, Maki Śetti, son of Era Śetti, attacked them, slew many, recovered the cows and gained the world of the gods. In the lowest panel is drawn the battle scene, showing foot soldiers with helmets, daggers, swords and shields, and warriors on horses and elephants. Bows are being shot and arrows flit from side to side. In the panel above this is shown a *vimāna* (heavenly cart) attended by winged nymphs, three on either side. The next higher panel shows a troop of celestial musicians playing drums and pipes and beckoning heavenwards, leading the way to it. Some of the divine damsels bear long staffs in their hands. The hero is seen sitting at one end with a young attendant who holds an umbrella over his head. In the next panel we are shown the hero in heaven. At the left, he is seated on a raised plank in an attitude of prayer. His hands are folded together at his chest, with an attendant at his side with a staff in his right hand. Next there is a *liṅga* being bathed by a priest, while another priest stands by praying. The last panel shows the sacred bull of Śiva with a lovely necklace of *bello* round his neck and a man standing by his tail end, apparently keeping guard. Above the central panel containing the *liṅga* is shown the upper portion of the heavenly abode, with the enthroned figure of a decorated cow with an attendant before it. Apparently this is intended to signify the successful exploit of Maki Śetti in rescuing the stolen cows. On either side of this panel, at the top, are the figures of the sun and the moon. The *vīrakala* is headed by a *siṃha-lalāṭa* (MG 2: 176).

Satī stones are called *māstī* (< *mahāsatī*) in Kannada. An inscribed hero stone in Kannada language with three panels was found at Tripurāntakam. The upper panel depicts a *Śiva-liṅga* in the middle, on the left of which are carved *Nandi* and the moon, and on right, a devotee, a *nāgabandha*, and the sun. The middle panel contains the inscription, in Kannaḍa language. The lower panel depicts a running horse and beneath it, two soldiers fallen down on the ground, and at the extreme right three warriors with staffs in hand. The whole *pāḷiyā* is beautifully carved.

The Inj[illegible]du sculptured hero stone set up in the Kalamdoddi of Karrpu Se[illegible]i Reddi (Tal. Koilkuntla, Andhra Pradesh), with an inscription written in archaic Kannaḍa characters of the 8th or 9th century A.D., refers to the fight between Pāleyaṇṇa, son of Prabhukāma and Revaṇṇa, son of Choreya (ARIE 1952-53, p. 22, no. 40).

A stone-pillar inscription of the middle of the 5th century A.D. has been discovered in the Bhumara region of Central India, referring to the setting up of a *bala-yaṣṭi* in the following words: *svapuṇyāpyāyanārthaṃ yaśaḥkīrttipravardhamānagotraśailikā balayaṣṭir pratiṣṭhāpitā vargagrāmikeṇa*. This was a memorial pillar apparently raised in honour of several dead relatives of a *grāmika* (village headman) named Varga. This is why the *bala-yaṣṭi* appears to be described as a *gotra-śailikā* or "family stone". The *Medinīkośa* recognises the word *bala* in the adjectival sense of *bala-yukta* "strong, stout". *Bala-yaṣṭi* may thus indicate a strong or stout (i.e., everlasting) pillar (EI 33, p. 172). In this connection, reference may be made to a late pillar inscription from the former Rewa state, now preserved in the Allahabad Municipal Museum. The inscription refers to a memorial pillar, raised by some persons in memory of a dead man named Mahārāja whose two wives apparently committed *satī* in V.S. 1417, Jyeṣṭha ba. di. 13, Budha (= May 13, A.D. 1360) during the reign of Vallaladeva, as a *gātra*. The word *gātra* in the sense of "pillar" is unintelligible. Perhaps it should be read as *gotra* rather than *gātra*, which can be taken as a contraction of what is called *gotra-śailikā* in the previously mentioned inscription of the Gupta period. The use of the term *gotra-śailikā* in the sense of a memorial pillar has so far been found only in the aforementioned records of the Rewa region (EI 33, p. 172).

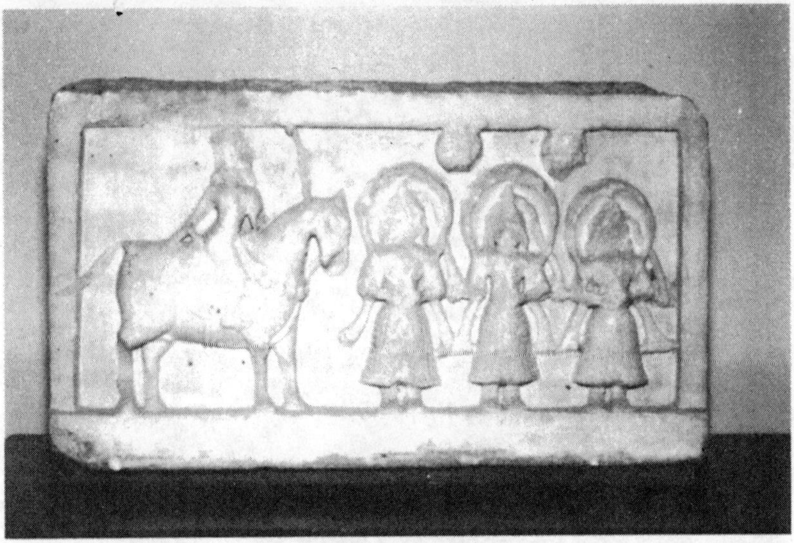

FIGURE 1 Marble satī stone from Dudheśvara, Ahmedabad

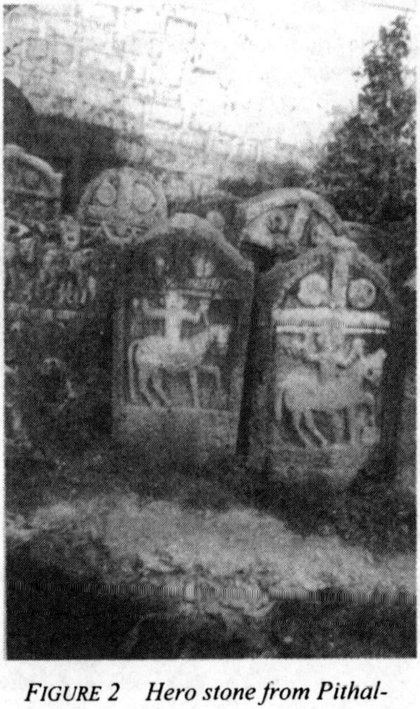

FIGURE 2 Hero stone from Pithalpura, near Bhavnagar, Saurashtra

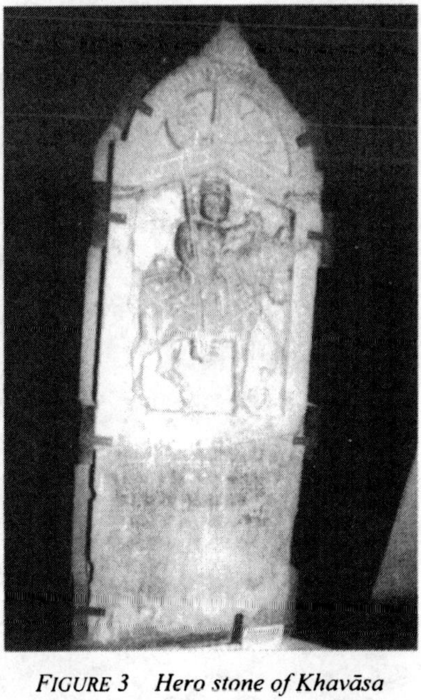

FIGURE 3 Hero stone of Khavāsa Govardhana, Bhuj Museum, Kutch

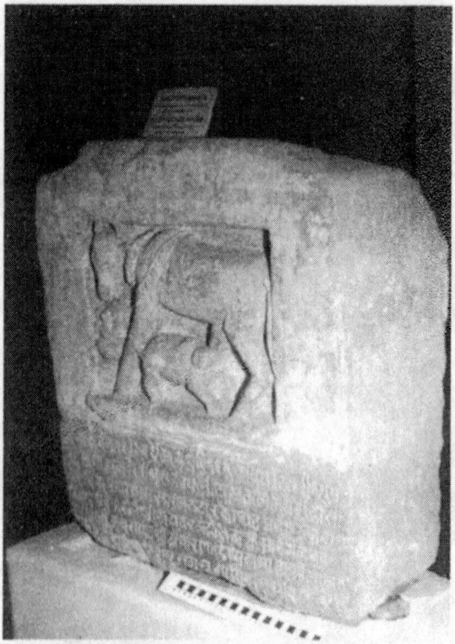

FIGURE 4 Savatsa cow pāḷiyā,
Bhuj Museum, Kutch

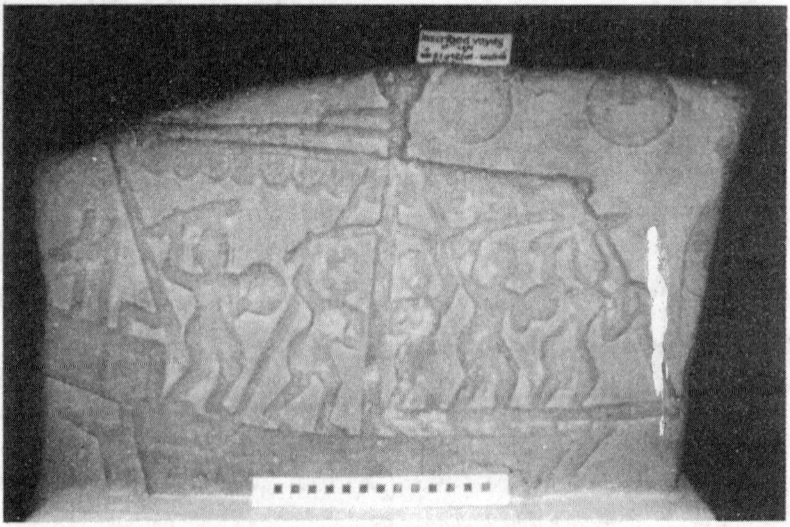

FIGURE 5 Sailor's pāḷiyā, Bhuj Museum, Kutch

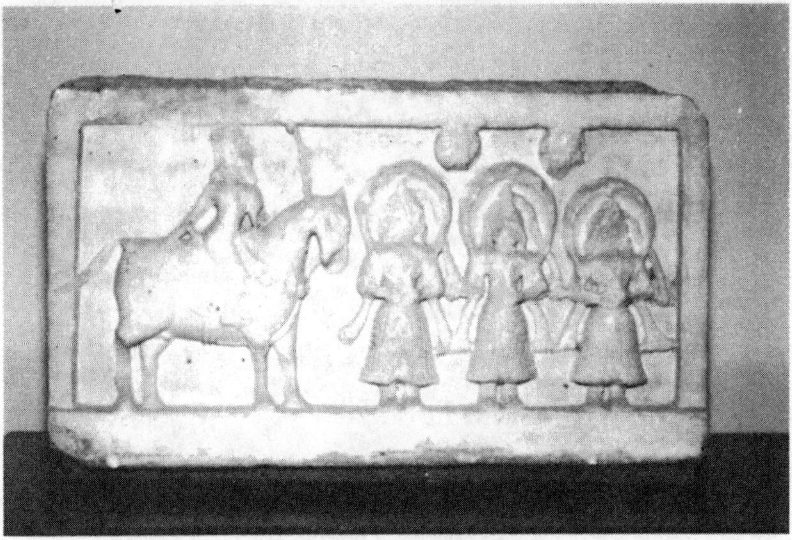

FIGURE 1 Marble satī stone from Dudheśvara, Ahmedabad

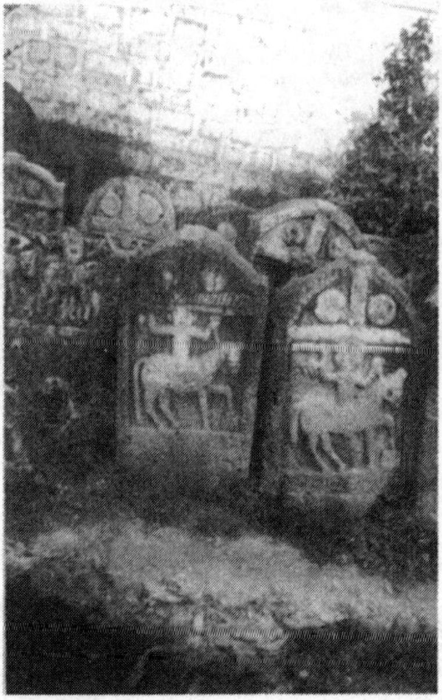

FIGURE 2 Hero stone from Pithalpura, near Bhavnagar, Saurashtra

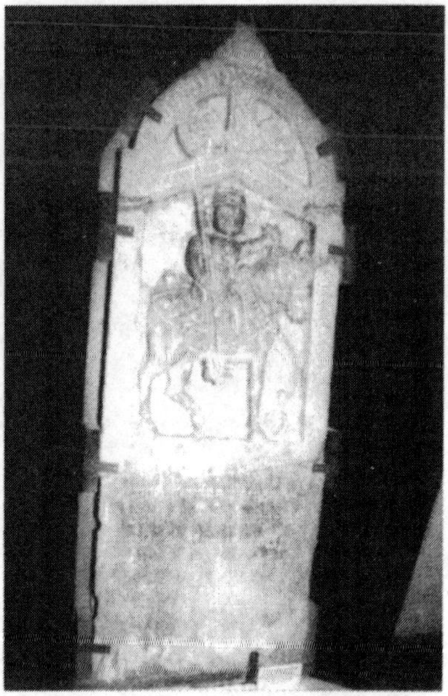

FIGURE 3 Hero stone of Khavāsa Govardhana, Bhuj Museum, Kutch

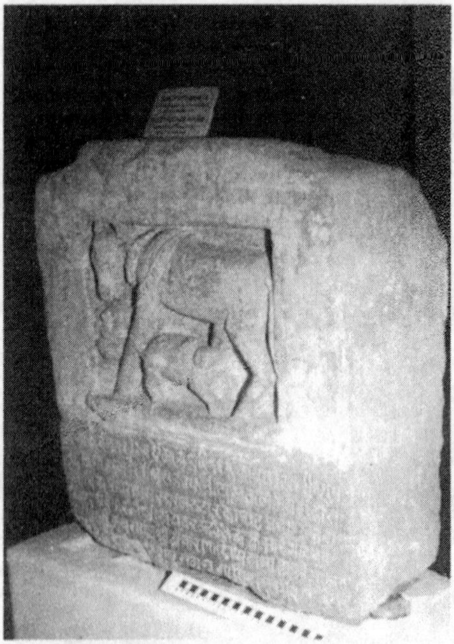

FIGURE 4 *Savatsa cow pāḷiyā, Bhuj Museum, Kutch*

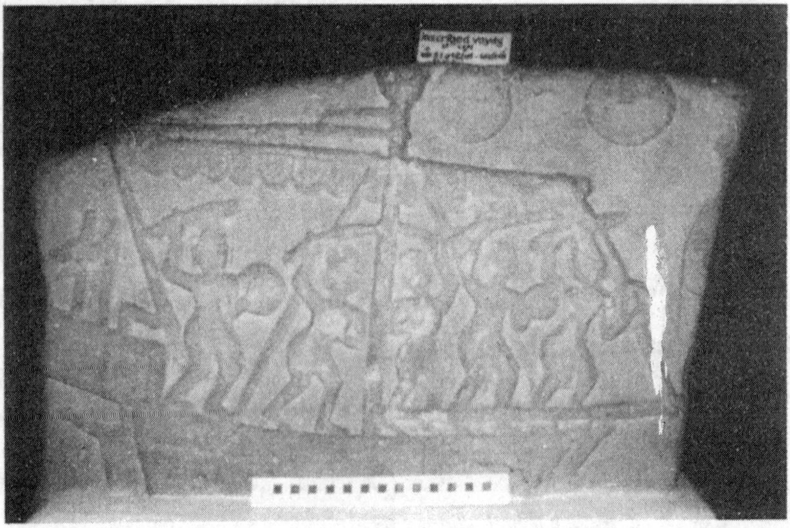

FIGURE 5 *Sailor's pāḷiyā, Bhuj Museum, Kutch*

INDEX OF SUBJECTS